WAITING FOR LIGHTNING TO STRIKE

The Fundamentals of Black Politics

WAITING FOR LIGHTNING TO STRIKE

The Fundamentals of Black Politics

Kevin Alexander Gray

CounterPunch
PETROLIA

AK
PRESS
EDINBURGH · LONDON · OAKLAND

First published by
CounterPunch and AK Press 2008
© *CounterPunch* 2008

CounterPunch
PO Box 228, Petrolia, California 95558

AK Press
674A 23rd St, Oakland, California 94612-1163

ISBN 978-1904859918

A catalog record for this book is available from the Library of Congress

Library of Congress Control Number: 2008929305

Typeset in Minion Pro, designed by Robert Slimbach for Adobe Systems Inc.; and Futura, originally designed by Paul Renner; and Amplitude Black, designed by Christian Schwartz for The Font Bureau, Inc.

Printed and bound in Canada.

Index by Jeffrey St. Clair.
Cover Design by Ja'maal Mosely and Tiffany Wardle.
Design and typography by Tiffany Wardle.

To my mother and father,
Sandra, Brian, Camille and my grandchildren,
my sisters and brothers — blood and otherwise
and
M.R. Burgin and R.P. Dawkins of Lincoln High School
who loved and encouraged all they taught.

"…It is my sympathy with the oppressed and wronged, that are good as you and as precious in the sight of God…. You may dispose of me easily, but this question is still to be settled — the negro question — the end of that is not yet." — John Brown, 1859

Contents

Acknowledgments

THERE ARE MANY INDIVIDUALS WHOM I OWE A DEBT OF gratitude and thanks. First and foremost — Frances Close and David Marsh who have been there for me throughout many years with not only their financial support but with their friendship, input, critique and editing on many an occasion. My high school "Afro-American" history and guidance teacher M.R. Burgin who was black and very, very classy, distinguished, proudly middle class but radical, and Dr. Joseph Killian my college black history professor who is white. I credit them both with helping shape an intellectual framework and giving me books to read. I write about what's happening around me and with the people around me. I start out most of my essays with a problem or concern that someone mentions. I then talk to as many people as possible, as I think a problem through. Some of the names of those people appear in my work, some don't.

The formal studies the "Intensification of Racial Solidarity" published by the *Harvard Journal of African-American Public Policy* and "A Call for a New Anti-War Movement" which appears in *How to Legalize Drugs* edited by Dr. Jefferson Fish of St. John's University were both team efforts. Efia Nwangaza, former University of South Carolina professors Glenn Harrison and Eva Elisabet Rutström, former American University professor Dr. Elizabeth Cook, Dr. Adolph Reed, Marjorie Brittain Hammock, Sasha Kennison, David Kennison, Cheryl Epps, Paul Ruffins, Dr. Michael Dawson, formerly of the University of Chicago, and Dean Robinson, formerly of the University of Massachusetts at Amherst, were all instrumental in my writing and publishing my first scholarly journal article which captures the bedrock of my beliefs. The "anti-drug war" piece is intended to show the everyday effects of the war on drugs on the African-American community. My drug policy reform work has been enhanced by the support of Jeff Fish who was courageous enough to pull together a book with the title *How to Legalize Drugs*. I can't thank him enough for asking me to participate in what has become in many folks' estimation "the Bible of drug policy reform." Meeting Dr. Fish and a host of others in the drug policy reform community was made possible through my friendship with Eric Sterling of the Criminal Justice Policy Foundation in Washington D.C. Eric, Drs. Ruth Lane, James Lynch and Ron Shaiko of the American University and Dr. Dawn Days of the Dogwood Center were all valuable resources for hard statistical data on the effects of the drug war in communities of color. My drug policy piece owes much of its academic girth to Lynch's "Building Data Systems for Cross-national Comparisons of Crime and Criminal Justice Policy: A Retrospective" and Eastern Kentucky University's Peter B. Kraska and Victor E. Kappeler's "Militarizing American Police: The Rise and Normalization of Paramilitary Units." I thank them for their work.

I met Dr. David Bositis of the Joint Center for Political and Economic Studies in Washington in the late 1980s while I was working with Jesse Jackson's Rainbow Coalition. We have been friends from day one. David is the activists' political scientist, keeping track of voter attitudes as well as being an open minded sounding board for both my personal and professional life. Bositis' contribution can be seen in "Identity and Race Politics: The Million Man March" which appeared in the American University *95/96 Graduate Review*. My thanks to Leslie Brown and Eleanor Addy-Binnings who edited the essay for publication.

There are those allies whom I have come to respect for their ideo-logical consistency and willingness to be bold. Alexander Cockburn and Jeffrey St. Clair of *CounterPunch* fall into that category. *CounterPunch* is my writer's home. It is a place where you can say what needs to be said. The human rights community owes *CounterPunch* a debt of thanks for just being there for us. At the top I mentioned my close friend and mentor Dave Marsh but I would also like to thank our online writers' group the *Stratlist* and the 'Holla If You Hear Me' blog. In particular I would like to thank Daniel Wolff for his guidance in helping me develop my writing skills and for sending my mother a copy of his book *You Send Me*, the biography of Sam Cooke. Thanks also to Mark Jacobson who traveled the back roads of South Carolina with me and Al Sharpton during the 2004 presidential season. It was through Mark that I had the wonderful opportunity to participate in his and Jack Newfield's last book *American Monsters.*

Thanks to Matthew Rothschild of *The Progressive,* mostly for his cogent case against the Iraq war before the fiasco began. Matthew's work was the catalyst for "Outlaw Nation" which appeared on *Counterpunch* and in black newspapers across South Carolina and many other venues. Matthew also gave me the opportunity to write a review of Barack Obama's *Audacity of Hope* which appears in this collection.

Although a child of the sixties the refinement of my political development came in the seventies and eighties. I started out like many marching against police abuse, or in support of civil rights for people like me. My first taste of big-time politics came through my involvement with Jesse Jackson's presidential campaigns in 1984 and 1988. At times I have written or said some harsh things about Jackson's politics in the years following the Rainbow Coalition's demise. But I do so with the recognition that my relationship with Jackson — both personal and professional — had a huge impact on my life and development. I will always be grateful for the opportunity Jackson gave me and the lifelong friends I have because of the Rainbow's efforts. Friends like Frank Watkins who constantly reminds me to "keep building the contradictions." Maybe one day the house of cards will fall and we can build something better. Thanks to my buddy Steve Cobble, who looks out for a brother from time-to-time. To Jack O'Dell, one of the first to stand besides Dr. King. Jack is the standard of class, humility and depth. Joe Beasley, who regardless of what I had to say, supported my right to say it. Joe is one of those folk who is doing community building for all the right reasons.

Thanks to Jan Phillips and the Davis-Putter Scholarship Fund, Gwen Patton, Wendy Brinker, Michael Watts, Jamaal Mosely, William "Shane" Felder, Jr., Glenn Gray, Sami Sekou Sanders, Sam Sanders, Kamau Marcharia, Glen Ford of the *Black Agenda Report,* the Harriet Tubman Freedom House Project and the many folks at the Thomas Cooper Library at the University of South Carolina. Lastly, I'd like to thank my friend and comrade JoAnn Wypijewski for all her help and encouragement.

Preface

I BELIEVE THE RULE THAT YOU CAN'T WRITE ABOUT WHAT YOU DON'T know about. So, I write about what I see and experience, which I hope to convey in this collection of essays. I make no claim to be an expert on things relating to race. My life's experiences are not particularly unique. I do believe that I am a bit more conscious of and sometimes combative about race issues than a lot of the folks around me — black and white. I try to understand why we relate to one another the way we do, why we say the things we say and do the things we do, and what it may lead us to. This collection of pieces written over the past fifteen years boils down to my efforts to understand race relations.

The essays in this anthology (with the exception of the "Introduction — The Fundamentals of Black Politics", "South Carolina's heritage of slavery — Part One" and "The Soul Will Find a Way") have appeared in various magazines or books. The opening essays give a rudimentary history lesson on the race divide and black politics in the United States. Other essays examine political ideology, where it comes from and what flows from it, with emphasis on the inconsistencies. The remaining essays tackle policy, party politics, cultural politics and internecine race politics. The styles vary from the academic to story telling to exposé.

The introductory piece and the subtitle of this book — "The Fundamentals of Black Politics" — suggest that there are some fundamental things people should consider in the fight for rights and freedom. It is followed by "South Carolina's Heritage of Slavery — Part One" which makes its debut in this book. The piece was written during the 2000 debate over the flying of the Confederate flag on the Statehouse dome in Columbia, South Carolina. I, along with others, set the flag ablaze on Confederate Memorial Day 2000, as the state legislature was voting to move the flag down from the dome to the Statehouse grounds. I had a few things in mind when I wrote this brief history lesson on what the

Confederacy means to today's political environment. First, the neo-con-federate, neo-conservative opposition — then and now — had a better grasp of their history then many of those fighting to have the flag removed from the dome. They plan with history in mind and the flag and confed-erate history is integrated into their actions. For example, when the flag was removed from the dome and placed on the Statehouse grounds on July 1, 2000, it was the anniversary of the day that Edward Rutledge of South Carolina refused to sign the Declaration of Independence due to its anti-slavery clause. Though the neo-confederates may explain their reverence for the "Stars and Bars" under the theme "heritage not hate," I believe that's more for convenience than honesty. The rocky history of race in the United States starts with the issue of African enslavement, regardless of how many attempt to dismiss it. Lastly, I wrote the piece as a primer for blacks in general, and for black college age kids in particular with the intent to distribute the essay in pamphlet form to black colleges across the state of South Carolina. I wanted to give black kids a sense of perspective on the flag and their history. The piece covers the period from the Africans arriving in the New World up to Reconstruction. Needless to say, the politics and history of South Carolina shapes my political, social and cultural values, dysfunctions and battles.

In the decade of the nineties, the breakdown or lack of understanding of the fundamental goals of black political struggle in America fed nos-talgia for a more radical black leadership embodied in the pop culture resurgence of Malcolm X and the political ascendancy of the Nation of Islam's Louis Farrakhan. "The Intensification of Racial Solidarity in the 1990s in the Guise of Black Nationalism," published in 1996 by the *Harvard Journal of African-American Public Policy*, probed the distinction between racial solidarity and black nationalism. The study uses survey and polling data for indications of the existence of racial solidarity and/or black nationalism; explores the validity of polling responses interpret-ed as black nationalism; and identifies and examines factors which may or may not substantiate radicalization among blacks with a suggestion as to where it leads black politics in the 1990s. The piece also gives an account of what black nationalism is and has been throughout American history. I completed the Harvard Journal study before "Mumbo Jumbo:

The Million Man March — Identity & Race Politics," which appeared in the American University Graduate Review in October 1995. Ten years later I find my conclusions in both pieces have proven right. The idea behind "Mumbo Jumbo" is the dead end road of religious, demagogic, self-righteous fanaticism. Both pieces are presented to show us where we don't want to go.

Before there was a war in Iraq, there was the power structure in America training for war in communities of color under the banner of the "war on drugs." The war on drugs has proven to be a war on people of color. Whenever I see an American soldier kick in a door in Baghdad I think about the TV show COPS. Better still, I think of the no-knock searches that the U.S. Supreme Court has ruled permissible in neighborhoods all across America. They are most commonly conducted in communities of color under the guise of drug or immigrant searches. And when I think of the scandal of Abu Ghraib or the Guantánamo Bay gulag, the maxi-max and super-max prisons in America also come to mind. "A Call For An Anti-War Movement" was written in the mid-nineties and first published in Jefferson Fish's *How to Legalize Drugs*. The only difference between the time I wrote the anti-drug war appeal and now is that things have gotten worse. The police have more power and there are more black males in jail. I wrote the anti-war piece sometime between 1994 and 1996. Way back then, 1 in 4 black males between the ages of 16-24 were under some type of criminal justice supervision. Now, ten years later , that number is 1 in 3. If the trend continues it will be 1 in 2. Ten years ago, "A Call For An Anti-War Movement" painted a picture that today is only darker. Like Dr. Fish's entire collection, the essay helps provide a framework for positive drug policy reform. It exposes the injustice of the situation and offers an alternative. "A Call For An Anti-War Movement" is an appeal for political action on the disastrous effects of the war on drugs on the African-American community, and also a call for an anti-war movement.

Now on to more treacherous ground. I was nervous about adding "Big Daddy and the Plantation" to this collection for a number of reasons. I wrote it while Jesse Jackson was having personal difficulties. I probably wrote it in anger over my disappointment, not so much with his relationship travails, but with the failure of the Rainbow Coalition. I said in the beginning that I generally write about what I experience. This does not lead to detachment. The downside of writing about what you experience is rereading what you wrote long after the experience is over and maybe understood differently. A large part of who I am politically stems from my experiences with Jesse Jackson and the "Rainbow Movement" we were trying to build. It was a disappointment that doubtless colored my experience. "Big Daddy and the Plantation" is about a bad model of leadership, not someone's personal foibles. The movement model of mission, comradeship and coalition that Jesse Jackson came up through is the best and perhaps the only model that keeps any of us politically viable. It's about spreading a message, building bottom up, not top down, extra emphasis on building. Reverend Jackson and I are part of the same community, we just don't always agree. I decided to include the piece because it's meant to be instructive not destructive.

It also segues nicely into "Soul Brother? Bill Clinton and Black America" since we're on the subject of bad models. Originally published online on *CounterPunch*, it was later included in Alexander Cockburn and Jeffrey St. Clair's book *Dime's Worth of Difference*. Bill Clinton is a master player in the political game but he is nothing more than a product and functionary of Reaganism, a Reagan Democrat.

Or better yet, a Dixiecrat. "The Legacy of Strom Thurmond" is the racial reckoning of Thurmond. Published in Jack Newfield and Mark Jacobson's *American Monsters* the essay covers the contradictions and accommodations of Southern life at the apex of segregationist power. There's an unbroken line between the politics of Strom Thurmond and those of Bill Clinton. Race and race politics are the thread of that line.

I've written a number of anti-Iraq war pieces. "The Sun Never Sets: How Did We Become an Outlaw Nation?" was the first. Nothing that has happened as a result of the Iraq invasion and occupation is a surprise. A lot of people laid out the scenario before the war began. As I write, more than 4000 American troops have died and the number is destined to climb. There are more than 50,000 wounded soldiers in V.A. hospitals across the country. Thousands of soldiers have been given bad conduct discharges for refusing to do a second, third, fourth or fifth tour of duty in occupied Iraq. On the Iraqi side conservative estimates from the first Gulf War to the present reveal that the United States has directly or indirectly contributed to the deaths of an estimated 1.5 million Iraqi people in the past 17 years. Over 2 million Iraqis have been forced out of their country in the past 5 years and the number rises monthly by the tens of thousands. The U.S.'s deadly policies toward the Iraqi people did not start with the George W. Bush Administration. It started with his father and continued through the Bill Clinton Administration. Still, George Bush, Dick Cheney, Condoleezza Rice, Richard Perle, Paul Wolfowitz, Donald Rumsfeld, Colin Powell and their apparatchiks must be held accountable for lying about the reasons for invading Iraq. As musician Gil Scott-Heron mocked, "Haldeman, Erlichman, Mitchell and Dean. It follows a pattern if you see what I mean" during Richard Nixon's Watergate scandal. Maybe the new chant can be, 'Cheney, Rumsfeld, Powell and Rice, helping Bush kill innocent people ain't so nice' or 'Cheney, Wolfowitz, Rice, Rumy and Perle, if we don't watch out they'll use Bush to destroy the world."

In "The Packaging of Obama" published in *The Progressive* in February 2007, I tried to write an unbiased review of Barack Obama's second book *The Audacity of Hope*. Most of the feedback I received was positive, though I got some letters from folks aiming to set me straight. Obama defenders questioned my blackness and race loyalty. The Obama book review and "The Black Primary" piece reveal the underlying theme of this anthology. I am a progressive, I believe in certain things and I've given my time and effort to encourage those things. I managed both Jesse Jackson's and Al Sharpton's presidential campaigns in South Carolina. "The Black Primary" is not about Obama per se. It's about how black voters are treated in the political process these days. It's about the issues facing African-Americans and whether or not they are being addressed by the candidates and the process. The essay gives an account of the stresses on the black community. It connects to the very first essay in the collection in that the political history of South Carolina shapes the political, social and cultural values, dysfunctions and battles of today.

"Race, Class and Art: Hustle and Flow" is a piece I wish I had promoted better because I thought Craig Brewer's film deserved more credit than people gave it. It deserved more than one Academy Award for the lead rap song "It's Hard Out Here For A Pimp." Some didn't like it for the misogynic lead character or the drugs or nakedness. But sometimes folks have to be reminded of what needs to be changed and that even the despised have a sense of humanity. We lose our own if we forget that. Culturally, Brewer captures the South and an inner culture that I know all too well. The people in Brewer's movie represent 250,000 New Orleans residents displaced by Hurricane Katrina and disbursed across the nation. "The Black Primary" describes politicians flashing the words "Hurricane Katrina" as a cue to blacks that they're on their side. Are the candidates, especially those who claim to be reaching out to the poor and lost, seeing and responding to the needs of the people portrayed in Brewer's film?

"Richard Pryor's Mirror on America" is my favorite piece because I love Richard. It's the most popular piece I've written in the last 5 years. That brother was alright even when he wasn't alright. The Pryor piece is a tribute to someone who made a lasting impact on culture and comedy. Pryor spoke the comedy and stories of the people in Brewer's film, people who once lived in the poor wards of New Orleans or the backwaters of the south, or in the ghettos of the cities. There was tragedy and messiness in Pryor's life. But it gave his stories and characters — such as Mudbone the Wino — a richness and honesty. He gave humanity to characters that some people wish would just shut up or disappear.

I guess I'm just a raunchy guy. Richard Pryor and James Brown are my favorite entertainers. Pryor's genius was his honesty. And, what can't you say about James Brown — good or bad? He was "Superbad!" When Brown was jailed in the late eighties in my home state of South Carolina I was one of those who looked out for the brother. In my role as editor of a local weekly newspaper, I got to meet and talk with Brown one-on-one while he was in prison. His funeral was one of the greatest public events that I've ever attended. "The Soul Will Find a Way" is about why we love Brown so much, his impact on music, culture and politics. It's my tribute to "The Godfather."

The Fundamentals
of Black Politics

I N THE SIXTIES I WAS AN ACTIVE PARTICIPANT IN THE SCHOOL
desegregation experiment. During the seventies I hung out with
the peace and love crowd and the holdouts of a dying civil rights
movement. In the mid and late eighties I participated in mainstream
Democratic Party politics with Jesse Jackson's Rainbow Coalition.
Political conditions have deteriorated from there for me.

Blacks in America are enduring stormy times. Even with more black
officials than at any time in history, many African-Americans feel that
things have been moving in the wrong direction for awhile now. When
things go bad, blacks get it first and worse; or as the well-worn saying
goes, "when America gets a cold, black America gets pneumonia." From
high infant mortality rates to low life expectancy, the black misery index
is acute. At present, the majority of black kids are stuck in poorly func-
tioning, segregated schools. To add insult to injury, many see the recent
U.S. Supreme Court decision, in the *Meredith* case, regarding school
desegregation as marking the end of the *Brown* decision mandating that
race be taken into account when determining the composition of the
public schools. *Meredith* was a victory for the opposite view. Yet regardless of their racial composition, in an overwhelming number of school
districts the majority of black kids don't graduate from high school.

If a kid is male, chances are he is going to jail, most likely for selling
drugs. If a parent has done time their offspring have a better than 60 per
cent chance of ending up behind bars.

Some of us seem to be waiting for a bolt of lightning to strike somebody, somewhere, who will rise up like Martin Luther King to lead us
through the rising waters. Maybe some are waiting for a bolt to strike at
the hearts of those in power, causing them to release their hold on power
voluntarily. Or for an Almighty surge from the clouds to eviscerate white

supremacy and everything that holds it together. But what do you do when you get tired of waiting?

The subtitle of this book — The Fundamentals of Black Politics — is a rewording of an earlier title I once planned to use — *The Death of Black Politics*. Someone beat me to it, which turned out to be a good thing. The title reflected my disappointment with black political life over the past twenty years. Now I believe it's better to write about rebirth and the possibilities of the future. The past has to be instructive. Where I'm from they call that "flippin' the script" or turning things upside down, or in this case turning a negative into a positive. I am hopeful about the future, despite my personal political depression. I have to be hopeful because I have grandchildren. If America actually survives another 20 or 25 years, as things are going now it will be waging war against my grandkids in particular and people of color in general. If the current incarceration trend continues, most of my male grandkids will have some type of criminal record. If the educational trends continue, it is unlikely that many of my grandkids will have a high school diploma. If they do graduate, but are thinking and grasping information on a less than eighth grade level, it's not much of a future for them anyway.

I'm hopeful that we will overcome and reverse these and other disheartening trends. I hope my grandkids and yours don't have to live in fear of a no-knock search or a dead end life. That they will have some control over their own lives and destinies. That they won't have to rely on somebody to give them a little bit of patronage to make it. I hope they will have meaningful freedom. Because when you get down to it, that's what's at stake.

Some may think it a big jump equating politics to freedom. But politics is like air. Politics determines who gets what. It plays a part in all aspects of living including macro and micro economics. Everything we do, where we live, what we wear, where we go to school and work — all involve politics. You have to decide how much or whether to allow others to make decisions that affect your life without input or challenge. You can act on things or wait and just let things act on you. But you ignore politics at your peril. Politics is how you protect your freedom without resorting to violence.

The huge number of black citizens under the direct control of the state through the criminal justice system has led to diminished voting rights and participation. The effect of this cannot be overstated. Nationally, one out of three black males between the ages of 16-24 are under some type of criminal justice supervision. Ten years ago it was one out of four. At the current pace it will be one out of two in ten years or less, and one in one in 20 years. So, it boils down to whether we wait for criminalization as a norm to be fully accomplished or take political action to reverse the trend. Think about it. A society where just about all the men of a particular race either go to prison or have some type of criminal record.

The subtitle of this book 'The Fundamentals of Black Politics' suggests that there are some fundamental things to consider in the fight for rights and freedom. Political action doesn't start with a mass epiphany by the people which leads them to storm City Hall or some other government building. It starts with people changing the way they think about things — their consciousness. Whenever I'm in a discussion about the many dilemmas of being black in America and I start talking about consciousness, that's usually when folks' eyes glaze over. Yet sometimes you need a consciousness or understanding of history to get directions on how to move forward.

For blacks that direction comes from the Abolitionists and the Civil Rights Movement of the 1950-60's which were both freedom and rights movements. What black political focus ought to be about now and in the future is what we were about then — freedom and rights. This simple core consciousness is where it all starts.

Now, I am not talking about the resurrection of some sort of "black consciousness" kick. Identity politics, the politics of *what* or *who* you are pretty much amounts to defining yourself against your attackers by wearing the label that was pinned on you by them. What I am talking about is a working understanding of some very basic things. Like the meaning of equal rights. Or an understanding of equal treatment by government. And an understanding that the freedom and rights agenda has no expectation of "extra" rights, only "equal" rights under the law, equally applied as a core principle that we defend for ourselves and for

3

others such as gays, Latino immigrants and even those accused of being "terrorists" or "enemy combatants."

During the fight against a state constitutional amendment in South Carolina to ban gay marriage or gay civil unions, National Association for the Advancement of Colored People (NAACP) board chairman Julian Bond made a public pitch against the discriminatory bill, despite the fact that his organization was not formally weighing in on the matter. Bond never raised the issue with his board fearing "they would be on the wrong side of history." Bond was well aware of the widespread and unrelenting homophobia throughout the black community. Homophobia is particularly acute among black religious leadership. There also exists among many blacks the patently ignorant notion that "civil rights," or particular Amendments to the Constitution, are the exclusive franchise of blacks.

There are some new faces on the present political scene talking about turning the page on the past, like Barack Obama whose call comes at a time of diminishing influence of many older national black political figures. But before we turn the page, we should read and understand it. It's also fair to ask where new leadership leads us.

The underlying thrust of this book is to compare what people say and what they do in regards to black political, economic and social advancement in America. Are folk just "talking the talk" or are they "walking the walk." Even if you disagree with what I have to say or don't like how I frame, interpret or tell the lessons of my experiences, at least you'll have some idea where I'm coming from and going to.

Many of these essays are a critique of political and cultural behavior. Let me clarify certain terms I'll use, for example, the admittedly confusing and tricky term *black politics*. The gathering of this anthology was sparked by the frequent question, "what's wrong with *black politics* these days?" The question implies that black leadership is doing something wrong or doing nothing, which is also wrong.

In my opinion, the simplest use of the expression *black politics* denotes the advocacy of African-American political and economic rights. Accordingly, advancement of these rights impacts the social and psychological well being of blacks. Political scientist Rickey Hill gives the best operating definition of *black politics* as "...the purposeful activity of black people to acquire, use, and maintain power. The dimensions of black politics are internal and external. They characterize a struggle for power, that is, the realization and defense of black people's interests and volition. This struggle for power reflects historical tensions and constraints between and among black people and white people. These tensions and constraints, concerning optimum strategies for control and liberation, are grounded in the dominant-dominated relationship of the two groups."[1]

I would add that *black politics* seeks to change how whites think and respond to supremacy and dispossession. Success or "walking the walk" is measured by conscious, recognizable, race-specific changes in politics and policies.

So, I wouldn't measure the political progress of blacks by, let's say, a black man being considered as a realistic presidential candidate, unless the outcome resulted in conscious, recognizable, race-specific changes in politics and policies. Abraham Lincoln's Emancipation Proclamation meets these criteria. So does Lyndon Johnson's Great Society Programs and his initiation of what is now commonly referred to as 'affirmative action." Which, by the way, Johnson described as "conservative reparations."

Now, none of what I've said is new stuff. Much of it was part of our understanding of why we did our first sit-in, march, boycott, protest, or walk-out. It's why we support certain organizations and people and are against others. *Black politics* has a goal. It is the dominated group's response to the dominant group's racism and white supremacy. The impact of structural white supremacy and racism was and is evidenced by the presence of group disparities. So change, as it relates to *black politics*, begins from a deficit caused by white supremacy and racism. Change is the advancement of equal citizenship and economic rights of blacks and a measurable erosion of individual and group dispossession.

Thus, *black politics* can be viewed as the countermove by the dominated class/group in reaction to *anti-black* politics. *Anti-black* politics and the resulting policies and laws revolve around maintaining dominant structures and institutions of white privilege and hegemony. *Black politics'* ultimate goal is a condition of economic, social and political parity with the dominant group. The phenomena of disproportionate poverty, lack of business ownership and opportunities, premature death rates and other social maladies will hopefully lessen under conditions of parity. Political parity can be proportional representation in electoral and governmental bodies. Economically it may be achieved by equal and fair access to capital, credit and wealth and limitations on predatory or exploitative lending, income and neighborhood redlining and obtainable and sustainable home mortgages. Black advancement starts in a deficit and progresses toward parity. Inculcated in the idea of parity is the elimination of privilege, which is unearned opportunity. For example, under the current setup government gives builders, developers and banks the privilege to exploit the dream of owning a home without a care as to whether or not homeowners can sustain the cost of shelter and hold their families together. A new setup would have government focused on keeping people in their homes and keeping families and communities stable. That might require another American Homestead Act. At the very least, it immediately requires a legislative revisit to the dramatic anti-consumer changes in the bankruptcy and foreclosure laws enacted under the Bush Administration. Or, consider a rollback on the number and types of credit card and bank fees. Or end special tax privileges to the national banks that have replaced their domestic workers with a cheaper foreign work force or just enough automation to insure you'll never reach them on the phone to complain. These instances where government protected the privilege of a few to make huge profits versus promoting sustainable communities have not only economically weakened the black community; whites now feel the blows as well.

Achieving parity is not a silver bullet solution. It's merely a step in the right direction. Parity would provide more resources to blacks. Out of desperation in the face of the present public school system's failure, many black legislators are lobbying for parity meaning 'funding equity' or equality. It means on balance (on a cost per student average) that all public schools are equally funded. Who can argue with equality of school district funding? But a story I once heard Jesse Jackson tell gives a cautionary note. He spoke about one of his kids when he was younger asking him did he love all his kids equally. Jackson responded, "I love each of ya'll adequately." Given that many schools and kids start with a deficit we might want to consider adequate funding as opposed to equal.

As president, Bill Clinton supported various pieces of crime legislations that had a negatively disparate effect on blacks. In the course of his career Clinton supported and passed a number of initiatives and laws that could be considered *anti-black* in effect and rejected measures to ameliorate problems. Clinton turned his back on his friend and law professor Lani Guinier for a post at the Justice Department over the issue of proportional representation and cumulative voting. Then and now, many believe that the voting schemes advanced by Guinier will lead to greater voter participation by blacks. Clinton called the plan "anti-democratic." But in reality, Clinton was probably more concerned with the method's impact on the selection of white Democrat office seekers. This is what anti-black politics is all about. *Anti-black* politics is how the institutionally and structurally dominant group protects its turf.

Anti-black politics results in an erosion or denial of (1) equal protection or treatment, (2) due process of law, and (3) equal opportunity or access to publicly-owned institutions and organizations to individuals based on their group status. *Anti-black* politics with its restrictive covenants limited where blacks could live. It kept blacks from applying for HUD home loans. Now it's coding black and working class families out of the city while giving whites incentives to move in. It is present whenever a criminal defendant has to make roll call at the courthouse day after day until he is forced to plea bargain. *Anti-black* politics is there when a prosecutor strikes a black or black sympathizer from the jury box. It's in the government-run lottery, where a hopelessness tax on blacks, the poor and desperate, funds the college educations of upper income white kids while the majority of black kids can't even get a high school diploma.

A*nti-black* politics also results in a denial of justice — both economically and constitutionally. Justice is the state achieved when wrongs are righted. Justice (and peace) is maintained when people are protected from wrongs. Nonetheless, if the first 3 rights — equal protection or treatment, due process of law, and equal opportunity — are withheld, diminished, ignored or eliminated, and restitution is still owed, one lives in an unjust society. Fighting for instatement or observance of these rights and the injustices and consequences caused by these denials, are what black politics and its predominant social movements — Abolitionism and the Civil Rights Movement of the 1950-60s are about. Effectiveness in securing or protecting core citizenship rights is how we measure the everyday work of black political organizations and actors. Securing or protecting those core rights is surely more important than trying to stop people from saying the word 'nigger' and having mock funerals for the same.

Anti-black politics and racism are synonymous. For example, the law in many localities can, and often does, require certain criminal defendants to make roll call. The law as written does not say so, but most of those defendants will be black. Same as with state-run lotteries. The lottery is a legal game. The fact that the players are disproportionally poor and black and there is no significant economic return to the group makes the scheme anti-black.

I differentiate between the terms *race politics* and *black politics*. *Race politics* is just one of the many tactics of *anti-black* politics used to protect white supremacy. The term *race politics can also be applied to other racial or ethnic groups*. But American history suggests that blacks were the original target for codified, structural dispossession and disenfranchisement as a group. No doubt, in the past, white women were denied the right to vote and suffered other structural inequities. Although they may have been treated like slaves in their homes they were never codified by law as chattel. They also retained some property or inheritance rights. Blacks are the prototype for the denial of rights and the idea of being less than human in an American context — the genocide of the Native Americans notwithstanding. In my usage, *race politics* is a negative tool of electoral politics as in the indictment, "he [or she] played *race politics*" — openly and consciously playing on race fear by the use of racial cues or to intermix such issues as crime, poverty and welfare with race, with the intent to inflame white opinion or shame blacks.

Another term to consider in discussions of *black politics* is "equal opportunity" — what does it mean and how can it be achieved. Equal opportunity is the legal right — of all citizens, regardless of group status or race, to fulfill their economic, educational, social potential, etc., free of artificial or contrived legal impediments.

The current equal opportunity deficit faced by African-Americans is linked to the property rights debate. The argument goes that enslaved Africans, and later, African-Americans, were denied the equal opportunity to inherit, produce, consume and bequeath property or wealth, resulting in an inheritance of disparity. Black children in effect start life with an economic and social deficit that makes "equal opportunity" meaningless. Obviously, equal opportunity would not be a problem if blacks equal protection or treatment and due process rights were observed. "Reparations" or "restitution" to descendants of enslaved Africans might or might not solve the problem. Black support for affirmative action and to a lesser degree, reparations for slave descendants, has remained constant through the decades. When asked do I support reparations my answer is yes. To believe no debt is due the descendants of slaves is to believe that the promissory note that King spoke of has been paid. In reality America hasn't made good on the bounced check that King demanded payment on years ago.

America must decide what kind of country it wants to be. Will the future promise a diverse and inclusive nation, or a sectarian and separate one? Do we want a public school system or a proliferation of church and private schools? We have to choose. For me, it's simple. If you're inclusive you open up the process, if you're exclusive you shut people out. Education is the 'great equalizer'. Benjamin Franklin put it best when he offered that the goal of public education is social "mobility, not nobility."

No doubt, the need for radical educational reform persists. When speaking about integration Malcolm X joked, "Now, you can sit down next to white folk on the toilet. That's no revolution." The victory isn't black kids sitting next to white kids in class. Public school desegregation was an attempt to dismantle a facet of structural dispossession. Contained in dispossession is denial of a group's history and value to a society. Consequently, a psychological goal is to insist that black kids have value, not as undeveloped "whites," not as "at risk", but as humans. As a black man in his sixties said to me when we spoke on the subject,

"Whites have to learn to understand that while you may be ahead of me you are not over me."

So here's the recap. *Black politics* and the organizing that takes place around it is about political self-defense in a broader sense. It involves protecting the rights and self-interest of the minority against the whims and biases of the majority. I believe that notion is at the core of the human rights agenda. That's why it is important to have an appreciation of the Constitution. There are a number of things that separate us, such as race, gender and religion, but the Constitution is what we all have in common as Americans. The Constitution remains the civil and human rights community's most potent organizing document.

There must be an acknowledgement of the power relationship between the dominant and dominated as the root organizing perspective. As political scientist Rickey Hill states, *black politics* operationally is "the purposeful activity of black people to acquire, use, and maintain power." I add that it is the counter to anti-black politics. *Anti-black* politics is denial of core citizenship or human rights. We judge the effectiveness of black leadership based on what they extract from the dominant group or how effective they are in eroding white privilege and the disparities caused by it. We cheer or boo white politicians based on their responses to *anti-black* measures or laws or legislation that has a disparate, negative racial impact. *Black politics* in its most positive sense continues to revolve around fighting white denial and privilege and its impact on racial disparities.

My model of *black politics* relates to my experience and my understanding of black political struggle. I hope the model can be applied to other group of individuals who find their core human and citizenship rights under assault. Simply replace black with human or gay or Latino or those of Arab descent or Native American. But the critical thing that must happen before the human rights movement in America can be re-started is for the dominated to realize a common struggle and band together in coalition. Then we can turn a page or two.

Lastly, my political orientation is rooted in the history of it all. It comes from living in the South and being black. It comes from cheering Thurgood Marshall, Oliver Hill, the NAACP and others as they fought the desegregation battles. It comes from my mother who chucked me in the middle of it. It comes from seeing my father walk the Steelworkers' Union picket line in the South in the late-sixties when it wasn't a safe thing to do. As a young boy I was proud of seeing him with a sign demanding better pay. My feelings about the criminal justice system stem from an inestimable number of visits to chain gang camps and work farms, city and county jails, state and federal prisons, courtrooms of all types — traffic, magistrate, city and county bond, bankruptcy, General Sessions, preliminary hearings, police hearings, public hearings and a million government hallways along the way. You name the proceeding or type of facility and I've been in it. I've sat, stood, hugged, held back and spoken for countless family members, relatives, friends and folks just needing support. I've soothed and counseled folks accused of just about every type of charge in the books. Knowing death row inmates and their families, having family members who have killed, and seeing the dead bodies of young black men killed under suspicious circumstances — either by the police or the Klan — have only reinforced my opposition to violence, be it state-sanctioned or in any other form.

I am haunted by the memory of many friends who shot, hung or poisoned themselves rather than face themselves and the homophobia of people in their communities. And friends who all of a sudden disappeared from the scene only to read in their obituaries that they died of pneumonia, kidney failure or some other form of death more socially acceptable than AIDS.

I can't remember a specific moment when I declared that the civil and human rights battle was the one I wanted to spend my life fighting. In the beginning I had a modest desire to work with people who worked with King. In the late seventies, Ralph Abernathy (father and son) and Golden Frinks as the SCLC breathed its last breathe started me on the quest that ended me with Jesse Jackson and the Rainbow effort in the late eighties.

I tell people on the stump that my politics are rooted in family. That when you approach a political problem with love instead of scorn the people you hope to change or influence accept the admonitions with a different heart and mind.

Endnotes

1. Rickey Hill, "The Study of Black Politics: Notes on Rethinking the Paradigm," in
   Black Politics and Black Political Behavior, edited by Hanes Walton, Jr. (Westport:
   Praeger, 1994), p.11.

Dixie 101: South Carolina's Heritage of Slavery

THROUGHOUT AMERICAN HISTORY, SOUTH CAROLINIANS HAVE led the fight to preserve and defend slavery, white supremacy, racial segregation, and race fear. This is the "heritage" that African-Americans see defended by modern day neo-Confederates. Although Virginia had the largest population of enslaved Africans and Richmond was the capital of the Old Confederacy, South Carolina was and is the soul of the old and new Confederacy. South Carolina gave birth to Dixie. It is a matter of pride to many South Carolinians living today that their home was the first to secede from the Union on December 20, 1860, and that the first shot of the Civil War was fired by Citadel cadets at Fort Sumter in Charleston harbor on April 12, 1861.

South Carolina's singular role in United States history is as a conduit for the growth of slavery. Between 1700 and 1775, forty per cent of all enslaved blacks came to America through South Carolina. As Ellis Island in New York was the first stop for many Europeans entering the New World, Sullivan's Island was the first stop for many Africans who were brought here against their will.

During the early colonial period North and South Carolina were simply Carolina. Old Carolina extended from the southern border of Virginia to the northern border of what is now Florida and as far west as the Mississippi River. The area became separate colonies in 1729. Later, the states of Mississippi, Alabama and a significant portion of Georgia were ceded from South Carolina. So it was essentially the territory of Old Carolina, along with Virginia, that left the Union to form the Confederacy. Slavery extended across the southern United States following the boundaries of and out-migration from Old Carolina. The Civil War eventually erupted because plantation owners and other enslavers — to include breeders, merchants, insurers, pirates, advocates, politicians and the like — wished to protect and promote that particular type of growth.

South Carolina played a leading role in providing enslaved Africans during the westward expansion. The state provided over 20,000 enslaved blacks to the territory secured after the Louisiana Purchase in 1803. Prior to the Civil War, as many as 179,000 black Carolinians went west with their masters creating more slave states and territories. After the importation of enslaved Africans was prohibited, South Carolina and Virginia carved out niches as slave-breeding states to keep up with the demand. Research reveals that fully a third of the profits of planters in the older regions of the South were derived from breeding slaves for sale in the interstate trades. Consequently, southern plantation owners encouraged the westward expansion of slavery to increase their wealth.

Many of the Founding Fathers held the belief that slavery would die a natural death over time. While many of the signers of the Declaration of Independence held enslaved blacks, at least they kept the bar high by declaring that "all men are created equal...," In both the Declaration and the Constitution, the words "white" and "slavery" were consciously omitted from the documents. Still, economic realities negated any hope or claim that slavery would have died a natural death. From an ideological viewpoint, most whites believe blacks to be inferior. Economically, slavery and the plantation system provided the South with a high rate of economic growth between 1840 and 1860. Slave plantations were more efficient than free farms. The mythic notion is that Southerners fought the Civil War to "defend the land" — a notion linked to an irrational attachment to agriculture as opposed to manufacturing. The reality is that planters were "profit-oriented, premeditated and rational in their exploitation" of enslaved blacks. Slavery concentrated economic power in the hands of the few. The few wanted the federal, state and local government to protect their privilege and wealth. John Caldwell Calhoun openly hoped that the "Nation of Carolina [would] continue to hold Negroes and plant cotton til the day of judgment." He called slavery a "positive good" and declared, "It is a great and dangerous error to suppose that all people are equally entitled to liberty." Fellow South Carolinian James H. Hammond affirmed, "Society must have a class to perform the drudgery

of life..., a class requiring but a low order of intellect..., a class that constitutes the very mud-sill of society." Today, Hammond Academy, a popular
private school in Columbia, bears Hammond's name and continues to
educate the children of the state's economic elite.

Today's race politics in America owes much to South Carolina. In
the 1800s, South Carolinians Thomas Cooper and Calhoun provided
the pseudo-intellectual framework for slavery. Calhoun always deserves
special mention in any account of race in America. He instigated the
"myth of Mandingo" which still lives today. The big, black, rebellious,
Mandingo buck stereotype underlies current racial apprehensions,
criminal justice practices, law enforcement policies and foreign policy.
Calhoun, who served as Secretary of War under James Monroe and Vice
President under both John Quincy Adams and Andrew Jackson, was the
leading intellectual of the Southern gentry. The Abbeville native used the
myth of the rebellious black to advance harsh slave codes, the ideology of
white supremacy and racial fear. In the myth of Mandingo, some white
slave owners were led to believe that Mandinkas were the fiercest warriors of Africa. Calhoun invoked the specter of the "Mandingo" slaughtering white masters as justification for perpetuating slavery. Calhoun
and others conjured Caribbean rebellions, such as the overthrow of the
French by Toussaint L'Ouverture and his fellow Haitians in the 1790s, as
the spawn of the unmanageable "Mandingos." This fed the southerners'
fear of blacks brought in from the Caribbean. While communism is often
used as a reason for poor relations, one can trace racism in United States'
foreign policy toward both Haiti and Cuba to fears of slave revolts, rebellious blacks, racial supremacy and plantation economics. United States'
hostility towards Cuba and Haiti is an extension of Calhoun's influence.
For some, this partly explains why black Haitians are routinely denied
access to the United States and why America remains at odds with Fidel
Castro's Cuba.

In the 1970s, the myth became the movie "Mandingo" in which one-
time heavyweight champion Ken Norton played a noble savage who
burns down the white man's plantation and escapes to freedom with
the lovely blonde lass in his arms. Rap music fantasies of the ruthless
and fearless gangsta are an incarnation of the "Mandingo" myth. 1990s

criminal justice legislation provides an excellent illustration of how the Mandingo specter still haunts our politics. Why else would something as ridiculous as taking exercise equipment out of prisons be included in supposedly serious legislation? Representatives acted on the hysterical fear that all black criminals do behind bars is pump iron, get big, then go out and beat up police. Translation: Mandingo!

Slavery, white supremacy and racial oppression are deeply woven into the fabric of South Carolina's history and daily life. The names of those who initiated the slave economy, Confederate heroes and those who dismantled Reconstruction adorn counties, buildings, roads, schools, monuments and the like. For most South Carolinians, the names of white southern patriarchs are integrated into their daily travels. The average citizens may not know the exact words or deeds but the names are engraved in their minds. Henry Laurens secured the state's status as a national and international slave market in 1748. Robert Rhett Barnwell and General Wade Hampton promoted and defended secession and the Confederacy. Governor Francis W. Pickens ordered the batteries to fire on Fort Sumter. Benjamin Ryan Tillman, a virulent white supremacist, constitutionally (and otherwise) reinstituted white rule after Reconstruction. "Pitchfork" Ben, as a member of the Sweetwater Sabre Club, drove black militiamen out of Aiken and his home county of Edgefield at gunpoint. Seven blacks died in the episode. Tillman and his fellow Red Shirts' murderous exploits in the summer of 1876 are enshrined in South Carolina history as "the Hamburg Riot." The white shirts stained in red and worn by Tillman's compatriots represented the blood of black men. But there were not just riots in Hamburg that year. The Red Shirt and other anti-black campaigns produced race riots in Charleston, Cainhoy and Ellenton where five whites and thirty-nine blacks were killed. The tension and terror prompted federal troops to be sent to the state. In 1881, over 5,000 blacks left Edgefield for Arkansas in a mass exodus because of labor exploitation and racial violence. Tillman's heir, James Strom Thurmond, rose to prominence in 1948 with the emergence of the States Rights Democratic Party — Dixiecrats. As Governor, Thurmond stood for segregation and against race-mixing. He warned that the Truman Administration was "demanding abrogation of our state laws providing for the separation of the races." Throughout his career Thurmond opposed almost every major civil rights initiative put forth. All these men hold a place of honor in the hearts and minds of many white South Carolinians. Statutes of Hampton, Tillman, Thurmond and a Confederate soldier guard the Statehouse grounds.

Long before the Tuskegee syphilis experiment on 399 black men from 1932 to 1972, there was James Marion Sims, the "father of gynecology" who established America's first women's hospital. Sims founded the Women's Hospital of the State of New York and the Cancer Hospital now known as the Sloan-Kettering Cancer Center. The doctor and slaveowner was born in Lancaster County in 1813 and died in 1883. The inscription on his Statehouse memorial reads:

> He founded the science of gynecology, was honored in all lands and died with the benediction of mankind. The first surgeon of the ages in ministry to women, treating alike empress and slave.

Yet before Sims treated the white and wealthy, he experimented on enslaved black women. In 1845, Sims was an Alabama plantation physician who took an interest in the female reproductive tract. Behind his home office he built a small hospital to perform his experiments. Enslaved women unable to perform work were granted to his custody by plantation owners. Over the course of four years, he performed some 40 operations for fistula repair mainly on three women: Anarcha, Betsy and Lucy. Anarcha, 17 years of age when she was sent to him, was Sims' main subject. Historical records reveal that Sims performed over thirty-four experimental operations on her for a prolapsed uterus without anesthesia or antiseptic. As the operations became more horrendous, local doctors refused to help Sims. Sims resorted to having the sufferers themselves help with the operations. He maintained that enslaved black women were willing collaborators in his work although the women who submitted left no account of their ordeals.

The Statehouse grounds are crowded with statutes of white men but the memory of the rebellious black haunts modern Confederates. The Citadel, the state-run military academy in Charleston that was recently forced to accept women, was built in 1825 after the Denmark Vesey insurrection of 1822. Construction of the Citadel arsenal (officially founded as a military academy in 1841) was to protect whites from "an enemy in the bosom of the state." In 1999, a majority-white committee was given the task of coming up with a memorial for the Statehouse grounds that would recognize the legacy of slavery. The Vesey conspiracy was one of the most elaborate slave uprisings on record. It involved thousands of blacks in and around Charleston. In the end thirty-seven blacks were hanged. Vesey and his five aides were hanged at Blake's Landing in Charleston on July 2, 1822. To many, Vesey is in the tradition of Revolutionary War hero Patrick Henry who shouted "give me liberty or give me death." In spite of that, the committee refused to recommend that a statute of Vesey serve as that recognition because "he advocated killing whites."

As Confederate heirs pass on the myths, legends and symbols of southern heritage, there is an attempt to revise or rewrite history in a way that erases, clouds, distorts and denies the truth of South Carolina's foundation. The truth of the Civil War is not all that obscure. The war's fundamental cause was about the right to breed, own and sell enslaved humans throughout the United States. Slave owners believed enslaved blacks to be property and that the national government was infringing on their right to do what they wanted to do with that property.

The 21st century began with an effort to fortify the symbols of the Old South. Throughout the course of the last century, the Confederate battle flag of Northern Virginia, or the "Naval Jack," has increased in popularity as a symbol of rebellion and white solidarity. Its supporters claim that it represents chivalry, honor and "defending the land." They say that it represents the "Southern way of life." This group often maintains a nostalgic vision of plantation life as grand and elitism as good. Others simply believe that the flag stands for a rebellious spirit, being against big, tyrannical government and for the underdog. Many in this group say, "my ancestors did not own slaves" or, "it was a rich man's war and a poor man's fight." Their farmer ancestors "fought because they had to — not because they wanted to," but, "they bravely fought." This is perhaps true for some, as many were drafted into service. Some yeoman farmers and middle-class whites complained that they were paid and treated the same as "niggers" — the Confederacy paid a slave owner $11 per month for the use of a slave's labor — the same pay as a white private. Yet South Carolina's enlistment rate was extremely high. In 1860 there were only 60,000 white males of military age (eighteen to forty-five). Records show that by 1864, 60,127 responded to the Confederacy's call.

Furthermore, slavery was widespread in South Carolina. The state had the highest percentage of slaveholders in the nation. In 1860 almost half (45.8 per cent) of all white families in South Carolina owned enslaved blacks. Thus, it is likely that many with ties to the state who protest that their ancestors did not own enslaved blacks are wrong. This is not to suggest that all whites in the South, numbering around 8 million at the time of the Civil War, generally enjoyed the benefits of slave labor. Three-fourths of white southerners did not own slaves. The highest concentration of enslaved blacks (and wealth) was in the hands of a relatively few number of slaveowners. In 1860 there were 384,884 slaveowners, 26,701 lived in South Carolina. 200,000 owned five enslaved blacks or less. Over one-half of enslaved blacks worked on plantations with holdings of more than twenty enslaved blacks, and at least 25 per cent of enslaved blacks lived on plantations with an excess of 50 slaves. 1,646 South Carolina planters owned more than fifty enslaved blacks; in the fifteen slave states only 13,770 did.

There was a direct relationship between slave ownership and wealth. The number of enslaved individuals held was included in the measurement of wealth. Enslaved blacks were counted as stock just like cattle or horses. It is estimated that two-thirds of the slave owners' wealth was in enslaved blacks and one-third was in land and buildings. The ten richest districts in South Carolina were more than 60 per cent black; the ten least prosperous districts were all-white. The cost of slaves varied from region to region, state to state and year to year depending upon demand and availability. In 1860, the average price of an enslaved black in the South was $900-1,200 ($16,350-$21,800) and the price of a prime field hand was $1,600 ($29,100) — [numbers in parentheses represent the cost today]. "Fancy girls" (who were most likely mulatto) sold for $1,600 ($29,100) or more. If an enslaved African could be used for breeding it often increased their value by $200. Slave merchants received a five to thirty per cent commission on each sale. And of course, the enslaved black was

valued per the amount of product yielded less the cost of feeding, clothing and shelter, which was minimal. The brutality and immorality of the
master class and the slave industry speaks for itself. Estimates set the life
expectancy of enslaved blacks at 30 years at age 20. Competition caused
many masters to push the slave to the limits of endurance and to pinch
on food, clothing and shelter.

Poor whites, or "crackers," "white trash" or "po buckras" as they
were scornfully called, were most often squatters or sharecroppers
who depended on the planters for work. If they were lucky they might
manage to get a job as an overseer on the plantation or as a slave catcher.
In spite of that, poor white conscripts fought to maintain the system that
they were competing against. The proudly proclaimed reason to fight
for many southerners not of the planter class certainly links to their
sense of racial superiority or the hope of one day becoming a member
of the planter class and owning slaves themselves. For the poorest white
dirt farmer, unable to compete against the plantation and slave labor,
his sense of pride and self-worth was based on "being better than a
nigger." The "abolitionist" north — the Yankees invaders — were going to
take that away that false pride and give blacks "equal" rights. Abraham
Lincoln, the "black Republican," as he was mockingly called in the South,
was going to deny any and all white southerners of the hope of one day
owning slaves.

South Carolinians' participation in the war and the resulting casu-
alty rate was extraordinarily high. Many states offered exemptions from
service as early draft laws permitted the hiring of substitutes. 7,050
Georgians and 15,000 Virginians paid others to fight and die for them.
Although South Carolina had more categories of exemption from service
than any other state — including the "twenty-nigger" exemption, which
excused from service an owner or overseer on plantations with twenty
or more enslaved blacks — only 791 South Carolinians sought exemptions. By the war end over 21,146 men had died — 35 per cent of South
Carolina's 1860 adult white male population (by contrast, only 4,129, or
1.05 per cent of the state's male population died in World War II). One
out of every nineteen white southerners died in the Civil War while
one in every fourteen South Carolinians was killed. Obviously, nobody

wants to believe or accept the fact that their ancestors fought the wrong fight. It is easier to say that they "fought bravely," "defended the land" or that their cause was "noble." Noble or not, South Carolinians promoted, then embraced, the cause of the Confederacy as fiercely as modern Confederates perpetuate the Cult of the Lost Cause.

Blacks and others insist that Confederate flags represent the states that fought to preserve slavery and racial oppression. To them the flags symbolize a privileged, landed class and white supremacy. They say that for whatever reason, those who fought for the Confederacy and under any of the many flags were against freedom. Moreover, since the end of the Reconstruction, through the Jim Crow era and even today, the "Naval Jack" has come to represent the hatred and terror of groups such as the Ku Klux Klan and the policies of bigoted politicians and demagogues. To African-Americans the flag signifies a "white man's country." Sadly, there are still many people shameless enough to attempt to promote such a vision.

White Man's Country

America (and South Carolina) has only been "a white man's country" as a matter of law, never as a matter of population. South Carolina's history is red, black and white. Indigenous people occupied the lands long before they were "discovered" by European invaders. Moreover, blacks were part of the earliest white or European incursions into the New World. Christopher Columbus is generally credited with initiating the Atlantic slave trade when he sent Taino Indian captives back to Spain to the displeasure of Queen Isabella who had not yet approved of the natives' enslavement. Nevertheless, Alonso Pietro, a mulatto, was pilot of the *Niña,* the ship on which Columbus returned to Spain on the first voyage. A free black African and enslaved Africans accompanied Columbus on his second and third voyages to the Caribbean. Most historians surmise that blacks reached the New World before the end of fifteenth century. Others, such as Leo Wiener and Ivan Van Sertima, insist that Africans came to the Americas between 800-700 BC (or earlier) and again in the 13th century. They point to the Egyptians, Malis and Mandinkas (among others) as being early explorers to the New World.

In the 1990s, a law enforcement practice known as racial profiling entered the public consciousness. Racial profiling is the practice of picking people out by race. Yet it is safe to say that the practice has its origins with the first enslaved Africans. The Portuguese get credit for beginning the wholesale enslavement and trade of Africans (although Africans were also the sellers of slaves). International commerce in Africans was initiated in 1441 when a Portuguese ship commanded by Antam Goncalvez kidnapped 12 Africans in a raid off the north Atlantic coast of Africa. The captives were given as gifts to Prince Henry the Navigator. The European slave trade began in earnest on August 8, 1444 when a cargo of 235 enslaved Africans was delivered to Lagos on the southwest point of Algarve, Portugal. The practice quickly spread to Spain, Holland, England and other European countries.

Portugal was the first European country to engage in the African slave trade and the last to abolish it. Yet, it did not become one of the principal countries to reap great profits from the trade in North America. The Portuguese Company of Cacheo was organized just as the British monopoly took hold. Others include the Maranhão Company and Pernambuco Company. The Portuguese involvement, under the auspices of the Pernambuco Company, is most noticeable in Brazil. The current Afro-Brazilian population, estimated at 70 million out of Brazil's 158,200,000 current residents, is indicative of the scope of the trade.

Enslaved Africans were with the Spanish conquistadors in the Caribbean as early as 1501. Nuflo de Olano and thirty enslaved blacks were with Vasco Núñez de Balboa when he reached the Pacific Ocean. Hernando Cortéz took blacks with him to Mexico and one of them planted and harvested the first wheat crop in the New World. Blacks were with almost every Spanish and Portuguese expedition to the New World — Alvarado, Coronado, Pizarro in Peru, de Vaca, de Soto, Ponce de León and Menéndez de Avilés in Florida, and many others. Estevanico (Little Stephen) is perhaps the best known of the early black explorers. He explored what is now the western and southwestern United States (New Mexico and Arizona) for the Spaniards.

In 1526, a Spanish expedition, which included enslaved blacks, landed on the South Carolina coast and founded the town of San Miguel de Gualdape. The failed settlement was the first European colony in what is now the United States. Port Royal and St. Helena, two early French and Spanish settlements in South Carolina, respectively, also had blacks in the population. The Spanish settlement at St. Augustine, Florida, used enslaved Africans from its founding in 1565. Spanish rulers granted direct license to individuals and groups such as the Cádiz Slave Company to sell slaves. The impact of African importation is evident in the racial composition of the Caribbean and Central and South America. The African heritage is profound in Cuba, Hispaniola (Haiti and the Dominican Republic), and Jamaica — three of the largest islands in the Caribbean. The Cuban population of 11,096,395 is 51 per cent mulatto (mixed-black, Spanish and native) and 11 per cent black. Hispaniola, Haiti, with a population of 6,884,264, is 95 per cent black, and the Dominican Republic, with a population of 8,129,734, is 11 per cent black and 73 per cent mixed. Jamaica, with a population of 2,652,443, is 94 per cent black.

Blacks-free and enslaved — were with the French as they explored Canada and the Mississippi Valley. They accounted for a substantial portion of the pioneers who settled the Mississippi Valley in the seventeenth century. Jean Baptiste Point du Sable, a French-speaking black, erected the first building in the place that became Chicago around 1790. French involvement in the trade is evident in the Caribbean where individual companies formed to sell slaves into the plantation economy.

The Slave Trade

> "We cannot forget that America was built on Africa. From being a mere stopping place between Europe and Asia or a chance treasure house of gold, America became through African labor the center of the sugar empire and the cotton kingdom and an integral part of that world industry which caused the industrial revolution and the reign of capitalism." — W.E.B. DuBois

The trade in Africans that grew into a big and essential business in the seventeenth and eighteenth century was dominated by the Dutch, French and English. The anchorages where slaves were obtained from Africa over the years extended from opposite the Canary Islands, all the way down the west coast of Africa, around the Cape of Good Hope (South Africa), to include Mozambique and Madagascar. Most of the ruling families of Europe licensed holding companies and received a share of the profits. The Dutch West India Company controlled the monopoly in the Dutch colonies of New Netherlands in the Hudson Valley, New Amsterdam and Manhattan Island (New York). Consequently, New York and New Jersey had the largest number of enslaved Africans of all the northern colonies. English control of the area led to a dramatic increase in the number of enslaved blacks.

At first, the English proprietors recruited poor whites to populate areas and cultivate crops in the New World. When the supply of those whites who voluntarily indentured themselves dried up, they resorted to kidnapping them. England quickly realized that white servants were unsatisfactory and insufficient. That is when they profiled blacks. Because of their color they could be easily apprehended and the supply from Africa seemed inexhaustible. In 1660, the Royal Adventurers was founded in London to take advantage of the profits in slaving. When the Royal Adventurers folded, the Royal African Company was chartered in 1672 by King Charles. For more than a half a century, this company dominated the English slave trade. The RAC brand was burned into thousands of slaves entering the colonies.

Money was the root of slavery. England came to dominate the slave trade and the success of its slave trading techniques is why it is most associated with the trade. The British had a system of trading posts around the world. Slaves were investment property. Consequently, the more slaves that made it to the plantation alive the better. The slave system was utterly brutal and inhuman. Still, the longer the slave lived the better. Insurance policies were taken out on the slave cargo. It is difficult to estimate (and there is wide dispute) the number of Africans imported into the colonies. Some place the overall figure slightly above 11 million; others guess the number to be higher. Nevertheless, getting the cargo to America as intact as possible meant greater profit. The agony of the middle passage from Africa could last as long as six weeks. Conditions on slave ship were monstrous. Enslaved Africans were packed in the

cargo hulls of slave ships like sardines in a can. Some captives committed suicide, some jumped over board the slave ships, parents killed their
children and husbands killed their wives. There was disease and the brutality of the ship's captain and crew. One in six died along the way. Once
in the New World, the plantation offered the most efficient use of slaves.
The French and Spanish plantation system in the Caribbean became
the model for the British. The plantation system produced rice, cotton,
sugar, tobacco and other goods for trading around the world. Except on
the rice plantation in coastal areas were enslaved blacks were given specific tasks each day, the gang system was used. Gangs of enslaved blacks
worked the fields under the direct supervision of an overseer or owner.
One slave was used per three acres of cotton. Consequently, the colonies
became the cornerstone of the English economic system and the slave
trade was the foundation.

Jamestown, established in 1606, was the first English settlement in
North America. Thirteen years later in 1619, twenty Africans were put
ashore at Jamestown by a Dutch man-of-war. The blacks who disembarked were indentured servants (although some believe a number were
enslaved — possibly kidnapped by pirates). Most of the transplants had
Spanish names like Antoney, Isabella and Pedro. According to records,
Antoney and Isabella married and in 1623 or 1624, Isabella gave birth to
the first black child born in English America. The child, William, was bap-
tized in the Church of England. In 1621 the *James* arrived from England
with a number of immigrants to include a black man named Antonio. In
1623 the *Swan* arrived with another black named John Pedro. According
to the first census of 1624-25, blacks constituted about 2 per cent of the
total population of 1,227. The twenty-three black settlers — eleven males,
ten females, and two children — lived in six of the twenty-three settlements in Virginia. Early black settlers owned land and servants, some
of whom were white. Anthony Johnson, who came to America around
1621, worked his indentured term and was granted 250 acres of land on
the basis of the headright system, which permitted planters to claim fifty
acres of land for each individual brought to the colony. In the following
years, Johnson and his relatives established one of America's first black
communities on the banks of the Pungoteague River.

Yet, by 1640, some Africans in Virginia had fallen into bondage for life. The statutory recognition of slavery in Virginia came in 1661 (although blacks were allowed to vote until 1723). In 1662, Virginia law set that enslaved status was according to the condition of the mother. Although the black population numbered 23 at first, by 1708 there were 12,000 blacks and 18,000 whites. By 1756 there were 120,156 blacks and 173,316 whites. Virginia had a larger population of enslaved blacks throughout the period of slavery (South Carolina had the second largest slave population) than any other state. Virginia also had its share of slave conspiracies, rumors of conspiracies, rebellions and individuals murdering their masters. The most noted revolt was that of Nat Turner in Southampton County in 1831. In the Turner insurrection sixty whites, including women and children, were killed. Fear of rebellion permeated the South. As a result, the slave codes were enacted to control the captive population.

Black slavery came into existence in Maryland around 1634. There were discussions in the legislature on the issue around 1638; and in 1641 the governor owned a number of slaves. Then, in 1663, the legislature attempted to declare as slaves all Negroes in the colony, even those free. It sought to impose slave status on blacks regardless of the status of the mother. It was not until 1681 that the law was brought back into accord with established practice. It declared that black children of white women and children born of free black women would be free.

Slavery existed in the New England colonies, but, the South's economy was far more dependent on slaves. Massachusetts was the first colony to give statutory recognition to slavery in December 1641. Other colonies followed: Connecticut, 1650; New York and New Jersey, 1664, Rhode Island and Pennsylvania, 1700; North Carolina, 1715; Georgia, 1750.

Slavery was protested and challenged from the start of the trade. It was protested in Europe, the Caribbean and South America. With the enforcement of legal slavery in the United States came legal protest from blacks and whites — both free and enslaved men — before, during and after the American Revolution. The first black legal protest in America was filed in 1644 by eleven blacks who petitioned the Council of New Netherlands (New York) for their freedom. They protested that they had "served the Company seventeen or eighteen years" and had been "long since promised their freedom on the same footing as other free people in New Netherlands." Their petition was granted by the Council. But in the years following the Revolution, racism, colonialism, religion and the ideology of white supremacy became validation for the practice of black enslavement.

Clearly, South Carolinians did not invent the slave trade. However, the state and its leaders served a pivotal role in the development of a trade that help finance the industrial revolution and the advent of world-wide capitalism. In 1846, Karl Marx contended that direct slavery is as much a pivot of industry as machinery, credit, etc.:

> Without slavery no cotton; without cotton no modern industry. It is slavery which has made the colonies valuable; the colonies have created world trade; world trade is the necessary condition of large-scale machine industry. Thus, before the traffic in Negroes began, the colonies supplied the Old World with only very few products and made no visible change in the face of the earth. Slavery is therefore an economic category of the highest importance. Without slavery, North America, the most progressive country, would be turned into a patri-archal land...

It was predestined that slaves would be introduced into the Carolinas as soon as possible. The proprietors received the territory by the royal charter of Charles II on March 24, 1663. The lord proprietors of the colony — John Colleton, William and John Berkeley, Anthony Ashley Cooper, George Carteret, George Monck, William, Earl of Craven and Edward Hyde, Earl of Clarendon, were in it for the profit. The examples of Maryland and Virginia convinced them that Carolina could prosper with plantation slavery.

In 1663, the original investors and settlers received twenty acres for every black male slave and ten acres for every black female slave brought into the colony that year. Anthony Ashley Cooper established the first successful settlement in the region that came to be South Carolina around 1669. In 1680 the settlers moved to the present site of Charleston (called Charles Town until 1783). The first settlement, made up of 130 English and a handful of Barbadians, was twenty-five miles from the sea on the south bank of the Ashley River. Over the course of the next two years about half the white settlers and more than half of the enslaved blacks came from Barbados. Twenty years after the original settlements, the black and white population was even. By 1715 the black population outnumbered whites, 10,500 to 6,250. Then in 1719, a rebellion in Charles Town overthrew the last proprietary governor. Five years later, in 1724 there were three times as many blacks as whites.

Royal governments were provided for both North and South Carolina in 1729, each with a governor and council appointed by the king and an assembly elected by the landowners.

By the time of the American Revolution, there were nine European ethnic groups represented in the state — English, Scots, French, Irish, Germans, Welsh and Jews. There was also a scattering of Dutch, Swiss and Swedes. Enslaved blacks helped them to drive out and exterminate the Catawba, Cherokee, Edisto, Etiwan, Santee, Savannah, Wateree, Waxhaw, and Westo natives (although many slaves ran off and consequently intermixed with some natives).

South Carolina whites were also particular about the ethnicity of their slaves. In Virginia, the only concern was whether or not a slave was an African or a Negro (Virginia born). In South Carolina though, there was a preference for what we now refer to as Sudanese who had been enslaved in the past by many other nations and people throughout history and were skilled in cotton cultivation. Still, Angolans accounted for 40 per cent of Africans imported into South Carolina over the years. Enslaved Africans were brought from seven regions of Africa; Senegambia, Windward Coast, Gold Coast, Bight of Benin, Bight of Biafra, Congo-Angola and Guinea. The ethnic groups and areas include Gambia, Mandingo, Jolanka, Bambara, Fulbe, Araba, Limba, Temne, Bola, Kisi, Coromantee, Fantee, Popo, Whydah, Nago, Ghari, Somba, Ibo, Calabar, Congo, Angola, Malimbe, Wollonga and Badongo.

It was English philosopher John Locke, who lived from 1632-1704 that provided a legal framework for enslavement. Locke is often credited with providing the Founding Fathers with the intellectual framework for the Declaration of Independence, Articles of Confederation and the Constitution. Locke also served as Thomas Cooper's secretary. In his *Fundamental Constitutions of the Carolinas* he wrote, "Every freeman of

Carolina shall have absolute power and authority over his Negro slaves, of what opinion or religion so ever." Although *Fundamental Constitutions* was never ratified, Locke's pronouncement not only sanctioned slavery but it protected it against future challenges that the conversion of slaves to Christianity might invoke.

As in Virginia and Maryland, South Carolina enacted slave codes to control their captives. South Carolina adopted the Barbadian slave statute in 1688. Under the code, blacks could not travel without permission of the master, although early on they could carry weapons and fought in the early Indian wars. Masters were cautioned against undue cruelty lest they spark a revolt. They were also prohibited from working slaves more than 15 hours per day (or dawn to dusk although it was common to work slaves overnight during certain months). Slaves wore proscribed clothing. Whites assumed that if the slave dressed like a white man the clothes were stolen. Still, the master, and whites in general, held total dominion over blacks. The master's rule and rules were often based on whim.

Africans opposition to their enslavement was natural and as early as 1711 there was white concern over slave revolts. In 1720, several slaves were burned alive after being implicated in a revolt near Charles Town. In the Stono Rebellion of 1739, twenty miles west of Charles Town, enslaved blacks killed two warehouse guards, secured arms and went on a full scale drive to destroy slavery in that area. It just so happened that Lt. Governor William Bull encountered the rebels on the road, outran his pursuers and spread the alarm. The uprising was crushed but not before thirty whites and forty-four blacks lost their lives. After the Stono uprising, masters were required to carry their guns to church on Sunday. A street in Columbia is named after Bull, and until recently was known to most South Carolinians as the location of the state mental hospital.

The large black population was a constant source of fear and apprehension for whites. By 1750, census estimates list the black population in South Carolina at 39,000 and 25,000 whites. The black population explosion was aided by those such as Henry Laurens. Laurens and his partner George Austen served as early agents for the Royal African Company collecting a 10 per cent commission for their services. Laurens, after having made his fortune, repented of his involvement in the trade and withdrew

Waiting for Lightning to Strike

from active trading in 1764. Still, by 1775, the eve of the Revolution, the black population of South Carolina was 104,000 compared to 70,000 whites.

The American Revolution and the Compromise of Slavery

Blacks were involved in the struggle for American independence from the beginning. Crispus Attucks, a former slave, was the first to be shot down in the Boston Massacre of 1770. However, when the Continental Army was formed, blacks were kept out. It was not until the British declared that all slaves who joined their side would be freed that most colonies changed their policy of exclusion. In 1779 the Continental Congress recommended that 3,000 Negroes be recruited in South Carolina and Georgia. The Congress was to pay the owners a sum no greater than $1,000 for each slave recruited; and at the end of the war the slave was to be set free and given $50. Georgia and South Carolina rejected the plan. Thus, each lost about 25,000 slaves, who ran off with the British, many settling in the Maritime provinces of Canada. Of the 300,000 soldiers who fought in the American Revolution, 5,000 were black.

The large black population gave South Carolina and other slave states plenty of reason to oppose measures to end the slave trade and slavery. If the slaves were freed and granted citizenship rights in South Carolina, they would represent a larger voting bloc than whites. It would also mean the end of the huge profits and a disruption of the plantation system. The slave states argued that they were "sovereign" and the decision whether or not to join the new Union was optional. This is the foundation of the states' right argument — an argument that modern Confederates routinely use to promote "heritage," and far-right and conservative politicians use to advance state autonomy or to limit the role of the federal government. Autonomy and limited central government are certainly legitimate concepts in spite of racial dynamics. But its first application was in the context of slavery.

> He [George III] has waged cruel war against human nature itself, violating its most sacred rights of life, liberty and property, in the persons

30

of a distant people who never offended him, captivating and carrying them into slavery in another hemisphere, or to incur miserable death in their transportation thither... Determined to keep open a market where men should be bought and sold, he has prostituted his negative for suppressing every legislative attempt to prohibit or to restrain this execrable commerce.

On July 2, 1776, this paragraph was removed from the Declaration of Independence at the insistence of Edward Rutledge, delegate from South Carolina. Rutledge threatened that South Carolina would fight for King George — against her sister colonies. He asserted that he had "the ardent support of proslavery elements in North Carolina and Georgia as well as of certain northern merchants reluctant to condemn a shipping trade largely in their own bloodstained hands." Prior to the Revolution, Rutledge moved in the Continental Congress to discharge all Negroes in the army.

Fearful of postponing the American Revolution, opponents of slavery, who were in the clear majority, resorted to compromise. Thomas Jefferson removed the anti-slavery language of the Declaration "in complaisance to South Carolina and Georgia, who had never attempted to restrain the importation of slaves and who, on the contrary, still wished to continue it." Thus, on July 4, 1776, the Declaration of Independence was signed in its fatally fragmented final form. The irony for African-American celebrants on Independence Day is that they, in essence, celebrate their ancestors' enslavement. Years later in 1787, during passage of the Constitution, James Madison reported to Jefferson that "South Carolina and Georgia were inflexible on the point of slaves." The only point where southerners showed flexibility was on the "three-fifth rule." To determine taxation and representation, five enslaved individuals were equivalent to three free men. Many argue that the Constitution, while not specifically mentioning slavery, validated the practice with the rule. Some see this as the reason behind the South's acceptance of the rule. Throughout the years, black leaders have proclaimed that the Founding Fathers tainted the American experiment by declaring "all other Persons" "three-fifths" human. In reality, Article 1, Section 2 of the Constitution limited the representative power of the southern states. The slave states wanted to count enslaved blacks as whole persons. Coincidentally, it would have created the condition whereupon enslaved blacks would have unwittingly aided in the expansion of slavery. The South would be able to send more pro-slavery representatives to Congress had enslaved individuals been counted as whole persons.

Various anti-slavery societies sprang up after the Revolution and a number of northern states moved to prohibit the traffic in slaves. In 1777, Vermont was the first colony to abolish slavery. By 1783, slavery was prohibited in Massachusetts and New Hampshire. Pennsylvania passed a gradual emancipation act in 1780. Connecticut and Rhode Island barred slavery in 1784 and were followed by New York (gradual emancipation) and New Jersey in 1799 and 1804, respectively. Still, the southern states, lead by South Carolina, Georgia and Virginia, sought to institutionalize the industry and spread it across the West. The south's reaction to northern industrial progress and westward expansion was to insist on strict enforcement of the Fugitive Slave Act of 1793. The 1793 act was the first federal fugitive slave law enacted by Congress. The measure made it a criminal offense to harbor a fugitive slave (even in free states) or prevent his or her arrest. Congress eventually banned the importation of enslaved Africans into the United States after January 1, 1808. Soon after, many southern states responded with illegal importation and breeding. As late as 1856, the governor of South Carolina, James Hopkins Adams, demanded a legal revival of the African slave trade. South Carolina began as a slave colony. After independence it became a slave state.

Looking at the past, it is easy to understand why South Carolina, Georgia and other Southern states cling to the Confederate flag. In 1961, the "Naval Jack," was raised over the South Carolina Statehouse. Georgia incorporated the battle flag into the design of its state flag in 1956. At the dawn of the modern civil rights struggle when racial change was one again in the air, Confederate descendants raised a symbol to remind us all of what their struggle was and is about. The flag represents a core belief in the supremacy of one race over another. Racial domination and separation is an undeniable part of the "South way of life." It is little wonder why the Confederate flag flew over the South Carolina capitol dome under government authority. This has been South Carolina's legislative history. There is very little difference in Klan rhetoric and that of heritage supporters inside or outside of government. If there is a difference it is of sophistication and costume.

States' Rights and the Civil War

Many African-Americans are familiar with the terms "interposition and nullification" through Martin Luther King's "I Have A Dream" speech. The words reach back to Calhoun's opposition to federal efforts to impose taxes and curb the slave trade. In King's 1963 speech, he speaks of the governor of Alabama, "his lips dripping with the words of interposition and nullification..." King was referring to southern opposition to desegregation and the southerners' claim that compliance to federal school and public accommodations desegregation orders were voluntary due to "states' rights." During the modern Civil Rights Movement white southerners maintained that they had the right to reject, or nullify, federal efforts to desegregate the South. Calhoun and his "Nullifiers," as they were called helped pave the way to the 1950s-60s conflict. They insisted, as did their predecessors, that the states were "sovereign" entities that had voluntarily agreed to form the Union. The "Nullies" saw the states as separate and independent. Calhoun was their standard bearer and he argued that if Congress exceeded its delegated power, say by imposing a tariff or placing limits on slavery, a state might interpose its authority to block enforcement of the law. This is nullification and the core of the states' right argument. In 1832, at the states' righters' insistence, the South Carolina legislature adopted its Ordinance of Nullification. In addition to codifying the "right to nullify," it required elected officials, military members and others to take an oath to obey and enforce the "Carolina Doctrine." The doctrine was invoked to defend and protect slavery in the 1800s and government-sanctioned segregation in the 1900s. It should come as no surprise that modern Confederates would oppose state and federal holiday efforts to honor Martin Luther King given his denunciation of states' rights and the principle of nullification.

Some take the autonomy or "sovereignty" claims a step farther. They argue (then and now) that if states have the power to declare themselves sovereign then local governments, even individuals, can also declare themselves free from the authority of government. Thus, the legitimacy to impose any tax, such as a property tax, is questionable. Much of the contemporary debate on property taxes (along with the legitimacy and enforcement power of the Internal Revenue Service) rest on this assumption.

Calhoun believed that if the Congress had the authority to pass protective tariffs, then there would be no limit to what else it could do. He was clear on the link between taxes and slavery — much clearer (and honest) than modern Confederates. He saw tariffs as the "occasion rather than the real cause of the present unhappy state of things." Southern economic and social institutions were based on the idea that a race of human beings was property. Blacks had no rights — human, civil or property. The Nullifiers wanted to use the power of the state to impose and enforce white privilege as a right.

Calhoun began his career as a federalist and if the federal government had protected slavery he probably would have remained a loyal nationalist. In 1846, Calhoun led the protest against the Wilmot Proviso. The amendment prohibited slavery and involuntary servitude in parts of the western territories (namely California and New Mexico). Calhoun, with his brand of federalism, contended that the territories were the common property of all the states. He argued that Congress had no power to deprive citizens of their right to migrate with their property to include enslaved blacks. Only the Compromise of 1850 saved the Union from an earlier civil war. The compromise was based on the notion of "popular sovereignty." This policy subsequently resulted in the Kansas-Nebraska Act of 1854. Both deferred the slave question to the residents of the new territory. Also included in the compromise, at South Carolina's vehement insistence, was the passage of the Fugitive Slave Act of 1850. The act, which called for more strict federal enforcement of existing fugitive slave laws, was nothing more than reaffirmation of the Fugitive Slave Act of 1793. Both set the precedent for the Dred Scott Decision of 1857. In the ruling, Supreme Court Chief Justice Roger B. Taney wrote that enslaved blacks "being of an inferior order" had "no rights which any white man was bound to respect."

South Carolina's role in strengthening, promoting and defending slavery did not stop in Congress and the courts. Across the state, thousands of dollars were raised to assist pro-slavery settlers in the territories. Companies of armed Carolinians shipped out for Kansas. In 1856, the "South Carolina Bloodhounds" of Beaufort, participated in a raid on the free-soil capital at Lawrence, where they seized the Free State Hotel and raised the Palmetto flag over it. The incident was a contributing factor in abolitionist John Brown's attack on Harpers Ferry, Virginia in 1859.

Throughout the contemporary debate over the Confederate flag flying on public property, proponents constantly profess their defense of heritage. Of course, there are the racists who enthusiastically promote race slavery and racial supremacy as good. But the [sophisticated] heritage defender is quick to say that the Civil War was about states' rights and sovereignty, not slavery alone. Some altogether dismiss slavery as a contributing factor to the war. There is a sense of denial and irrationality as they contend that the flag commemorates the idea of independence over a tyrannical, majoritarian government. Still, to understand what the Civil War was about, one need only read the Declaration of the Immediate Causes of Secession adopted by the secession convention in December 1860. South Carolina leaders made the preservation of slavery their main concern. States' rights are claimed to defend slavery. Slavery was "the cornerstone" of the Confederacy and the succession convention concluded with an invitation to form "a Confederacy of Slaveholding States."

On February 8, 1861, delegates from the seceding states of the South met in Montgomery, Alabama to set up a new government. The convention established a provisional government with Jefferson Davis as President and drafted a Constitution (enacted March 11, 1861). The most striking feature of the Confederate Constitution is the degree to which it resembles the Constitution of the United States and the ways in which it differed from the document. Added to the Confederate document was the language sanctioning slavery. Thomas Jefferson and other the Founding Fathers choose to omit language sanctioning slavery from the Declaration and subsequent historical documents. Whereupon the Founding Fathers used grand language such as "all men are created

Waiting for Lightning to Strike

equal," the Confederates felt no compulsion to be high-minded in their constitution.

> [Art. I, Sec.9] 1. The importation of Negroes of the African race, from any foreign country, other than the slaveholding States or Territories of the United States of America, is hereby forbidden; and Congress is required to pass laws as shall effectually prevent the same.
>
> 2. Congress shall also have power to prohibit the introduction of slaves from any state not a member of, or Territory not belonging to, this Confederacy...
>
> 4. No bill of attainder, or *ex post facto* law, or law denying or impairing the right of property in Negro slaves shall be passed.
>
> [Article. II, Sec. 1] The citizens of each State shall be entitled to all the privileges and immunities of citizens of several States; and shall have the right of transit and sojourn in any State of this Confederacy, with their slaves and other property; and the right of property in said slaves shall not be thereby impaired...
>
> 3. No slave or other person held to service or labor in any State or Territory of the Confederate States, under the laws thereof, escaping or unlawfully carried into another, shall, in consequence of any law or regulation therein, be discharged from such service or labor; but shall be delivered up on claim of the party to whom such slave belongs, or to whom such service or labor may be due.
>
> [Article. IV, Sec. 3.]3. The Confederate States may acquire new territory; and Congress shall have power to legislate and provide governments for the inhabitants of all territory belonging to the Confederate States, lying without the limits of the several States; and may permit them, at such times, and in such manner as it may by law provide, to form States to be admitted into the Confederacy. In all such territory, the institution of Negro slavery, as it now exist in the Confederate States, shall be recognized and protected by Congress and by the territorial government; and the inhabitants of the several Confederate States and Territories shall have the right to take to such territory any slaves lawfully held by them in any of the States or Territories of the Confederate States...

Both the Declaration of the Immediate Causes of Secession and the Confederate Constitution were clear on the importance of slavery. Just as clear was the ideological mindset for the design of the "official" banner of the Confederacy. There were many Confederate flags used during the war, as well as numerous regimental and company flags. In South Carolina, the red banner of secession flew over public buildings immediately after the secession announcement was made. The first unofficial flag (used in 1861) was the "Bonnie Blue," a single star in the center of a blue background. "Big Red," a red variation of the current state flag, was carried by Citadel cadets when firing the war's first shots as the federal ship *Star of the West* months before the attack on Fort Sumter. It remains the Citadel's flag. Up until 1980, Citadel cadets had adopted the "Naval Jack" as their flag. During sporting events, the rebel flag was waved as "Dixie" played to stir up the crowd. Public disapproval led to a discontinuation of the use of both, thus, many Citadel cadets and alumni now display "Big Red" on their cars, homes and businesses. Some are familiar with the "Stars and Bars" which looks like the American "Stars and Stripes." The "Stars and Bars," the first official Confederate flag, was used from 1861-1863. It was dropped because it was often confused with the "Stars and Stripes" on the battlefield. The "Stainless Banner" and the "Third National Flag" are official flags and their meaning was unambiguous. The "Stainless Banner" adopted in 1863, has a white background with the Southern Cross — an adaptation of the Scottish Cross of St. Andrews — in the corner. Of course, the lone Southern Cross was adopted as the "battle flag." Still, the white-background flag was chosen to represent "the fight to maintain the Heaven-ordained supremacy of the white man over the inferior or colored race…" The "Stainless Banner" was hailed as "the white man's flag" by those who promoted its adoption. The "Third National Flag" is a modification of the "Stainless Banner." A red bar was added to the design so that it would not look like a flag of surrender in the smoke-filled, pitch of battle. Adopted in 1865, it remains the official flag of the Confederacy. While contemporary controversy swirls around the "Naval Jack," it has never been officially adopted to represent the Confederacy. Its use was primarily as a naval flag during the war.

Figure 2-1 — 1st Confederate Flag — The Bonnie Blue

Figure 2-1- First National Confederate Flag
Adopted March 4, 1861

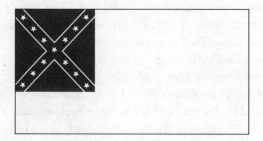

Figure 2-3 — Second National Confederate Flag
The Stainless White Banner
May 1, 1863 to March 4, 1865

Figure 2-4 — Third National Confederate flag
Since March 4, 1865

Figure 2-5- Battle flag

Figure 2-6 — Confederate Navy Jack after May 26, 1863

The Civil War began following southern secession. Consequently, Northern policies regarding emancipation evolved as part of the war strategy as did the use of black troops. Lincoln generally supported abolition throughout his career. Prior to the war Lincoln declared, "A house divided against itself cannot stand" and, "If slavery is not wrong, nothing is wrong." But like most whites he viewed blacks as inferior. He saw only race-conflict in America's future. Lincoln's solution to the black-white dilemma was to propose colonizing Central America, Haiti or Liberia with blacks. His primary concern was not the enslavement of blacks but the survival of the Union. He argued that slavery threatened white labor because it interfered with "the right to rise." He said that "advancement, improvement in condition — is the order of things in a society of equals." Lincoln favored homestead legislation that would provide small, cheap tracts of land (160 acres) within the common person's reach to help them gain economic independence. Plantation owners were against such legislation. In addition, Lincoln noted that other countries thought Americans to be "hypocrites" who touted freedom but practiced slavery.

On the one hand, Lincoln opposed slavery as a moral wrong. On January 1, 1863, three years into the war, he issued the Emancipation Proclamation. Now on the other hand, he privately claimed that the proclamation — a landmark in United States history — was merely a measure to help the North win the war. At first, Lincoln was opposed to the use of black troops. But it soon became apparent that "no human power" alone could crush the rebellious South "without the use of the emancipation policy." Abolitionist Frederick Douglas said, "The Negro is the key of the situation — the pivot upon which the whole rebellion turns... To fight against slaveholders, without fighting against slavery, is but a half-hearted business, and paralyzes the hands engaged in it." Abolition of slavery was a "military necessity." Lincoln used the phrase as he changed his policy. He also worried that the South would force slaves to fight on their side and that the additional black forces could change the course of the conflict to the South's favor. The Proclamation asserted freedom for enslaved blacks in areas under Confederate control and left slavery untouched in those areas under Union control. Lincoln wanted to maintain support in the slave-holding border states and court support from slave owners loyal to the Union in Kentucky, Delaware, Maryland and Missouri, therefore, he did not free their enslaved blacks. He also did not free enslaved blacks in New Orleans, Northern Virginia (the area later became West Virginia), much of Tennessee, parts of the South Carolina coast, and other areas of the southern states already under federal control. Several of Lincoln's generals attempted to emancipate enslaved blacks in their districts but each time Lincoln countermanded their orders. It was not until June 1864, four years into the war and a year after the proclamation, that Congress finally repealed the Fugitive Slave Act. On December 18, 1865, after Lincoln's death, Congress ratified the Thirteenth Amendment which abolished involuntary servitude. It was followed by the Fourteenth Amendment, ratified on June 28, 1868. It grants blacks citizenship rights. The Fifteenth Amendment, ratified on March 30, 1870, grants blacks the right to vote.

Both the North and South had black troops. Two regiments of free blacks formed in New Orleans — one fought on the side of the South and the other with the North. There were only a handful of blacks in the rebel army and navy because southerners were afraid to arm enslaved blacks. As the war progressed, some blacks simply walked off the plantation. Others sought refuge with Union troops. To prevent such occurrences, planters moved their enslaved black around and to the interior of the southern colonies to prevent runaways. Confederates used enslaved blacks to work in factories, mines, repair railroads and build fortifications so that able-bodied whites could be drafted in the military. Some of the wealthier Confederate officers took enslaved blacks to war with them but relying on the skills of enslaved blacks was risky. Case in point is the story of the black pilot and future member of Congress, Robert Smalls. On May 13, 1862, Smalls sailed with his family out of Charleston harbor on the Confederate steamer, *The Planter,* and delivered it to the Union navy. There was a later effort by the South to recruit free and enslaved blacks with the promise that enslaved blacks would gain freedom after the war. Confederate General Robert E. Lee approved of the plan and the Confederate Senate in the winter of 1865 passed a measure calling for the call up of 200,000 black troops. But the call was too late. Some argue that if the South had called or compelled blacks to fight earlier, a great number would have fought for the rebels. However, considering the numbers who ran away to fight for the North or the thousands of "contraband" — freed slaves — who left the plantations to greet Union troops, and the masses that followed behind the troops as they left an area, it is clear that enslaved blacks knew that the war was about their freedom.

The larger number of blacks fought for the Union and freedom. The first regiment of black soldiers came out of South Carolina in 1862. The First South Carolina Volunteers were under the command of General "Black David" Hunter. Hunter also issued a proclamation "forever" freeing enslaved blacks in South Carolina, Georgia and Florida but Lincoln revoked the early proclamation. By the war's end approximately 186,000 blacks had enrolled in the Union army. Ninety-three thousand came from the seceded states, 53,000 from the free states and 40,000 from the border slave states. To distinguish them from white soldiers blacks were organized into 166 all-black regiments (with 4 exceptions to include the 54th and 55th Massachusetts Volunteers) called the United States Colored Troops. The movie *Glory* with Denzel Washington and Morgan Freeman tells the story of the 54th Massachusetts Volunteers and their attack on Battery Wagner in Charleston. For his actions at the battle for Wagner, Sgt. William H. Carney became the first black to receive the Congressional Medal of Honor.

Black Union soldiers performed the same tasks as enslaved blacks did for the Confederates. They built fortifications, railroad lines and performed other wartime activities. When captured by the Confederates they were often killed as an example to enslaved blacks. Lincoln responded by issuing the "eye for eye" order. It warned the Confederacy that the Union would shoot a rebel prisoner for every black prisoner shot, and would condemn a rebel prisoner to a life of hard labor for every black prisoner sold into slavery. Blacks also spied for the Union army. Abolitionist Harriet Tubman, most known for her activities with the Underground Railroad, was a Union spy. Working in South Carolina and others states, she organized slave intelligence networks behind enemy lines and led scouting raids. Enslaved blacks hid Union soldiers who had escaped from Confederate prisons, sabotaged the war effort with work slow downs and told Union troops where valuables and equipment were hidden.

More than 38,000 black soldiers lost their lives in the Civil War. The estimated mortality rate among black soldier was nearly 40 per cent greater than among white troops. The high mortality rate was due to excessive fatigue, poor equipment, bad medical care, the haste and recklessness that they were sent into battle, and the "no quarters" policy (which was the refusal to regard them as soldiers fighting under acceptable rules of war) with which Confederates fought them. Confederates ordered thousands of captured black soldier killed.

Obviously, the North with more resources and men won the war. But prior to the war's end, Union General William Tecumseh Sherman and his 62,000 man army swept through Georgia and South Carolina. On November 15 1864, the day he left Georgia, Sherman wrote, "Behind us lay Atlanta, smoldering and in ruins..." He had occupied Atlanta for 10 weeks while his army rested and refitted. The beaten Rebel army had given up the city and headed for Tennessee. The Union Commander, General Ulysses S. Grant, had agreed to let Sherman march to the Atlantic Ocean. Sherman's aim was to make Georgia "howl" and to "purify South Carolina." His military objective for the area was clear — "the utter destruction of its roads, houses, and people will cripple their military resources." Sherman said that his army was "burning with an insatiable desire to wreak vengeance upon South Carolina." South Carolina and Georgia were the hard-liners that had to be broken. Many of those confronted by the Union troops were civilians, old men, women and children who could not fight, but who had supported the Confederacy with their resources and kin. The Yankees set out from Atlanta with wagons full of ammunition and cannons. They took most of their food from those they encountered in their sweep east towards Savannah. The soldiers took what they wanted and burned or destroyed the rest in a swath that sometimes reaches a width of 60 miles. The destruction Sherman's army wreaked on the way to Savannah made Georgia howl but it was mild in comparison to what a despised South Carolina faced. After leaving Savannah on February 5, 1865, the Union army took a direct line to Columbia burning property all the way. One soldier joked that the town of Barnwell should change its name to "Burnwell." Union soldiers reached the Congaree River and Columbia on the night of February 15. On the next day they began shelling the city. After a day of bombardment, the mayor of Columbia surrendered the city under the assurance that the city and its inhabitants would not be harmed. The city was burned to the ground, but not a single Columbian was killed. Sherman's army left Columbia on February 20 marching towards North Carolina. Their path of "purification" took them through Winnsboro, Camden, Chester, Cheraw and Florence.

Charleston, which surrendered on February 17, 1865, also experienced the torch. Most of the occupying force came from the 21st United States Colored Regiment. Black Charlestonians greeted the black troops with joy as they entered the city. But no scene was as dramatic as the thousands of blacks who followed behind Union General Edward H. Potter and his troops as they made their sweep from Georgetown to Sumter destroying the railroad and its rolling stock and burning cotton.

Adding insult to injury, and validating southerners race fears, Sherman issued his Field Order 15 setting aside "the islands of Charleston, south, the abandoned rice fields along the river for thirty miles back from the sea, and the country bordering the St. John's River, Florida," for the exclusive settlement by blacks. The order provided that "each family should have a plot of not more than 40 acres of tillable ground...in the possession of which land the military authorities will afford them protection until such time they can protect themselves." Later, the South Carolina Freedman Bureau settled some 40,000 blacks on 40 acre tracts in the area. This is the genesis of the restitution/reparation claim, or debt —"40 acres and a mule"—that many African-Americans argue remains unpaid.

Robert E. Lee surrendered to Ulysses S. Grant on April 9, 1865 at Appomattox Court House in southern Virginia. Black troops were with Grant that day as they had been throughout the siege of Richmond and Petersburg. Then, five days later on April 14, Lincoln was assassinated at Ford's Theatre in Washington by John Wilkes Booth.

Gray burns a Confederate flag and a Nazi swastika on the South Carolina Statehouse grounds to protest the flying the Confederate flag on the Capitol dome on May 10, 2000 — Confederate Memorial Day — photo by Mary Ann Chastain, AP

In a bit of irony, 135 years after his death, some "new" southern Republicans — who have more in common with the democrats of Lincoln's time, still see Lincoln as a race traitor. While campaigning in 2000, South Carolina Republican presidential candidate John McCain hitched his wagon to Confederate flag supporters. The editor of one of the many "heritage" publications that have sprung up in the past decade served as McCain's spokesperson in South Carolina. In the magazine, a full page is dedicated to Abraham Lincoln. Under Lincoln's picture are the words — "*Sic Semper Tyrannis,*" *("As Always to Tyrants")*. These are the words that John Wilkes Booth is said to have shouted after he assassinated Lincoln.

References

Lerone Bennett, Jr., *Before the Mayflower*
John Blum and et al. *The National Experience, A History of the United States, 2nd edition*
W.J. Cash, *The Mind of the South*

Waiting for Lightning to Strike

Walter Edgar, *South Carolina, A History*
John Hope Franklin, *From Slavery to Freedom*
John Locke, *Fundamental Constitutions of the Carolinas*
Karl Marx, *Letters of 1846-1860*
Milton Meltzer, Slavery: *A World History*
William Lee Miller, *Arguing About Slavery*
Kenneth O'Reilly, *Nixon's Piano*
David Robertson, *Denmark Vesey*
Ivan Van Sertima, *They Came Before Columbus*
Harold C. Syrett, *American Historical Documents*
Hugh Thomas, *The Slave Trade*
Leo Weiner, *Africa and the Discovery of America*
Arnold Whitridge, *No Compromise!*
C. Vann Woodward, *The Burden of Southern History*

The Intensification of
Racial Solidarity in the 1990s
in the Guise of Black Nationalism

"There's going to be dancing in the streets in black America because we have defied forces who sought to divide us." — Benjamin Chavis, [now former] Executive Director, NAACP[1]

URING A NATIONAL RAINBOW COALITION STAFF MEETING IN preparation for the 1992 Democratic National Convention, Jesse Jackson commented on what he saw as a possible outcome of the election of either Ross Perot, Bill Clinton, or George Bush: "All these candidates play the race card — which polarizes people. When people are afraid of what the future holds and unsure of their position in society, they retreat to something that is familiar and safe, they retreat to race."[2] It would seem that resurgent American pop culture's interest in what some have attempted to define as black nationalism might tend to support Jackson's assertion. However, in examining nationalism as the building of a geographically separate black nation, with a clear view of the ideological and programmatic implications associated with advocacy of a nation-state, one has to apply a more appropriate description to what may be occurring in African-American politics.[3] This study asserts from the onset that "intensification of racial solidarity" is the appropriate terminology for that which is occurring due to the radicalization of the African-American polity in the 1990s, not "increased black nationalism."[4]

This essay probes the distinction between racial solidarity and black nationalism. In describing the distinction, the study: (1) examines recent survey and polling data for indications of the existence of racial solidarity and/or black nationalism; (2) explores the validity of polling responses interpreted as indicative of black nationalism, and; (3) identifies and examines factors which may or may not substantiate radicalization, and seeks to suggest where it may lead black politics in the 1990s.

Measuring Nationalist Attitudes, Racial Solidarity, and "Discontent" Methods

To measure the depth and breadth of radicalization and its effect on racial solidarity, we examine the results of "Black Discontent: The 1993-1994 National Black Politics Study" (NVPS) by Michael C. Dawson of the University of Chicago and Ronald E. Brown of Wayne State University and the *CNN/Time* telephone poll of African-Americans conducted February 16-17, 1994. Both surveys were conducted exclusively with African-Americans.

In their quantitative study, Dawson and Brown attempt to identify indicators of discontent and growing nationalist attitudes among blacks in America. Released in April 1994, the NBPS consisted of a 45-minute telephone interview of over 1,206 randomly selected African-Americans from a national sampling base.

504 African-Americans participated in the *CNN/Time* national telephone poll. The sampling error for the poll is ± 4.5 percentage points. For some questions, results are given for a group described as "Those familiar with Farrakhan." This group includes all 364 respondents who did not say on Question 10 of the *CNN/Time* poll, that they were "not familiar enough" with Farrakhan to have an opinion of him. The sampling error for this category is ± 5.0 percentage points.

For additional support data, this study also uses the *CNN/USA Today*/Gallup Poll #5: "*Brown versus Board of Education* Retrospective" for its polling data on racial attitudes concerning the impact of public school integration.

This essay posits black nationalism as the territorial separation of blacks and whites, with the belief that the two races will never reach common ground or mutual respect. Separatism is synonymous with nationalism under this state. Black nationalism as an ideological construct involves demonstrative nation-building. It is against the ideology of separatism that we measure whether or not support for nationalism exists. While this study concurs with many of the NBPS's findings, the existence of separatist ideology begets a fundamental contradiction in expressing black political radicalization, and/or a desire for community control, as black nationalism. This essay aims to address the conceptual confusion that the terms black nationalism, racial solidarity, community control, and separatism, so often provoke among scholars, and in policy discussions and popular interpretations of survey data.

Racial Solidarity and Black Nationalism: Preliminary Considerations

Racial solidarity fundamentally has no ideological or programmatic implications beyond the desire of people (1) to organize themselves on the basis of their common color and their shared perception of an oppressed or threatened condition, and (2) to move in some way to alleviate that condition. For African-Americans, this forms the basis for what many attempt to define as the black community. Community control becomes akin to participation. Racial solidarity becomes evident when a racial or ethnic group makes electoral and/or socio-political decisions based primarily (but not solely) on racial group identification. In this light, racial solidarity can be interpreted as an irrational response to race-based oppression or tyranny. It is irrational because it is an acceptance of the very foundation of the oppressor's misconceptions and stereotypes of his victim. The foundation for the misconception is the misidentification of the victim's essence as being his color rather than his humanity. Liberation comes when the victim rejects color as the foundation of his identity and reclaims humanity as the essence of his self-concept.

Nationalism has ideological and programmatic characteristics. It entails nation-building in a demonstrative sense — economic, linguistic or geographic. The nationalist structure has seemingly consistent political outcomes because it most often contains an ideology accepted by its adherents. Comparatively viewed, the results of solidarity are politically inconsistent due to the lack of structure.

John Bracey, Jr., August Meier, and Elliott Rudwick provide the most often used topology of black nationalism [see Appendix A page 71 for complete topology]. They describe it as a body of social thought, attitudes, and actions ranging from the simplest expressions of ethnocentrism and racial solidarity to the comprehensive and sophisticated ideologies of Pan-Negroism or Pan-Africanism. Between these extremes lie many varieties of black nationalism of varying intensities.[5]

This inquiry uses the Bracey *et al* categorizations solely for the purposes of comparative analysis. The authors posit *racial solidarity as the simplest expression of racial feeling that can be called black nationalism*. It was Bracey *et al* who originally stated that racial solidarity fundamentally has no ideological or programmatic implications. One can agree that racial solidarity is an essential feature of black nationalism. However, since nationalism is only sometimes born of solidarity, nationalism is not an essential feature of solidarity. Solidarity distinguishes itself as a transitory state, not proto-nationalism. The difficulty arises when the authors attempt to define solidarity solely as a form of nationalism, leaving any or all actions of a group exposed to the charge of being *nationalist* in nature. This charge could and does give rise to an oppressive nationalistic response by the dominant political and social culture. Even if one were to accept the notion that being a member of an oppressed class brings with it a structured oppressed ideology or pedagogy[6], the acceptance of structure invokes nationalism. Acts of solidarity are observable, but those actions are not necessarily nationalist actions. In the absence of the nation-building prerequisite, defining a manifestation of racial solidarity as nationalism becomes invalid.

A multitude of contradictions can be raised as to the identity of nationalism, but advocacy of the nation-state is a necessary condition. Segregation, *de facto* or *de jure*, may create and support the conditions of a dual society. However, without nationalistic control of the sub-structure, nationhood can hardly be asserted — only segregation.

Identifying Racial Solidarity

Racial solidarity is perhaps a more utilitarian term for contemporary political and social scientists. Racial solidarity often manifests itself as support for a particular political candidate based solely on race, ethnicity, or shared membership in an oppressed class. It is often reflected in public opinion polls which highlight the vast socio-economic, cultural, and political differences that separate blacks and whites in America.

One of the most profound examples of racial solidarity is observed in the black press defense of Washington, D.C. Mayor Marion Barry as he faced drug possession charges. Washington political essayist Paul Ruffins is critical of the city's black newspapers for their lack of objectivity and accountability in covering "the tragedy of how a once progressive activist had been so corrupted by power, blinded by hubris, and disoriented by drugs that he gave his sworn enemies more than enough rope to hang him".[7] Ruffins accuses the black press of engaging in "reactive skin-color nationalism" and ignoring Barry's failings in favor of concentrating their fire on the racism of whites.

Ruffins's assertions are validated by comments from members of the Washington black press. Frances Murphy, the publisher of *The Afro-American*, stated, "Yes, we bend over backwards to give Barry the benefit of the doubt because so many others are bending the other way". The *Capital Spotlight* editor Barry Murray stated, "I'm a nationalist and I just don't accept the idea that I should be bound by the same editorial standards as *The Washington Post*."[8]

Ruffins argues that their blind support was motivated by a "bourgeois black nationalism that refuses to engage in critical analysis of black leadership" — however, Ruffins concedes that, given the substantial racism on the part of the mainstream media and the prosecution in the Barry case, there could be an argument for solidarity with Barry against a common enemy.[9] Ruffins correctly identifies racial solidarity as a component of support for Barry. However, he goes beyond the bounds of common sense when he ascribes the term nationalism to supporters of Barry. *Nation-building was not and is not a feature of the Barry administration* — the Barry administration represents governance and participation in the dominant political structure with financial support from the traditional mainstream business community.

The 1994 re-election of Barry, bolstered by democratic primary support from a lower socio-economic constituency base (i.e. inner-city blacks), illustrates the reality of racial solidarity against a common enemy. It was Barry against the political establishment — the "haves" versus the "have nots". Barry flirted with symbols of black nationalism throughout his resurrection process, inviting Louis Farrakhan to attend his trial, wearing Kente cloth and other African garb, and playing the role of the outsider. Without a doubt the political resurrection of Barry, consciously imbued with nationalist metaphors and symbolism, can be interpreted as a manifestation of the intensification of racial solidarity.

The distinction between racial solidarity and black nationalism concerns the existence of structure. Solidarity is transitory and lacks ideological or programmatic construct. Therefore, political outcomes can appear to be contradictory or dispersed. In the case of the Barry election, distinct racial economic and socio-political goals remain obscure. Barry elicited support by manipulating black nationalist symbolism to create a "who is blacker" aura around the election, however, it was not nationalism. Black nationalism is demonstrative and indicative of a belief in separatism and nation-building. This study posits, as was the case with the Barry election, that racial solidarity is intensified during periods of discontent. Solidarity is evidenced by cursory support for race conscious solutions. Discontent is easy to observe in polling responses because it expresses itself as dissatisfaction with societal conditions. The results of Figure 3-1 — questions D1, D6D and F21, contained in "Selected Indicators of Black Nationalism"[10] on the NBPS, provide clear illustrations of racial solidarity and the inconsistency it can produce.

Figure 3-1 — Selected Indicators of Black Nationalism
[Racial Solidarity]

1. (D1) Do you think what happens generally to black people in this country will have something to do with what happens in your life?

	%
A lot	36
Some	32
Not very much	10
No	22
Valid cases	1147
Missing cases	59

2. (F21) Do blacks form a nation within a nation?

	%
Blacks Another Ethnic group like Irish-Americans, etc.	46
Blacks form a nation within a nation	49
Valid cases	1089
Missing cases	117

3. (D6D) Blacks should support the creation of all male public schools for black youth?

	%
Strongly agree	26
Agree	36
Disagree	29
Strongly disagree	9
Valid cases	1144
Missing cases	62

American society suffers from the myth of the monolithic black community as a consequence of solidarity. Responses in Questions D1 and F21 go directly to the heart of a shared identity in a racially segregated society. Seventy-eight per cent of the respondents felt connected solely by race. Queen College professor Andrew Hacker attributes the phenomenon of racial solidarity to racism and racial stereotypes, and calls it the defining feature in American society. "In the eyes of white America, being black encapsulates your identity. No other racial or national origin is seen as having so pervasive a personality or character... Your people have had a long history of being divided and conquered. At the same time, you have no desire to be held responsible for what every person of your color thinks or does. You cannot count how many times you have been asked to atone for some utterances of Louis Farrakhan or simply to assert that he does not speak for you."[11]

In response to the creation of all-black male schools, Question D6D highlights the inconsistency and irrationality solidarity often presents. The plight of "the endangered black male" has been widely reported for 10 years; young (18-25) black males are more likely to die by homicide than any other group, and the U.S. black-male incarceration rate is higher than that of South Africa. Respondents' support for the proposition elicited in Question D6D at the 62% level is hardly surprising, but it stands in sharp contrast to the percentage of blacks in the *CNN/USA Today*/Gallup Poll on school integration, in which 84% of the black respondents stated that they would like to see "more done" to integrate American schools.[12] Also, in a country where the prevailing and most enduring racial stereotype of the black male has been that of a dangerous and violent creature, to support a structure which segregates by gender and race would seem to confirm racist stereotypes.

In Figure 3-2 — Selected indicators of Black Nationalism (continued) — the NBPS ask the following questions:

1. (D6A) Blacks should participate in black-only organizations?

	%
Strongly agree	20
Agree	36
Disagree	35
Strongly disagree	9
Valid cases	1184
Missing cases	22

2. (D6F) Black people should control the government in predominantly black communities?

	%
Strongly agree	24
Agree	44
Disagree	27
Strongly disagree	5
Valid cases	1154
Missing cases	52

3. (D6G) Black people should control the economics in predominantly black communities?

	%
Strongly agree	31
Agree	43
Disagree	23
Strongly disagree	3
Valid cases	1164
Missing cases	42

It should not be surprising that discontented ethnic groups in a pluralist society retreat to solidarity to attain socio-political and economic goals when the structures of government and politics seem unresponsive. This study takes exception to the implication posed by Questions D6A, D6F, and D6G of the NBPS. Under the subtitle: "Selected Indicators of Black Nationalism," the researchers asked: (D6A) Blacks should participate in black-only organizations?; (D6F) Black people should control the government in predominantly black communities?; and (D6G) Black people should control the economics in predominantly black communities?. It is important to note that the questions presented in this study were worded in the same way as they appear in the NBPS. Objections can be raised as to whether or not beginning questions with "Should blacks...," as opposed to "Blacks should...," may have resulted in differing responses. Phrasing the questions in such a manner [i.e. "Blacks should"] has the impact of affirming the consequence. This criticism aside, in all three cases, the results predictably favored community control. However, the NBPS should resist concluding that these constitute measures of nationalism. If the same three questions were posed to white Americans living in predominately white communities, Jewish-Americans, Italian-Americans, or others, one would probably find a significant percentage of *affirmative* responses in favor of community control. The questions posit that in order not to be considered a black nationalist, one must agree to be controlled by forces that may or may not serve one's best interest. If a group feels that its socio-political and economic needs are not being addressed, responses to the previous questions stand only as indicators of their dissatisfaction, not indicators of nationalism. Question (D6A) asks if blacks should participate in black-only organizations. This *presupposes* that they have a choice of participating in white organizations that meet the needs of a black constituency. Participation as an indication of nationalism places that same assumption on white Americans. The question asserts that any ethnic or racial group which celebrates its ethnic diversity and culture is practicing nationalism.

In Figure 3-3 are NBPS questions pertaining to support for an all-black party (D5A) and race conscious voting. They are also promoted as "Selected Indicators of Black Nationalism" by the NBPS. Also listed in Figure 3 are responses pertaining to support for Bill Clinton. On the NBPS, Question (B1) was listed under subheading — "Selected

Indicators of African-American orientation towards the political system." Comparison of the results raises extreme doubt as to conclusions of nationalism propounded by the NBPS.

Figure 3-3 — Selected Indicators (continued)

1. (D5A) Blacks should form their own political party?

	%
Agree	50
Disagree	50
Valid cases	1129
Missing cases	77

2. (D6B) Blacks should always vote for a black candidate?

	%
Strongly agree	9
Agree	17
Disagree	56
Strongly disagree	18
Valid cases	1182
Missing cases	24

3. (B1) Do you approve or disapprove of the way Bill Clinton is handling his job as President?

	%
Strongly approve	53
Approve	31
Disapprove	8
Strongly disapprove	8
Valid cases	1031
Missing cases	175

The contradictory nature of responses to Questions D5A, D6B and B1 should have alerted surveyors to the lack of reliability and validity of the responses. Respondents were split down the middle as to support for the formulation of an all-black political party while at the same time giving Bill Clinton a substantially higher percentage of support than whites. Respondents in the NBPS gave Clinton an 84% approval rating (B1). Buttressing the contradiction, the *Time/CNN* poll, taken in February 1994, shows Clinton with a 70% approval rating among blacks as opposed to a 53% approval in the general population. These results, combined with the fact that a majority of respondents disagreed with the idea of race-conscious voting, makes assertions of black nationalism spurious.

Such high levels of support for Clinton illustrate the paradoxical nature of interpreting support for a black political party solely as nationalism. It is only when Clinton is matched against Jesse Jackson as a possible presidential candidate that his support drops and perhaps this is where the inference to solidarity can be raised. In the aforementioned *Time/CNN* poll, Clinton receives 41% black support and Jackson receives 50% support, thus raising racial solidarity as a mechanism of discontent. The results indicate that blacks believe Clinton to be the best available representation from the dominant political culture; however, Jackson would be an expression of dissonance.

Discontent

The NBPS uncovers stark pessimism in the attitudes of African-Americans as to social and political conditions in this country. In Figure 3-4 — Selected Indicators of African-American Evaluations of American Society, the NBPS asked the following questions:

F9. Is American society fair to black people?
Fair   17%
Unfair   77%
Valid cases: 1161
Missing cases: 45

F23. Is the American legal system fair to black people?
Fair   17%
Unfair   79%
Valid cases: 1152
Missing cases: 54

F10. Is American's economic system fair to black people?
Fair   14%
Unfair   83%
Valid cases: 1171
Missing cases: 35

D7A. America has provided black people fair opportunity.

Strongly agree	13%
Agree	29%
Disagree	22%
Strongly disagree	36%
Valid cases:	1192
Missing cases:	14

F25. When will racial equality in America be achieved?

Has been achieved	5%
Will be achieved soon	30%
Not in my lifetime	42%
Never	23%
Valid cases:	1157
Missing cases:	49

D7B. American society just hasn't dealt fairly with black people.

Strongly agree	56%
Agree	30%
Disagree	10%
Strongly disagree	4%
Valid cases:	1191
Missing cases:	15

D7C. American society owes black people a better chance than they currently have.

Strongly agree	51%
Agree	30%
Disagree	12%
Strongly disagree	7%
Valid cases:	1176
Missing cases:	30

The results of the NBPS confirm the deep discontent felt by African-Americans. In Question F25 over 95% of those interviewed hold the opinion that racial equality has not been achieved, 23% responding that it will *never* be achieved, and 42% responding that it will not be achieved in their lifetime. Question F9 shows 77% of respondents believing that American society is unfair; Question D7B shows 86% of respondents believing that American society "just hasn't dealt fairly with black people". The *Time/CNN* polls also uncovers solidarity and discontent. Discontent is caused by the feeling of having no power. In Figure 3-5

Question 8 (Race and Power) respondents were asked about their feelings on who had power in American society:

Figure 3-5 — Race and Power

Question 8—For each of the following groups of people, please tell me whether you think that group has too much power in this country, not enough, or the right amount.

	Too much	Not enough	Right amount	Not sure
Whites	80%	31%	2%	5%
Big corporations	69%	9%	15%	7%
Jews	28%	22%	31%	19%
Catholics	26%	20%	34%	20%
Labor Unions	21%	52%	19%	8%
Blacks	2%	90%	6%	2%

Blacks intensely feel that whites have too much power (80%) and that they themselves do not have enough (90%) and/or feel powerless. Question 8 provides the most compelling evidence of discontent.

As political scientist Lucius Barker writes,

> It is sad but true that what the late Justice Thurgood Marshall wrote in the 1978 Bakke case remains as relevant today as it did then. 'It is unnecessary in 20th Century America to have individual Negroes demonstrate that they have been victims of racial discrimination; the racism of our society has been so pervasive that none, regardless of wealth or position, have managed to escape its impact.' Marshall's observation remains on the mark: statistics and conceptual models may provide information and explanation, but they cannot begin to give life to the hurt that flows from personal experiences that I, and many other African-Americans, encounter, no matter what our achievements of socioeconomic status.[13]

Contemporary Black Nationalism Identified

In defining black nationalism with its central ideological feature that of racial separation, measuring African-American support for the Nation of Islam and its leader Louis Farrakhan would seem to be the most logical place to start. While the formal nationwide membership of the Nation of Islam has been estimated to be in the range of 10,000 to 15,000, Farrakhan himself may command a larger following to include many middle-class blacks. Over 30,000 men attended a Farrakhan address in New York during the height of his 1994 press exposure and over 800,000 black men attended his "Million Man March" held in Washington in October 1995. No other black leader since the death of Dr. Martin Luther King, Jr. has been able to draw such numbers.[14]

The Nation of Islam was founded in the 1930 by a silk peddler named W. D. Fard Muhammad. After his disappearance four years later, he was succeeded by Elijah Muhammad, who led the organization for 41 years until his death at the age of 77. Muhammad preached that Islam was the natural religion of blacks, but its orthodoxy had been contaminated with whiteness; blacks belonged to the tribe of Shabazz, which landed from space 66 trillion years ago; and whites were a plague on the world created by Yacub, a mad scientist whose 600-year hybridization experiment produced devils who ruled for 6,045 years by "tricknology." Muhammad preached that the black man is the progenitor of all civilization and will inherit the earth.[15] After Muhammad's death in 1975, the Nation of Islam divided as Muhammad's teachings were repudiated by his eldest son Warith Deem Muhammad, who moved toward orthodox Islam and established the American Muslim Mission. In 1977 Farrakhan re-established the Lost-Found Nation of Islam in the Wilderness of North America, thus succeeding Elijah Muhammad. Like Muhammad, Farrakhan believes that blacks should form a separate nation with reparations paid by America for slavery.

Farrakhan was born Louis Eugene Walcott in 1933 to a West Indian domestic in the Bronx, New York. After hearing Malcolm X preach at the Harlem Mosque, he joined the Nation. Although brought into the Nation by Malcolm X, Farrakhan has been often negatively associated with the assassination of his mentor. In 1964, when Malcolm X accused Muhammad of fakery and adultery, Farrakhan counterattacked his mentor in the Nation's newspaper, which Malcolm X founded. Farrakhan wrote: "Only those who wish to be led to hell or to their doom will follow Malcolm X. Such a man is worthy of death...." Within three months Malcolm X was dead. Farrakhan, who replaced Malcolm X as Muhammad's spokesman, confesses to having contributed to the violent and murderous atmosphere of the time and adds, "Nothing that I wrote or said yesterday do I disagree with today — Not one thing! ... Anybody that rose up against the Honorable Elijah Muhammad in that way, I would rise up against them."[16]

From late 1993 to June 1994, a firestorm of media attention swirled around Farrakhan. On November 19, 1993, Khalid Abdul Muhammad, Farrakhan's national spokesman, gave a three-hour speech at Kean College, a state-supported institution in New Jersey. In his speech to a predominately black audience, Muhammad attacked whites, South Africans, homosexuals, Arabs, and black moderates, but his primary target was Jews. The Anti-Defamation League (ADL) and scores of politicians and civic leaders, black and white, condemned the speech as anti-Semitic, with the ADL subsequently taking out a full page ad in the *New York Times* condemning Muhammad. Farrakhan, then viewed as inching his way to mainstream acceptance with appearances on several television news programs, was urged to rebuke his minister. While removing Muhammad as his national spokesperson, Farrakhan supported the "truths" he spoke but admonished him for the "tone" in which the "truths" had been expressed.[17] The controversy renewed charges of anti-Semitism against Farrakhan. The National Congressional Black Caucus, through its chairman Rep. Kweisi Mfume (D-Md.), voided the "sacred covenant" between the Caucus and the Nation of Islam, placing pressure on national black leadership to distance themselves from the Nation of Islam, Farrakhan, and Muhammad.

In June 1994, the Reverend Dr. Benjamin Chavis, then executive director of the NAACP, invited Farrakhan to participate in the African-American Leadership Summit. Chavis then found himself in the hot seat, accused of taking the NAACP toward black nationalism and away from its integrationist roots. Harvard professor Cornel West defended the NAACP's inclusion of Farrakhan, stating, "Minister Farrakhan and the Nation of Islam — though far too patriarchal, homophobic and anti-Semitic for the vast majority of African-Americans — are in no way comparable to Adolph Hitler and the Nazis of Weimar Germany. They are simply one noteworthy black response, among hundreds of others, trying to understand and overcome pervasive black social misery...."[18] Black leadership coalesced for what they perceived as an attack against their right to associate with a faction of the community which appeared to have credibility with the urban underclass. The tempest surrounding Farrakhan produced a sense of racial solidarity against a common enemy, namely, white society. It was in this white-hot media environment, with Farrakhan on the cover of *Time* magazine being proclaimed "The Minister of Rage", that the *Time/CNN* poll and National Black Politics Study (NBPS) were conducted.

Is black support for Farrakhan indicative of black support of nationalism/separatism?

The February 1994 *Time/CNN* survey asked respondents questions concerning black leadership, race, power, and institutions. Responses reveal recognition of Farrakhan as a national leader; however, at the time of the surveys, by comparison, Farrakhan ranked behind Jesse Jackson in name recognition and popularity by 9% to 34% respectively. However, in order to understand why Farrakhan can attract thousands to a rally, one needs to examine what he represents to an ethnic group undergoing mass discontent and increased racial solidarity. The NBPS results in the questions listed in Figure 3-4 consistently register high levels of discontent among African-Americans, as do other polls. These results are especially revealing when juxtaposed against the *Time/CNN* survey Questions 13 and 14, which specifically address black attitudes toward Farrakhan as the projected image of dissonance.

Figure 3-6 — Louis Farrakhan

Question 13 — Do you think that Farrakhan represents the views of most blacks in America, the views of about half of blacks, less than half but a significant number, or the views of only a few blacks?

	Total	Those familiar *
Most	13%	17%
About half	23%	27%
Less than half	26%	30%
Only a few	22%	20%
Not sure	16%	6%

Question 14 — Thinking about your own views, do you generally agree with the positions of Louis Farrakhan, generally disagree, or aren't you familiar enough with his views to say for sure?

Generally agree	29%	38%
Generally disagree	22%	27%
Not familiar	38%	25%
Not Sure	11%	10%

*Those familiar with Farrakhan [Base=364]

Farrakhan is often portrayed as representing dissonance, a challenge to the status quo. With such high levels of discontent among the black populace, those offering dissonant views might tend to receive support not necessarily for the specific beliefs that they espouse, but because of *the mere act of challenging* the status quo. However, in examining Questions 13 and 14 of the *Time/CNN* poll of those familiar with Farrakhan, it is all but impossible to interpret the results without data identifying specific "views" associated with "blacks in America", and without data identifying specific "positions" associated with Farrakhan. To this end, the *Time/CNN* polling data tells us very little about the depth and breadth of support for Farrakhan. Thus, widespread mainstream reporting of the 38% of respondents who "generally agree" with Farrakhan can certainly be challenged as to its validity and reliability. Survey data on support for the notion of separatism goes to the heart of the depth and breadth question and takes us beyond the spurious application and analysis of popularity polls.

Black support for separatism

Figure 3-7 — Black Institutions

Question 11b. — Do you generally have favorable impressions or generally unfavorable impressions of the Nation of Islam, or are you familiar enough with the Nation of Islam to say?

Favorable	31%
Unfavorable	16%
Not familiar enough	49%
Not sure	4%

Question 12 — From what you know, do you think the Nation of Islam has been a positive force in the black community, a negative force, or aren't you sure?

Positive	39%
Negative	13%
Not sure	48%

Support for separation is measured against favorability and familiarity of the Nation of Islam among respondents. In regards to the claims of high levels of support for Farrakhan, it should be reasonable to assume that polling data concerning support for Farrakhan, the Nation of Islam, and separatism would be consistent with each other. As indicated by the *Time/CNN* poll, the majority of respondents (53%) were not familiar enough with the Nation of Islam to render an opinion one way or the other. Of those familiar with the group, 31% had a favorable impression (16% unfavorable) and 39% of those familiar with the group considered them a positive force in the black community. However, the 39% composed only 5.7% of the total respondents. This, of course, adds to the charge of spurious application of polling data. The percentage of those unfamiliar with the organization indicates an absence of support for separatism if we postulate that respondents who support black nationalism would have some idea as to those groups advocating the concept. This buttresses the previous assertion that pop culture attitudes of dissonance may possibly form the base of support for Farrakhan. As Adolph Reed points out, "Farrakhan has been attacked so vigorously... in part because he is black. He has been invented by whites as a symbol embodying, and therefore justifying, their fears of a black peril."[19]

Responses given in *Time/CNN* Questions 13 and 14 are illuminating in that a purportedly significant number of respondents stated that Farrakhan's views were held by about half (27%) or most (17%) blacks, even as a greater number of respondents (49%) were unfamiliar with the ideological views of the Nation of Islam or held unfavorable opinions of the organization (16%). Taken together (unfamiliar and unfavorable) those respondents represent 65% of the total. Once again, the inconsistency of the responses point to a polling mechanism that superficially interpreted Farrakhan as having more support than what actually may exist.

When asked on Question D6I of the NBPS: Black people should have their own separate nation? Fifty-seven per cent of the respondents disagreed and 29% strongly disagreed with the forming of a separate nation (combined 86%). Only 5% strongly agreed and 9% (52 missing cases) agreed that blacks should form their own separate nation. These results lead to the contention that the 49% who *affirmatively* responded to the assertion posed in Question F21: Do blacks form a nation within a nation? — responded to the reality of lingering segregation in America versus supporting the establishment of a separate black nation. Obviously, the NBPS results in the aforementioned questions contradict any assertion that there is high support for separatism. NBPS question D6I speaks directly to the depth and breadth of concerns that survey questions should seek to uncover. Thus, it gives us far more information than *Time/CNN* polling questions concerning Farrakhan as an indicator of support for separatism.

The results of the April 1994 *CNN/USA Today* poll on integration suggest that African-Americans would like the country to become more racially integrated, thus undermining any claim that black nationalism or the establishment of a nation-state is high on the political agenda of African-Americans.[20]

The apparent contradictory nature of the reported responses on both *CNN* polls — support for Farrakhan and simultaneous support of increased integration — could be used to support the assertion that the manifestations of solidarity can produce politically inconsistent results due to the lack of structure and ideology entailed in solidarity. However, the charge of spurious application and the lack of a survey mechanism aimed at depth and breadth analysis would leave any assertion based on the *CNN* data subject to claims of lacking validity and reliability.

Farrakhan and the dissonance factor — (Time/CNN Poll)

Figure 3-8 — Question 15 — In your view, which of these descriptions apply and which do not apply to Louis Farrakhan?

Waiting for Lightning to Strike

	Total	Familiar
a. Someone you personally admire		
Describes	32%	40%
Does not describe	47%	51%
Not sure	21%	9%
b. Good for the black community		
Describes	52%	62%
Does not describe	24%	25%
Not sure	24%	13%
c. A bigot and a racist		
Describes	29%	34%
Does not describe	46%	54%
Not sure	25%	12%
d. Speaks the truth		
Describes	54%	63%
Does not describe	19%	21%
Not sure	27%	16%
e. An effective leader		
Describes	57%	67%
Does not describe	21%	21%
Not sure	22%	12%
f. Someone who says things the country should hear		
Describes	60%	70%
Does not describe	18%	18%
Not sure	22%	12%
g. A good role model for black youth		
Describes	45%	53%
Does not describe	30%	33%
Not sure	25%	14%

Question 16 — From what you know, do you think Farrakhan has been a positive force in the black community, a negative force, or aren't you sure?

Positive	36%	46%
Negative	11%	14%
Not sure	53%	40%

Question 17 — Do you think Farrakhan is more of a racial moderate or a racial separatist who believes in keeping blacks and whites separate?

Moderate	22%	27%
Separatist	45%	53%
Mixed/Neither**	4%	4%
Not sure	29%	16%

Question 18 — Do you think Farrakhan's opinions and behavior improve relations
between blacks and whites in this country, make them worse, or have no real effect?

Improves	12%	14%
Makes worse	31%	35%
Has no effect	34%	37%
Not sure	23%	14%

** Volunteered response
* Those familiar with Farrakhan [Base=364]

The environmental discussion in *Contemporary Black Nationalism
Identified* is important in that portions of the *Time/CNN* poll have been
used to assert a claim of growing black nationalism by citing support for
Farrakhan as a barometer of that growth. The polling data cited most frequently have been Question 15f, to which 70% of the respondents agreed
that Farrakhan "says what the country should hear," and Question 15d, to
which 63% of the respondents said that Farrakhan "speaks the truth." The
two polling numbers have been juxtaposed frequently against Question
15c, which cites "only" 34% of the respondents seeing Farrakhan as a
"bigot and a racist."[21] Little mention is made of Question 18 in which
35% of respondents thought that Farrakhan makes relations between
blacks and whites worse. However, the most damning criticism of the
Time/CNN, as mentioned previously, is the extent to which respondents understand the views and/or beliefs of Farrakhan (i.e. the depth
and breadth issue) to accurately respond to Question 15d. What is the
"truth" that Farrakhan speaks? The "truths" would have to be isolated
and specifically associated with Farrakhan in order for responses to have
both reliability and validity. There is also the problem of the individual
respondents' definition of certain terms, such as: What is a role model?
What is a leader? What does the word "admire" mean? What are the
criteria for being a positive force? Superficial analysis and polling creates
ambiguity and inaccurate responses. In essence, the *Time/CNN* poll tells
us nothing about depth and breadth of feelings of discontent or *real*
support for the Farrakhan ideology. It fails miserably as a "snapshot" of
opinion and falls in the same category as fast food — it will fill you up,
but overall, it is unhealthy.

Mainstream media has portrayed Farrakhan as the image of "dissonance", and factoring in the environment in which the poll was taken leaves little doubt that poll numbers on Farrakhan would be skewed *positively* in his favor. In comparison to an overall 9% popularity rating as indicated by the results of Question 9, dissonance imagery appears to be the only explanation for the results in Questions 15c, 15d, and 15f. Farrakhan is promoted as the dominant dissonant voice penetrating the status quo. Still, the data cannot be interpreted as support of separatism in the form of support for Farrakhan. Question 17 shows 53% of respondents acknowledging that Farrakhan is a separatist; however, the 49% in Question 11b who were unfamiliar with the Nation of Islam and 16% who had an unfavorable impression (cumulative- 65%), would tend to contradict the notion that blacks support separatism.

On the day of Farrakhan's "Million Man March," he and Clinton traded barbs, Clinton charging that the foundation of the March was tainted by Farrakhan's message. Farrakhan responded by proclaiming that the foundation of the country was racist. Regardless of the public protestations, the march organizers and the attendees were making an appeal to the government of this country for inclusion. The *CNN* poll belies this assert with fifty-three per cent of respondents in their poll preferring to be called African-*American* (versus 36% — black), one would think that if blacks wished to separate from the United States, they would eschew the term American. Of course, the only true measure of Farrakhan's clout would be witnessed if he called for a million black men to begin the process of building a geographically separate black nation. One in which he was the leader, and his theology was installed as the primary doctrine.

Figure 3-9 - Black versus African-American:
Which do you prefer as a name for your race — African-American or black?

	Feb. 1994	April 1991	Feb. 1989
African-American	53%	39%	26%
Black	36%	48%	61%
Other [volunteered]	1%	4%	3%
No difference/Not sure	10%	9%	10%

Conclusion

At this point in American history, blacks are split down the middle in support of forming a racially based political party, but they overwhelmingly support community control of economics and politics in predominantly black areas. A 74% majority of those surveyed by the NBPS also say that they disagree with the notion of always voting for a black candidate and 86% majority still identify themselves as Democrats. These results appear consistent with discontent, but they still indicate a desire for political and social inclusion. It is in no way indicative of increased black nationalist sentiment.

The increased dissatisfaction of African-Americans, due to the lack of measurable political, economic, and social gains, has created a radicalized community. The result of radicalization is the intensification of racial solidarity without coherent and consistent political outcomes. In the absence of a structural response to the problems facing the black community, nationalism, in the form of latent support for the imagery of a dissonant voice and charismatic figure, has been invoked by mainstream media, issue entrepreneurs and others. Support for Farrakhan and his "Million Man March" is viewed as an indicator of growing black nationalism. However, the depth and breadth of that support is surely not supported by the *Time/CNN* poll, the *National Black Politics Study* or 800,000 black men in Washington.

The NBPS quantifies measures of black discontent; however, it would be troublesome to ascribe the term black nationalism to that discontent. Although oppressive economic, political, and social conditions have combined to maintain a feeling of joint oppression by the dominant culture, blacks continue to support their American status. African-Americans seek more equitable inclusion in American society, rather than the building of a separate nation-state. However, black discontent has resulted in a more radicalized polity. Operationally, radicalization of a racial community is the concomitant of diminished confidence in the ability of governmental and political structures and institutions to redress historically race-based political, economic, and social grievances. This radicalization, as the data indicates, manifests itself through increased racial solidarity (i.e., political and social decision-making using race as the primary causal variable). Under extreme conditions, it *can* lead to ethnic and racial conflict, polarization, and nationalism or nation-building.

For those who wish to see structural political, social, and economic gains by blacks, without an extreme and real drift towards separatist confrontation, a mechanism of inclusive social change must be developed. The organizing mechanism need not be nationalist in nature, but one that focuses resources on economic, political, and social equity, and creates the dynamic for a new social movement with more effective ethnic group participation in a pluralist society.

Andrew Hacker's contemporary observations on the long-standing moral and social paradox of race and racism in America serve as a premonition of the resurgence of some type of nationalism, or at the very least, an intensification of racial solidarity, polarization, and bifurcation. Hacker cites Alex de Tocqueville's prediction that "the abolition of slavery will, in the common course of things, increase the repugnance of the white population for the blacks."[22] The premonitions of de Tocqueville and Hacker bolster the contention by some that Pan-Africanism or separatism is an option for blacks in America.

Hacker's premonition is identical to that of Gunnar Myrdal, who alleges that the actions of blacks in America depend on the actions of whites. Thus, any solution, be it racial separation or racial inclusion, will be determined by the dominant culture: "It is thus the white majority group that naturally determines the Negroes' `place'. All our attempts to reach scientific explanations of why the Negroes are what they are and why they live as they do have regularly led to determinants on the white side of the race line. The Negro's entire life and, consequently, his opinions on the Negro problem, are, in the main, to be considered as secondary reactions to more primary pressures from the side of the dominant white majority."[23] If Myrdal, de Tocqueville, and Hacker are accurate in their common assessment, then perhaps America has arrived at a critical point in race relations. America could be in store for a more violent episode of black nationalism should the worsening economic and social conditions in the black community remain unameliorated, perhaps an episode that supersedes racial solidarity's confusion with nationalism, to a demonstrative or symbolic movement to create a black nation-state. As economic forces redefine black labor, the possibility seems to have a measure of validity in some quarters. Juan Williams writes, "...black liberal demands for more seats in Congress, more special programs for minorities, and more support for a black separatist movement have pushed black America out of the mainstream of the national dialogue. In effect, the black liberal strategy of the past three decades has backfired by inadvertently strengthening the hand of a group long considered the enemy of strong civil rights — conservative Republicans."[24] Williams cites Michael Meyers, executive director of the New York Civil Rights Coalition, who contends, "all the institutions we developed for the purpose of influencing the mainstream have become moribund, dysfunctional and self-destructive."[25] Williams' and Meyers' lamentations buttress the historical analysis of both Myrdal and de Tocqueville. However, in the absence of measurable depth and breadth support for a nationalist ideology and a viable structure to express that ideology, Williams overstates the significance for a black separatist movement at this point in history.

Appendix A: Models of Black Nationalism

Pop culture media has generated a great deal of attention on Louis Farrakhan and the Nation of Islam. Leonard Jeffries, an Africentric professor at City College of New York, and his support organization, the Association for the Study of Classical African Civilization (ASCAC), have support among upper-income middle-class blacks. Militant (revolutionary) nationalist groups, such as the Malcolm X Grassroots Movement, are growing in many low-and middle-income urban areas of the South. "It's Nation Time!" is seen as an expression of the political (reform) nationalism of Ron Daniels, 1992 independent presidential candidate and convener of the State of the Race Conference held in Baltimore in November 1994. These examples are termed nationalism by some and fundamentalism, pseudo-revolutionary nationalism, consumerism, and imperialism by others. But they are, to a lesser extent, representative of the movement characterized in the *modern* sense as black nationalism.

The typology provided by Bracey, Meier, and Rudwick posits that black nationalism takes many forms: the religious nationalism of the Nation of Islam, the Marxist revolutionary nationalism of the Black Panther Party, the economic nationalism of black capitalism, the political nationalism of the Republic of New Afrika, Pan-African nationalism, and cultural or Kawaida nationalism.[26] Bracey *et al* suggest an overlapping nationalism typology: racial solidarity, cultural nationalism, religious nationalism, economic nationalism (bourgeois and socialist), political nationalism (reform and revolutionary), territorial separatism, and Pan-Africanism.

University of Massachusetts researcher Dean Robinson exposes the contradictions and shortcomings inherent in the work of Bracey et al and is critical of the authors' terminology and creation of a black nationalist history and theory. "Certain behaviors are called black nationalist and not something else..., say for example, `separatist collective action`, for reasons the authors do not explain... If we consider any sample of older textual material Bracey, Meier, and Rudwick present, we can see how problematic the label black nationalist can be. With the exception of the Garvey Movement, which had as its central concern the founding of a Negro nation, black nationalism has contemporary connotations that generally seem to make less and less sense the further back the concept is projected into history."[27] Bracey, Meier, and Rudwick's terminology is also problematic in the present. Robinson argues that scholars who have treated more general manifestations of nationalism would argue that a nation is a community of people whose members consider themselves to be part of a nation. It is highly doubtful that nineteenth and early twentieth-century black Americans considered themselves to constitute a separate nation.[28] Robinson maintains that solidarity during the periods mentioned was more often a function of formal and informal barriers of segregation, blacks organized together because they "had no other choice."[29] In short, solidarity had very little to do with nation-building and more to do with the dominant culture imposing socio-economic and political segregation upon blacks in America.

Economic nationalism includes both capitalist and socialist outlooks. The capitalist, or bourgeois nationalist, advocates either controlling the black segment of the marketplace by attempting to establish black businesses and buy-black campaigns, or establishing a black capitalist economy parallel to the economy of the dominant society.[30] In a contemporary sense, Benjamin F. Chavis would fall at the top of Bracey's list. Ousted from his post as executive director of National Association for the Advancement of Colored People (NAACP) in the fall of 1994 amidst charges of sexual harassment, financial mismanagement, and perhaps organizational flirtation with black nationalism, Chavis attempted to reaffirm and expand the NAACP's Fair Share Economic Development Programs. The locus of his message involved traditional "buy black" campaigns, control of black dollars that flow through mainstream white businesses (such as the organization's yearly Susan B. Anthony dollar demonstration), corporate negotiations on hiring, and minority subcontracting with a focus on elite capitalism. In a speech at the NAACP's national convention in 1993 Chavis stated that economic empowerment "falls at the top of our priority list..., I think the NAACP can make an invaluable contribution to the overall civil-rights movement by becoming a leader in conceiving, defining, and implementing effective economic development projects and programs."[31]

Jesse Jackson falls under the bourgeois reformist model due to his advocacy of a national independent progressive party.[32] Jackson differs from other modern reformist to the extent that a quasi-black nationalist focus is not a central feature of his message (although racial solidarity is a frequent theme). Mobilization of voters through registration mechanisms, which focus primarily on a black voter base (i.e., solidarity) has been Jackson's stock in trade.

In contrast to bourgeois reformism, revolutionary black nationalism views the overthrow of existing political and economic institutions as a prerequisite for the liberation of blacks in America and does not exclude the use of political violence. Malcolm X, in his 1963 speech "Message to the Grassroots," defined black nationalism as building the nation-state:

"When you want a nation, that's called nationalism. When the white man became involved in a revolution in this country against England, what was it for? He wanted this land so he could set up another white nation. That's white nationalism. The American Revolution was white nationalism. The French Revolution was white nationalism. The Russian Revolution too — yes, it was — white nationalism. You don't think so? Why do you think Khrushchev and Mao can't get their heads together? White nationalism. All the revolutions that are going on in Asia and Africa today are based on what? — black nationalism. A revolutionary is a black nationalist. He wants a nation. I was reading some beautiful words by Rev. Cleage, pointing out why he couldn't get together with someone else in the city because all of them were afraid of being identified with black nationalism. If you're afraid of black nationalism, you're afraid of revolution. And if you love revolution, you love black nationalism."[33]

The Black Panther Party came closest to representing a true revolutionary ethos in the earliest phase of the party. Two factors combined to support the dominant culture's belief that the Black Panthers had an ethos and program to attack and dismantle. One, they expressed an interest in seeking support from countries desiring of the demise of the American government or wanting to ameliorate the oppressed condition of blacks in America. Second, they maintained a belief in self-defense. Those beliefs resulted violent attacks by the dominate culture in the form of J. Edgar Hoover's FBI and the exile by many of its members to socialist countries such as Cuba and the Soviet Union. Although the tenet of nation-building was central to the Black Panther program, contradictions within the Party's platform regarding the meaning of revolutionary nationalism proved vexing to its ideological homogeneity as a revolutionary movement. The "Black Panther Party's Ten Point Program" called for "freedom" and the "power to determine the destiny of the Black community"; however, the Panther platform, couched in socialist terms, called for the dominate political culture, characterized as the oppressor, to provide "full employment".[34] Full employment granted by the oppressor is not a revolutionary platform.

Adam Lively describes traditional nineteenth-century black nationalism as a conservative movement advocating racial self-improvement through the civilizing influence of Anglo-Saxon values, particularly

Christianity. Construing black nationalism as the assertion of group identity did not occur until the period 1914-1929 as the nature of the American black community changed. Lively juxtaposes Dubois and Marcus Garvey in an effort to show the continuities between traditional and modern black nationalism in an attempt to place the current movement in historical context.[35] Lively's group identity construct of nationalism forms the primary foundation on which Bracey *et al.* rest their typology.

Modern black nationalism focuses attention upon liberation movements within Africa struggling against various forms of white oppression or neo-colonialism. Lively asserts that these liberation movements serve as the vanguard of the black nationalist movement of today; thus, the movement as a whole becomes a *liberation* movement. For traditional black nationalists the vanguard were those in the black diaspora, especially Christians and traditionalists, who had received the benefits of European or American civilization, and affirmed the universal application of those values. It was they who would redeem Africa by bringing to it civilization and thus pulling it out of its state of backwardness.[36]

The second point of distinction that Lively makes between the traditional and the modern concerns the extent to which black national ism presents an attack on European/American values. Modern black nationalists attack European and American imperialism not only for the economic exploitation and political oppression it involves, but also for its accompanying cultural and intellectual arrogance. As a liberation movement, modern black nationalism strives for autonomy in the fullest sense — complete independence from "alien wills."[37]

Lively suggests Garvey as an example of a traditional black nationalist, describing him as a racial chauvinist who condemned the mixing of races as socially or genetically unnatural and as having a debilitating effect on racial solidarity. Contrary to popular belief, Garvey never envisioned a mass exodus to Africa. He did, however, make the comparison between "Africa for the Africans" and a homeland for the Jews in Palestine. The return to Africa would be led by elite elements and would be a symbolic homeland. Garvey believed the nation-state was the highest expression of a race's independence and separate development.

This central plank of his ideology makes him the continuing focus of research on black nationalism.

W.E.B. Dubois trumpeted the modern nationalist movement with his international view and pre-Lenin (1917) analysis of capitalism as the perpetuation of imperialism. For Dubois, the conflict between capital and labor in the modern world is the global conflict between the white and colored races. World democracy will only be achieved with the emancipation of the colored races from colonialism.[38] What separates Dubois and Garvey is not only their respective economic beliefs but also Dubois's notion of Pan-Africanism. To many, Pan-Africanism represents a return to Africa, but Lively asserts that Dubois also never advocated such a policy. Dubois specifically recommended African self-government; although development would be along the lines of the best western and colonial models, it would utilize existing patterns of local and/or tribal government. Lively also states that Dubois saw the relationship between African development and the future of American blacks as being purely expressive and symbolic. Pan-Africanism did not mean a missionary expedition to Africa or a retreat from the struggle for democracy in America, but rather a raising of racial consciousness that could be used in that struggle. Adolph Reed, Jr. states;

"We have to be careful of what we call black nationalism and if it can be called nationalism. Much of what was called nationalism from 1957 to the mid 1970s is nothing like the nationalism of the turn of the century. What Dubois was saying and, to some degree, what Marcus Garvey was saying, is nothing like the `pork chop' or consumer nationalism of Ron Karenga. Garvey and Dubois can also be questioned about what they were defining as nationalism — many call what they were advocating black imperialism. Farrakhan, who is advocating religious fundamentalism, is another good example. Though he is portrayed as a radical in the popular press, he really is conservative. Under this media attack, misguided calls for racial solidarity are confused with black nationalism."[39]

Appendix B – Black Leadership

Figure 3-10 — Black Leadership

Question 9 — In your view, who is the most important black leader today?

Jesse L. Jackson	34%
Martin Luther King, Jr.	9%
Louis Farrakhan	9%
Colin Powell	4%
Malcolm X	3%
Nelson Mandela	3%
Carol Moseley-Braun	1%
Other	7%
None [unsolicited response]	25%

Figure 3-11 — Race and Power

Question 10 — Is your impression favorable or unfavorable, or are you not familiar enough to have any impression?

	Favorable	Unfavorable	Not Familiar	Not Sure
Jesse Jackson	86%	10%	2%	2%
Louis Farrakhan	48%	20%	27%	5%
Clarence Thomas	42%	31%	23%	4%
Carol Moseley-Braun	42%	3%	53%	2%
Ron Brown	38%	6%	53%	3%
Al Sharpton	38%	25%	42%	3%
Doug Wilder	30%	5%	63%	2%
Benjamin Chavis	26%	3%	69%	2%
Bill Gray	22%	2%	73%	3%

References

Barboza, Steven. "A Divided Legacy," *Emerge*, V. 3, (April 1992, pp. 26-32).

Barker, Lucius. "Limits of Political Strategy: A Systematic View of the African-American Experience," *American Political Science Journal*, Vol. 88, No.1 (March 1994, pp. 1-13).

Bracey, John H. Jr., August Meier and Elliott Rudwick (eds.). *Black Nationalism in America.* New York: Bobbs-Merrill Company, Inc., 1970.

Breitman, George (ed.). *Malcolm X Speaks.* New York: Pathfinder Press, 1965.

Carmichael, Stokely and Charles V. Hamilton. *Black Power — The Politics of Liberation in America.* New York: Random House, 1967.

CNN/USA Today/Gallup Poll Report Card #5. "Brown vs. Board of Education Retrospective," April 22-24, 1994.

Dawson, Michael C. and Ronald E. Brown. "Black Discontent: The Preliminary Report on the 1993-1994 National Black Politics Study," University of Chicago, April 1994.

Dubois, W.E.B. "Striving of the Negro People," *Atlantic Monthly*, LXXX (August 1897, pp. 194-195).

Freire, Paulo. *Pedagogy of the Oppressed*. New York: Seabury Press, 1974.

Hacker, Andrew. *Two Nations: Black and White, Separate, Hostile, Unequal*. New York: MacMillan Publishing Company, 1992.

Lively, Adam. "Continuity and Radicalism in American Black Nationalist Thought, 1914-1929," *Journal of American Studies*, V. 18 (August 1984, 208-237).

Myrdal, Gunnar. *An American Dilemma: The Negro Problem and Modern Democracy, 12th Ed*. New York: Harper and Row, 1962 (1st ed. 1944).

Newton, Huey P. *Revolutionary Suicide*. New York: Harcourt Brace Jovanovich, Inc., 1973.

Reed, Adolph, Jr. (ed.). *Race, Politics and Culture: Critical Essays on the Radicalism of the 1960s*. New York: Greenwood Press, 1986.

Ruffins, Paul. "Rallying 'Round Mayor Barry," *The Nation*, V. 251 (July 30-August 6, pp. 121-124).

Tucker, Robert C. *The Marxian Revolutionary Idea*. New York: W.W. Norton and Company, 1969.

West, Cornel. "NAACP: Renewing an Old Tradition," *The Washington Post*. (July 9, 1994, A21).

Williams, Juan. "Blacked Out in the Newt Congress: The Black Caucus regroups as Jesse mulls a Third Party bid," Outlook Section, *The Washington Post* (November 20, 1994, C-1).

Yankelovich Partners, "CNN/Time Poll of African-Americans," February 18, 1994.

Endnotes

1. Kevin Merida, NAACP Leader Hails Summit as Victory Over "Forces Who Sought to Divide Us", *The Washington Post*, June 15, 1994:A21.

2. Rainbow strategy meeting at NRC Headquarters, June 1992, Washington, DC. As Jackson campaign worker in 1988, and southern political director for Iowa Senator Tom Harkin in 1992, I have often served in an advisory capacity to Jackson. In 1992, I served as an unofficial advisor to Jackson during the Democratic National Convention and participated in staff meetings.

3. Robert C. Tucker, *The Marxian Revolutionary Idea* (New York: W.W. Norton and Company, 1969) pp. 64-65.
"To account for the discrepancy between the real meaning of politics and what people believe about it, Marx and Engels invoked their theory of ideological thinking as false consciousness." From this perspective, the advocation of black nationalism, or the division of economic, social, and political issues primarily by race, represents the imposition of a false consciousness.

4. Ibid., pp. 181-185.
In Tucker's interpretation of Marx, he defines radicalism as:
1) Having an intense element of *negation* in it. Radicalism rebels against the existing order, repudiates the world as it stands or as the radical perceives it to stand.

"The radical is first of all someone who says 'No!' to the surrounding society." 2) Radicalism must be *visionary*. There must be a vision of an alternative universe, a *right* social order..., an idealized image of what the world ought to be. 3) Another general attribute of radicalism is *activism*. Radicalism not only rejects existing reality; it seeks to transform it..., "as Marx put it in the last of his eleven these on Fuerbach. '*The point is, to change it*.'" 4) There can be no radical movement without a radical *social doctrine* to serve as its inspiration and ideology.

By the definition of racial solidarity that we accept in this study, ideology is not necessarily a component of that definition, however, Marx would conclude that a period of growing racial and\or ethnic solidarity is merely a transition period before acceptance of ideology.

5. John H. Bracey, Jr. et al, *Black Nationalism in America* (New York: Bobbs-Merrill Company, Inc., 1970) xxvi.

6. Paulo Freire, *Pedagogy of the Oppressed* (New York: Seabury Press, 1974) p. 13.
    It is Freire's contention that every human being, no matter how "ignorant" or sub-merged in the "culture of silence" he may be, is capable of looking at his world in a dialogical encounter with others. Provided with the proper tools for such encounter, he can gradually perceive his personal and social reality as well as the contradictions in it, become conscious of his own perception of that reality, and deal critically with it.

7. Paul Ruffins, "Rallying 'Round Barry," *The Nation* V. 253 July 30-August 6, 1990: p. 121.

8. Ibid. p. 122.

9. Ibid.

10. Dawson and Brown use the term black nationalism. This study contends that it is appropriately termed racial solidarity.

11. Andrew Hacker, *Two Nations: Black and White, Separate, Hostile, Unequal* (New York: MacMillan Publishing Company, 1992) pp. 32,43.

12. In the *CNN/USA Today*/Gallup Poll #5: "Brown versus the Board Of Education Retrospective," a national poll which interviewed 1246 adults [whites-859, blacks-324], with a sampling error of ± 3 percentage points at the 95% confidence level, conducted April 22-24, 1994, *84% of black respondents felt that more should be done to integrate schools throughout the nation* — Question 34.
    Question 38 asked respondents — "Would you like to see the country more integrated in terms of minorities and whites living together in the same neighbor-hood — would you like it to become less integrated, or is it about right?" (Black respondents only)

More integrated	63%
Less integrated	2%
About right	31%
No opinion	4%

13. Thurgood Marshall, see *Regents of the University of California v. Bakke* 1978, p. 387. Qtd. in Lucius J. Barker, "Limits of Political Strategy: A Systemic View of the

African-American Experience," *American Political Science Review* V. 88, No. 1, (March 1994): p. 11.

14. Arch Puddington, "Black Anti-Semitism and How It Grows," *Commentary* V. 97, No. 4 April 1994: p. 21

15. Steven Barboza, "A Divided Legacy," *Emerge* V. 3, April 1994: p. 21.

16. Ibid., pp. 30-32.

17. Puddington, p. 19.

18. Cornel West, "NAACP: Renewing an Old Tradition," *The Washington Post* (July 9, 1994) p. A21.

19. Dean Robinson, "Black Nationalism", diss., University of Massachusetts, 1994, p. 5.

20. *CNN/USA Today* Gallup Poll #5.

21. Ibid., p. 21. Puddington cites the same polling data in his article.

22. Hacker. *Two Nations*, p. 215.

23. Gunnar Myrdal, *An American Dilemma: The Negro Problem and Modern Democracy, 12 Ed.* (New York: Harper and Row, 1962 [1st ed. 1944]) p. ii.

24. Juan Williams, "Blacked Out in the Newt Congress: The Black Caucus Regroups as Jesse Mulls a Third Party Bid," Outlook Section, *The Washington Post* (November 20, 1994), C1.

25. Williams, C1.

26. Jennifer Jordan, "Cultural Nationalism in the 1960s: Politics and Poetry," *Race, Politics and Culture,* ed. Adolph Reed, Jr. (New York: Greenwood Press, 1986) p. 29.

27. Dean Robinson, "Black Nationalism", diss., University of Massachusetts, 1994, p. 5.

28. Ibid., p. 5.

29. Ibid., p. 6.

30. Bracey et al, *Black Nationalism in America,* p. xxviii.

31. Sasha Kennison, unpublished research paper, George Washington University, May 1994. Kennison attended convention as a delegate.

32. Juan Williams, "Blacked Out in the Newt Congress: The Black Caucus Regroups as Jesse Mulls a Third Party Bid," *The Washington Post* Nov. 20, 1994: C1 and C4. Williams asserts that the Republican sweep of Congress in 1994 has pushed black America into a corner:
Williams: "The Congressional Black Caucus is politically impotent, its members stripped of key committee chairmanships and their voices weakened in the diminished choir of Democrats... And even as it pushed civil rights crusader Jesse Jackson farther from the nation's political center, it boosted his resolve to consider a third-party run for the presidency."
In an interview with Williams, Jackson stated, "It's not something I look forward to but something I may have to do to recapture the moral center... the burden, obligation and political risk of running for president will have to be seen as in the interest of our struggle."
Williams cites the national organizing effort of the Rainbow Coalition as it attempts to form a new "black political party.

33. George Breitman ed., *Malcolm X Speaks* (New York: Pathfinder Press, 1965) p. 10.

34. Huey P. Newton, *Revolutionary Suicide* (New York: Harcourt Brace Jovanovich, Inc. 1973) p. 116.

35. Adam Lively, "Continuity and Radicalism in American Black Nationalist Thought, 1914-1929," *Journal of American Studies* V. 18 (August 1984) p. 202.

36. Ibid., p. 208.

37. Ibid., p. 208

38. Ibid., p. 222.

39. Adolph Reed, Jr. personal interview, Jan 1994.

The Million Man March:
Identity and Race Politics

AN ACQUAINTANCE OF MINE ONCE CASUALLY REMARKED THAT the current civil rights leadership "is living in the past and the past is their future." The present day failure is rooted in the absence of a political strategy, direction, and measurable practical outcome to be achieved. The problems are compounded by the absence of a coherent political leveraging mechanism — as was the case with the multiracial, internationally-supported civil rights movement of the sixties. David A. Bositis describes the apparent paralysis of the nineties as the evolution of "The Rentier Left." He defines the *rentier* as:

> ...one who lives on the income from rents or investments, with no other occupation. More broadly defined, a rentier is one who lives on the past, including past actions, past successes, past patterns of behavior, and past ideas. A rentier is one who seeks to preserve past investments, and worries about future change endangering those investments. Included among the class of properties and investment to preserve are position and leadership status. (Bositis 1994)

In seeking to maintain rentier status, identity politics has predictable patterns. Identity politics is based solely on religious, sexual, physical, ethnic or some other singular characteristic or role. Simply put, it is the politics of what or who you are. The Million Man March in October 1995 provided a clear illustration of politics based on the traits of being a black male. Quite naturally, when community or personal politics are restricted to singular traits, the inward focus leads to the erosion of coalitions and the continuation of polarization on multiple fronts. The politics of what or *who* you are has led civil rights leaders in the nineties to resort to a form of sixties symbolism, pseudo-nationalism, paternalism and machismo, as evidenced by attempts to elevate Nation of Islam Minister Louis Farrakhan as the mythical national black spokesperson

(Guinier 1991, 1079). The sixties black nationalist/separatist movement which included groups like the Black Panthers ran concurrent to the multiracial civil rights movement. The drift to symbolism is consistent with rentiers who do not offer a cogent message as they seek to maintain their roles and image management. However, attempts to mobilize mass dissent around charismatic personalities, demagoguery, black nationalism, fundamentalist religious dogma and sexism can only have a debilitating effect on the traditional human rights coalition in America.

Race Politics and Religious Fundamentalism

> Many whites who fear the thought of so many black men standing in unity are actually experiencing — consciously or subconsciously — a guilty complex about their historical oppression of blacks and people of color. If they really free themselves, what will they do to us for our sins to them? they ask in their hearts.
>
> Blacks, who rabidly oppose the march, regardless of the purpose, suffer from a self-hatred inbred in blacks during chattel slavery. Anything called for and led by blacks can't be right, they assume. Most of these types — those with a level of wealth and status — have bought into the illusion of an integrated America where a black man or woman can get a fair shake and a fair share based upon his or her ability and desire to achieve their goals.
>
> On the other hand, supporters of the march cheer the thought of sober minded, focused black men participating in a Day of Atonement where they openly confess to Allah (God), their people and the world, their shortcomings as protectors and providers of their communities.
>
> — Louis Farrakhan, *Editorial, The Final Call, August 2, 1995*

In race politics, crime and violence have historically served as code words for black men. Thus, the debate predictably and rapidly disintegrated into the stereotyping of young black males as predatory. The crime debate feeds off the "family values" and cultural disintegration themes as propounded by the likes of former Vice President Dan Quayle, Pat Robertson, the founder of the Christian Coalition, and Empower America's Bill Bennett. In November 1993, President Bill Clinton went to Memphis on Martin Luther King's birthday to tell African-Americans how Dr. King would be "ashamed" if he were alive today (Jehl 1993). That same year the Reverend Jesse Jackson publicly and repeatedly confessed that seeing black males at night caused him discomfort. C. Delores Tucker of the National Political Congress of Black Women blamed it on rap music. Violent black men were marked as the cause of the national woes by all, black and white, left and right. The success of the conservative fundamentalist message of moral decay has also contributed to the leadership's paralysis and the acceptance of fanaticism. Thus, black leaders have adopted the politics of racial solidarity under the guise of pseudo-black nationalism in response to these societal attacks. The politics became a matter of circling the wagons to fight off attack. Black nationalism is identity politics under these conditions.

America remains a profoundly racist society. The Ku Klux Klan's violent and hateful rhetoric has been replaced by inflammatory radio and television personalities. Works such as *The Bell Curve* and *Alien Nation* seem to legitimize racist views. Affirmative action has been characterized as something which inherently victimizes white people in order to confer privileges on undeserving black people. There is also the perception that community assault and destabilization are taking place on and within the black community. Speaking at the Million Man March in October, Jesse Jackson railed against the injustices of the criminal justice system charging that prisons were becoming the "new form of public housing." But he failed to suggest a plan of action. Instead, consistent with rentier image management, he offered, "I am somebody!"

In a racially-polarized environment, the overwhelming response to the March was not surprising. The paralysis within the traditional civil rights leadership provided the community-at-large with the illusion that messianic leadership was the only leadership out there. The March was promoted as a "National Day of Atonement", although it is still extremely murky as to what that so-called "Atonement" entailed. The difficulty in building a mass movement lies in linking discontented masses to a coherent political strategy and message with attainable goals. The political goals of "Atonement" creates a myriad of problems too numerous to mention. Undaunted by the lack of measurable outcomes, defenders of the effort posited that "any attempt to bring people together is good." Cornel West of Harvard University speaking about the effort said, "The march is for anyone who has been disrespected, denigrated and disregarded. Moreover, it's about us coming together for the sake of the true, the beautiful and the good" (1995). After the event, there were anecdotal claims of an increase in volunteerism in the black community, but the political goals of the event remain elusive.

In addition, the moralist premise of Farrakhan's call of atonement exposes the influence of conservative fundamentalism on the politics of black leadership. The atonement theme was more reminiscent of the Christian Coalition's fundamentalist call to be "born again" than a challenge to a profoundly racist society to be just. The theological assertion of Washington as Mecca also gives one cause to wonder. Washington could be viewed as Babylon or Rome rather than Mecca or Jerusalem. Therefore, the suggestion of repentance in contemporary Babylon is tantamount to accepting racist stereotypes and second class status as true and deserved.

Benjamin Chavis, former director of the National Association for the Advancement of Colored People (NAACP), and Farrakhan said that they were calling black men "to spiritual repentance and responsibility along with reconciliation within the black community" (or the often proclaimed "Call for Unity!"). Farrakhan said that the March would allow black men to contemplate their condition as well as that of the race. He decreed, "The coldness with which we brutalize our women and abuse our children — this must cease... Black men will seek God's forgiveness for not fulfilling their roles as fathers and caretakers of the black family" (1995). Critics such as Willie Legette of South Carolina State University, maintain that such a "reactionary" message "blames black males for their own deprivation." Legette states, "You know how it goes. Black men just won't do right! The entire premise of the March and message is the result of a decade of the `endangered black man thesis'" (1995).

Beyond Legette's criticism lies another striking observation of the march: the social and economic makeup of the March attendees. The march organizers were making a call to the "disrespected, denigrated and disregarded." In trying to predict who would attend the event, Bositis cited Farrakhan's and Chavis' past overtures to young blacks and assumed that they would be the ones in attendance. Bositis stated, "Middle-class suburbanites don't need a march to get them to get out and vote. Mobilizing and getting people involved who have not been involved is a good idea" (Bositis 1995). The outcome surprised Bositis and others because the discontented participants were indeed middle-class suburbanites, union members, police organizations, black fraternities and the like (i.e. the economic mainstream of the black community). They were primarily working men — shattering the irresponsible, black male stereotype. Nonetheless, they were a group which perceived a threat to their status based on prevailing stereotypes.

Bolstering identity politics, Farrakhan and his supporters sought to silence critics of the event by using the street tactic of "calling people out." Anyone not with the program was "not black", they were in denial of who they are, they "don't want to be black", or they are "trying to be white." In terms of identity politics, unity is mandatory. Everyone is to be in lockstep or face ridicule. Failure to conform means you lose your identity as defined by the righteous. As if this were not enough, Chavis said that the March was in "keeping with God" as to imply that anyone not with the effort was not with God.

Chavis had the job of espousing the political sub-theme of the March which he said was a way "to send a message to government officials in regards to the deteriorating conditions in the U.S. for black people in general, and black men in particular." If the event had been connected to a clear political objective, a focus could have been the U.S. Sentencing Commission's recommendation to abolish the 100-1 crack-cocaine sentencing disparity (Mauer 1995), which has led to record imprisonment of black males. However, even after a rally of an estimated 800,000 black men on the steps of the Capitol where speakers denounced the United States criminal justice policy as racist, Congress and President Clinton felt no pressure to follow the Commission's recommendations. When Farrakhan arrived on stage to give his two-hour address to a world audience, his revolutionary cry was the novel exhortation to "register and vote." He did not present a plan to combat the structural, social, economic and political exclusion experienced by blacks and other ethnic minorities in America. Farrakhan asked black men to confess to being the cause of the disparity. This agenda, beyond its sexist edict, Legette adds, "concedes to the political right that we [blacks] are irresponsible and the state does not have a role to play in reducing inequality" (1995).

Sexism and Black Leadership

Farrakhan then instructed the marchers to return home and practice a similar discrimination. "…[I]t is time for the men to take their place as 'protectors' of 'our women.' Inherent in most religions is the sexism which historically excludes women from leadership roles. Farrakhan's sexism is fundamental to his religious beliefs. But sexism has also been the most glaring contradiction of a civil rights movement which habitually boasts a moral authority over an oppressive society. The failure of Chavis at the NAACP wasn't just about money and limousine activism. His failure was about sexism and abuse within the civil rights community. Legette adds, "Those brothers, like Harvard professor Cornel West, who rallied around Chavis after his sexist debacle at the NAACP tried to ignore the problem and blame the victim instead of dealing with the problem. They acted like [sic] it wasn't a problem at all, just a brother under attack and they responded with machismo" (1995).

Ella Baker, a woman who was crucial to the organization of the Southern Christian Leadership Conference (SCLC), is ignored by historians who give most of the credit to King. Similarly, although women in the NAACP raise the most money on the grassroots level through "Woman of the Year" fundraising contests, the leadership of the organization is still predominately male with women serving in only supporting roles. Within groups founded to advocate racial equality, sexism is an obstacle which has not been overcome.

From the beginning, the newly-formed, Chavis led, Nation of Islam sponsored National African-American Leadership Summit (NAALS), which organized the March, seemed overtly predicated on sexism, adopting the "woman from man's rib" sub-theme for its inaugural national effort. Barbara Reynolds, syndicated columnist with *USA Today*, was harsh in her critique of the effort: "I am insulted by attempts to make the black woman invisible again! We had the suffrage celebrations and although Sojourner Truth, a black woman, was instrumental in the

Women's Suffrage Movement, hardly any black women were asked to participate in the events. Now you have this march being organized by persons with histories of sexist behavior who are attempting to define blackness as black man. So what we now have is women's rights being defined as white women and blackness as black men. The black woman is once again invisible" (1995).

Still, black women from all walks of life supported the effort. Most cited the desperate need for *any* type of symbolic action in a hostile environment. In the Nation of Islam's newspaper, *The Final Call*, television host Bev Smith, of *Black Entertainment Television (BET)*, was quoted as saying, "I think that this is the first time that a man of God is calling men. And there is no way in the world a black woman cannot support a man of God calling black men to stand up this way in the world." This type of reasoning is certainly predictable but naive in its willingness to ignore or deny the inherent sexism in the call to march and to accept the lockstep nature of paternalistic unity as presented by organizers. To conclude that the problems of black women will be solved if God is on their side and black men "just do right" leaves black women dependent on the winds of chance with no power of their own. It also implies that, should the economic, social and political circumstances of women deteriorate further, the blame should go to God or to black men, not to an inherently racist and sexist society.

Where do we go from here?

A call for unity as a political strategy has appeal to blacks of all social and economic classes, but fundamentalist religious themes and symbolism cloud the effort. The traditional civil rights leadership has always been plagued by sexism, hypocrisy, and messianic protestations. Yet the rhetoric of the civil rights movement has been connected to enduring principles of love, justice, peace, freedom, social integration, due process, equal opportunity and protection — not on racial and gender separation.

At the foundation of the traditional civil rights ideology is the precept that unity is essential to the struggle. Under this construct, all men are brothers and all women are sisters. Unity as a strategy may not have eliminated the sexism in our homes, churches, and communities, political and civil rights organizations; however, respect for equal opportunity forced us to pursue a political agenda aimed at empowering the community regardless of the family structure. We would not have allowed society to blame the single black mother for her own poverty. Our assumption was that when economic conditions improve, relationships improve at every level of society. Gender and racial separation are non-issues under this premise. One million black men marching may be powerful; but many would have viewed one million people of both genders and many races as more powerful, especially when organizing around a theme of reconciliation and unity with a specific political agenda.

The March was sure to receive support in a community hungry for direction. Farrakhan's iconic popularity is not an indication of his qualities as a leader with a palatable message; it is merely a symptom of the failure of *rentier* leaders to effectively address the needs and anxieties of the black community and their failure to create an effective political front to counter the onslaught on black America. It is vexatious to argue against mobilization. Yet mobilization around charismatic personalities, political demagoguery, black nationalism, racial separatism, fundamentalist religious dogma, and paternalistic sexism can only have a debilitating effect on the human rights struggle.

References

Bositis, David A. 1994. "The Rentier Left." Washington, D.C.: The Joint Center for Political and Economic Studies.

Bositis, David A. 1995. Telephone interview by author. 19 September.

Farrakhan, Louis. 1995. Editorial. *The Final Call*. 2 August: 16.

Guinier, Lani. 1991. "The triumph of tokenism: The Voting Rights Act and the theory of black electoral success." *Michigan Law Review* 89:1079. ("Spokesmodels" are role models who speak in a representational capacity on behalf of others. In general, the notion of "spokesmodels" seem to apply only to the black community.)

See Reed, 1986. "The black revolution and the reconstitution of domination." In *Race, Politics and Culture: Essays on the Radicalism of the 1960s*. 61, 67-68. ("No 'white leaders' were assumed to represent a singular white population; social category 'black leaders' meant "certain blacks were declared opinion-makers and carriers of the interest of an anonymous black population.")

Jehl, D. 1993. "Clinton declares emotional appeal on stopping crime." *New York Times*. 14 November: A1.

Legette, Willie. 1995. Telephone interview by author. 18 September.

Mauer, M. and Tracy Huling. 1995. *Young Black Americans and the Criminal Justice System: Five Years Later*.

Washington, D.C. : The Sentencing Project.

Reynolds, Barbara. 1995. Telephone interview by author. 19 September.

The Final Call. 1995. 2 August.

West, Cornell. 1995. "Why I'm marching in Washington." *New York Times*. 14 October: A19.

A Call for a New Anti-War Movement

... The racists, that are usually very influential in the society, don't make their move without first going to get public opinion on their side. So they use the press to get public opinion on their side. When they want to suppress and oppress the Black community, what do they do? They take the statistics, and through the press, they feed them to the public. They make it appear that the role of crime in the Black community is higher than it is anywhere else.

What does this do? This message — this is a skillful message used by racists to make the whites who aren't racist think that the rate of crime in the Black community is so high. This keeps the Black community in the image of a criminal. It makes it appear that anyone in the Black community is a criminal. And as soon as this impression is given, then it makes it possible, or paves the way to set up a police-type state in the Black community, getting the full approval of the white public when the police , use all kinds of brutal measures to suppress Black people, crush their skulls, sic dogs on them, and things of that type. And the whites go along with it. Because they think that everybody over there's a criminal anyway... — Malcolm X[1]

ON THE STREET, WAR HAS DEHUMANIZING SLANG. THE "SLINGERS" are "shaking out" or selling to the crackheads, lunchboxes and fiends — the users. The "skeezers" sell their bodies for a crack rock. In years past these crack-addicted prostitutes were called "rock stars." To build a "rep," short for reputation, a slinger has to be willing to protect his "spot" or territory. His employers then elevated him to "banger," one "who works in blood and bullets." If a slinger is good in "putting in work" in the "game," whatever that "game" may be, he then becomes a "baller" or "high-rolling hustler."[2] Despite the language, the most common perception of the drug problem is that "it's a black thing!" or a "G [gangsta]-thang!" For white America, the drug problem has a black face. This provides the validation for the law enforcement targeting of blacks. Many believe that all the dealers are black because that is what they see on television. The language of the streets and office suites, politics, culture and media is that of dehumanized dark faces. Dehumanization strips away an individual's humanity and attempts to insert stereotypical, collective properties. It fosters the tyrannical and regressive policy known as the "war on drugs" to the exclusion of policies that focus on the public health implications of substance abuse. It also encourages the undermining of civil liberties and violations of human rights protections. Both the war on drugs and conventional wars practice dehumanization of victims in the mind of the aggressors. In addition, the drug war effects dehumanization of victims in the victims' own mind. As with dehumanization, often the combatants (as opposed to communities of innocent bystanders) share a lack of respect for human rights — life, liberty and property. Furthermore, the aggressors and the victims are united in their hostility to human rights just as drug dealers and users are united in their commitment to the eventual destruction of human life.

Television reflects, monitors and records where the government is waging its domestic war. Programs, such as "*COPS*" seldom, if ever, show police engaged in "dynamic entries" (kicking in doors) out in suburbia. They do not show some soccer mom laying face down on her living room floor wearing only her underwear. The faces on the floor, the hoods of cars, the pavement, in the dirt or up against the wall are generally black, Latino, or poor. This may account for the incredulousness and denial that white America feels toward reports that drug use is prevalent among their children.

Other forms of media, popular culture and even artistic expression also serve to reinforce the dehumanization needed to wage war. Popular culture images have advanced the notion of the violent and sexually promiscuous underclass; an example being the "gangsta" rappers' portrayal of young black men as angry urban guerrillas locked in a geno-cidal/suicidal/fratricidal lifestyle. The rappers are often surrounded by black women referred to as "hoochies," a contemporary twist on the myth of Jezebel, the promiscuous black woman. Douglas Kellner of the University of Texas posits that ideology (popular culture) can "seduce individuals into identifying with the dominant system of values, beliefs, and behavior. Ideology replicates their actual conditions of existence, but in a mystical form in which people fail to recognize the negative, histori-cally constructed and thus modifiable nature of society."[3]

The drug war has spread from the urban ghettoes and rural com-munities of color "across the tracks" to all neighborhoods of color. It is common to witness detained minority motorists with their car trunks open and their personal belonging spread on side of the road. Police road blocks are a way of life in neighborhoods of color. Often, when a police stop is made, a questionable search is conducted and if no con-traband is found, a motorist receives what is commonly referred to as a "nigger ticket"— issued to head off any possible legal action or formal complaint. Moreover, stories abound about routine traffic stops that become life threatening events. Additionally, many black motorists have experienced being surrounded by three or more patrol cars for the issu-ance of a traffic citation or warning.

The "war on drugs" particularly affects how children are viewed, valued and treated by society. First, the perception created by the war is that youth are abnormally violent. The dehumanizing portrayal of the current youth subculture as being more violent than past generations has resulted in a corresponding erosion of the rights of minors. Warrantless searches of lockers, drug sniffing dogs and urine testing for athletes have become commonplace in the public schools. Many state and federal laws now allow minors as young as 13 to be tried as adults. This is one of the few areas that society grants minors equal value to adults. It might be assumed that since many in the black community have a child, relative or friend under some type of penal supervision, they would eschew any attempts at dehumanization. However, it seems that tacit acceptance of the portrayal of youth as abnormally violent has taken place. Since the fear of youth is promoted, solving the drug abuse problem takes a back seat to control and containment. This promotion of fear gives irrespon-sible adults an escape from facing their responsibility for the problem of so-called incorrigible youth. Instead of dealing with the problems of youth one often hears stereotyping comments such as, "If you look at them [youth] hard they will cuss you out or shoot you." Fear also creates irresponsible parents. Fear lowers resistance to dehumanization and they surrendered parental responsibility to the state. The surrender takes the form of more police with an over-abundance of power, boot camps, regressive "youth-oriented" legislation, curfew laws, and schools that are more reminiscent of penal facilities than educational institutions. Lack of parental responsibility coupled with the increased reliance on control and containment has caused children to become resentful and lose respect for adults and institutions, especially in the face of the erosion and disrespect for their equal protection and due process rights. These are the dynamics that make for a more violent society.

Hereafter, the "war on drugs" will be referred to simply as the "war." Let's call it what it is. For many policy experts, the information, assumptions and conclusions of this essay are not new. This chapter is written for those living in an already hostile environment further exacerbated by the so-called "war on drugs." It offers ammunition in the struggle for justice and peace. The ammunition includes exposing the connection of history, politics, policy and personalities, and how each has fostered the war. A primary theme of this essay, as expressed in the foregoing quotation made by Malcolm X in 1965, is that those who harbor and advance the racist notion that the black community is a community of criminal deviants promote war. Consequently, racism is a primary ingredient in the drug war.

Throughout United States history, racial stereotypes have determined individual actions and interactions, public policy, and group and state conduct. In this context, the war is a continuation of attitudes that fostered United States participation in the *Maafa* (slave trade)[4], slave and Black Codes, Jim Crow laws, and state-sponsored segregation. Stated more strongly, the war reflects white supremacy, militarism or fascism and a total disregard for fundamental civil liberties and human rights. Drug warriors primarily aim these assaults at people of color but the war affect all citizens.

The racial disparity in sentencing overall, and drug sentencing in particular, is reminiscent of the Black Codes and Jim Crow laws — ethnic discrimination against blacks by legal enforcement to contain and control. The sentencing disparity is an obvious disregard for equal protection under the law. In California for example, records show that between 1988 and 1994 not one white defendant was convicted of a crack offense in the federal courts serving Los Angeles and six other southern counties since the federal government enacted mandatory sentencing in 1986. As reported in *The Los Angeles Times*, nearly all white crack offenders were convicted in state court, where sentences were less severe.[5] Blacks and Latinos were routinely referred to federal courts where jail sentences are commonly much longer than those meted out by the state. Further, the racial and ethnic composition of United States' jails and prisons and the categorizing within the prisons harks back to the days of segregation. Inmate discipline and rewards (for example, percentages of inmates, by race, in maximum security or super max facilities, solitary confinement or lockdown, prison work assignments, parole, pardons, probation, work release and job placement) can all be shown to have racially disparate applications.

American racism is economic in origin and effect. Slavery emerged for economic reasons and racism made inhumane violations of human rights palatable to a majority. The drug war is simply a continuance of the legacy of American economic racism. A steady depletion of inner city business capital and jobs has occurred over the past two decades. Manufacturing jobs have moved from the United States to cheaper labor markets abroad, and migrant laborers do much of the field or unskilled work.[6] This has made the lack of proper education and skills training among blacks obvious, and created large scale unemployment and underemployment. The poor, unskilled, underemployed and unem-ployed black has become the raw material for the unprecedented expan-sion of the prison-industrial complex. The poor and dispossessed are a recognizable, bountiful and an easily harvested raw material. They are the chattel. Many states and localities use inmate labor for a variety of tasks. This state of affairs is also tantamount to chattel slavery. In the past decade, the building of jails has outpaced the building of public housing and schools in many areas. Moreover, the government has demolished and not replaced many older public housing projects. This is not to imply that building more public housing or expanding the welfare-state is a solution to the economic problems of the poor. It is merely an example of public policy priorities that make jail one of the few places left for the poor to go.

The war provides a place for both semi-skilled and skilled workers. Many of those who once held professional positions and semi-skilled jobs in manufacturing now find themselves building and operating the infrastructure of the prison-industrial complex. They are the bail bondsmen, lawyers, judges, police, those who build and supply the prisons, prison guards, social workers, educators, instructors at the various criminal justice academies and criminal justice courses at community and technical colleges, private security officers, home security technicians and salesmen, and many others. Many states and localities depend on prison construction and operation as an integral part of their economies. According to the United States Census Bureau, federal, state and local governments increased their prison construction spending from $4 billion in 1975 to $30 billion in 1994. This represents a 612 per cent increase between 1970 and 1990. Furthermore, in 1994, spending on construction and operations of prisons increased twice as fast as the growth in overall state spending according to the National Conference of State Legislatures.[7] In many rural areas the prison has replaced the mill or the factory as the primary employer. In the coalfield region of southwest Virginia the unemployment rate hovers around 20% and it is difficult recruiting manufacturers. Building four prisons resulted in the creation of 800 - 1,000 jobs.[8] As with any industry, there must be a product that satisfies a real or imagined need. The product offered by the prison-industrial complex is the illusory and euphemistic promise of a "safe and secure quality of life" — threat reduction. For war supporters, successful threat reduction is measured by an increase in the black jail population [see Figure 5-1 — arrest rates for blacks and whites, age 18 and older], longer sentences for those convicted of a crime and, more punitive treatment while incarcerated. These increases have come as a direct result of drug arrest and prosecutions.[9]

The charge of conspiracy is raised in the drug debate. The conspiracy charge is not a new one. It is usually linked to the genocide of blacks and covers a variety of concerns. Whatever the concern may be, some blacks maintain the belief that there are small, secret, groups of white racists tucked away somewhere plotting policies deleterious to blacks. Awareness of the Tuskegee syphilis experiment evoked allegations of

conspiracy. Long before it was publicly revealed that political opera-
tives in the Richard Nixon White House used crime as an issue to attack
blacks or the Gary Webb's articles exposed possible Drug Enforcement
Administration (DEA) and Central Intelligence Agency (CIA) involvement in the drug trade[10], the cry of conspiracy percolated within the
black community. Many blacks now see conspiracy in the disproportionate spread of AIDS and the disproportionate drug arrests in the black
community. Business practices of corporate America have long been
suspect. The once secret, now public, actions of executives at Texaco oil
and Avis car rentals only validated the cries of conspiracy theorists. They
see conspiracy in the educational system and in a popular culture that
promotes what some feel is a sanitized, majoritarian portrayal of slavery
and history. It is felt that the portrayal reinforces the denial that many
whites have regarding the economic disparity unjustly created by slavery
and racial discrimination. However, historical interpretations, institutions and popular culture images are functions or outgrowths of supremacy. Fundamentally, with institutional white supremacy and white male
hegemony firmly in place, conspiracy is unnecessary. All that a white,
majoritarian society needs to endure is maintenance of the status quo.
Most people, of whatever race or ethnic origin, unless they are totally
disengaged from institutional society, knowingly or unknowingly participate in the maintenance of white supremacy. White supremacy is not
only the Ku Klux Klan with its white men in robes. White supremacy is
the unjust institutional and structural control by whites. In the American
context, it is generally control by those of Anglo-European descent,
although the definition of *white* has expanded throughout the years to
include almost everyone except those of African origin. To some extent
society and culture often view *white* more as an economic term than a
racial classification. White supremacy is the conspiracy. The war helps
to maintain and advance it as status quo. Thus, ending white supremacy
and curing dispossession are the primary issues to be addressed for
genuine reform to take place.

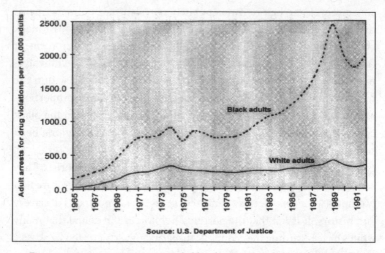

Figure 5-1. Among persons age 18 and older, the arrest rate for drug violations for blacks has grown much more rapidly than the arrest rate for drug violations for whites, 1965-1992

At the birth of this nation, the Founding Fathers dispossessed enslaved blacks. Racism was used to rationalize dispossession for the sake of white privilege. Dispossession is denial of capital and access to capital. The Founding Fathers legally defined enslaved Africans as property with no rights whites were bound to respect. They denied them equal opportunity, due process, equal protection and economic rights. The goal of abolitionism was to secure these rights for all and to repair the damage caused by denial of those rights. This goal has also long been the framework for the human rights struggle. At the signing of the Declaration of Independence the Founding Fathers betrayed the abolitionist cause with the codification of slavery. While the 13th Amendment ended the legal condition of chattel slavery, it failed to eliminate the effect that was dispossession. It is dispossession that causes and maintains racial economic disparity. Abolitionism was about ending dispossession, not just ending the treatment of individuals as property or ending the legal condition of slavery. Once one pulls a knife from a person's chest, one stops the hemorrhaging or eventually the victim will die. Ending slavery removed the knife. The United States government has yet to treat the hemorrhaging.

When addressing dispossession in America, inevitably one must also address denial. Denial is ignoring the obvious. It is in the expectation placed on African-Americans that they accept thirty years of affirmative action policy as restitution for 300-plus years of slavery and state-supported discrimination — the hemorrhaging. In a legal sense, restitution is making amends for an injustice. Affirmative action policy is a conservative remedy to address past and ongoing economic inequities and injustices. Many believe that affirmative action policy is restitution avoidance policy that has failed to redress the dispossession that epitomizes the phrase "justice denied." The outward expression of white denial is in such wide ranging comments as, "My ancestors never owned slaves" or, "They have had enough time to catch-up." While these comments seem to express very different sentiments, both share a denial of history and economics — current and past. As for the first comment, in most wars the rich and powerful use the poor to defend their interest. Such was the case with non-slave owning farmers and commoners who fought to defend the economic interest of the wealthy that included the institution of slavery. Many also fought for the possibility of themselves becoming slave holders.

Then and now, many whites also participate in supporting and creating institutions and policies that maintain the status quo of dispossession. The second comment is usually either a manifestation of ignorance or a racist view that assumes that blacks cannot catch up due to some genetic predisposition. Both sentiments deny that a horrific injustice occurred and that United States society and government incurred a debt because of that injustice. Government is the obvious focus of debt collection because the injustices were sanctioned and promulgated by government. Sentiments of denial also seem grounded in the belief that blacks have or are somehow benefiting at the expense of white entitlement to privilege. Entitlement to privilege simply means that one group believes that it is uniquely qualified or entitled to rule. The privileged group sees economic, social and political control as a birthright. Alternatively, its members view participation and power sharing with other groups as at the controlling group's disadvantage, pleasure, or "tolerance." Nonetheless, the reality is that the original injustice to blacks has enriched and continues to enrich many whites unjustly. The interplay of these issues is some-times referred to as the "cultural conspiracy." It applies to a laundry list of issues — from affirmative action, attacks on multiculturalism and racial diversity, welfare programs cutbacks to curfews in neighborhoods of color. The perception is that these issues, along with the politics and the popular culture environment that surrounds them, are somehow the result of conspiracy, inspired by denial and linked to genocide. Some theorists credit this conspiratorial environment with spawning so-called "hate-radio" and the notion of the "angry white male."

While many acknowledge the war's failure and others cry conspiracy, there has been an unwillingness to challenge the failure of the current drug policy beyond rhetorical attacks. The violence of the war will end when those most adversely affected decide that enough is enough. The war must stop at the front. Blacks, Latinos, and the poor, all those ground up in the onslaught, must resist the genocidal impact and implications of the war. Activists, reformers, and community intellectuals must support the resistance by providing a connected and cogent argument identifying and explaining the impact and implications. Current drug policy leads to further expansion of the prison-industrial complex, specifically to the detriment of people of color, and to society overall. Moreover, current policy has not eliminated or decreased drug usage. Therefore, the subject of legalizing drugs must no longer be taboo. Reformers need not feel embarrassment, shame or fear when engaging in advocacy for the com-plete legalization of all drugs. Debating which drugs should or should not be banned encourages confusion and obfuscation. Legalization is a tactic available to counter the mass criminalization and militarization of civil society that has been another by-product of the war. Legalization is the abolition of all illegal possession laws, criminal statutes and regulations concerning the production, distribution, possession or consumption of drugs — leaving only those laws that protect consumers from decep-tion and fraud. Some support a policy of decriminalization because it may be more palatable and socially acceptable. Decriminalization is the abolition of laws that make it a crime to use substances deemed illicit. Under decriminalization, the government maintains control of how they dispense a particular drug. Legalization infers that protecting one from oneself is not a legitimate function of government. There has been a noticeable silence on the issue of legalization for fear of advocacy being labeled as soft on crime. Supporting legalization attracts the new pejorative label of "liberal." When former Surgeon General Jocelyn Elders supported holding discussions on the issue of legalization, she had very little support from any quarter, including the black community. Legalization is not promoting or condoning drug use. The drug abuse problem is a health problem as opposed to a crime problem. Drug use is often very harmful to people. The problem is that the drug war is not stopping the harm from drug use but it is adding the harm from drug prohibition. In this respect, legalization, or ending drug prohibition, is a means of achieving a more constructive and humane drug policy. Citizens must ask the question, "are we winning the war on drugs?"

Direct and political action is essential in the anti-war effort. Opposition to current drug laws must take place at the local, state and federal levels. Opposition must be expressed at city and county councils, at the courthouse, the statehouse and at the White House. In addition, war opponents must consider direct action tactics such as jury nullification in drug cases. Jury nullification gives the individual juror the power to judge the law. Some declare that the criminal justice system is utterly racist and beyond reform. As a result, they advocate that black jurors set black defendants free no matter the crime. Jury nullification is not simply setting criminals free or setting a person free because of their color. Jury nullification signals public disapproval of the current policy and empowers individuals to act on the unfairness of current laws. Moreover, political action must take place. Policy reformers must educate the electorate on the cost and consequences of current drug policy. Political candidates who support policies that maintain the war must then face opposition from those seeking change. Opposition to candidates who advocate social policy that results in dehumanization must be vocal, organized and expressed at the ballot box.

This essay does not intend to provide justification or comfort for those who would assign blame for their drug condition solely on their status as a victim. Drug users, who happen to be black know that American society is racist; the scar of slavery and discrimination remains and they do not get a reasonable chance in the criminal justice system. Nevertheless, choices and consequences for individuals remain. Surrendering one's rights should never be a choice. One should make legal choices only after obtaining clear information . Those who do not have clear information and enter a plea out of ignorance have surrendered to the war. Volunteer recruits in the war are those who know the war is violating their rights but surrender their rights out of fear or convenience. While challenging a racist legal system is both difficult and dangerous, giving up one's rights implies approval of the conduct of the war.

The black elected officials and leaders who condemn the consequences of the war but continue to support the conduct of war are even more problematic. The war is a means of social control and containment and has led to an expansion of the criminal underclass. Support of the war in any respect, allows society to escape its responsibility for the dispossession created by the initial absence of justice.

Reformers should reject regressive policy measures wrapped in the language of justice and equality. Many "liberal" leaders call for the equalization of drug sentencing (which is nothing more than equalized suffering). Equalization to them means more whites in jail, not fewer blacks. This is another diversion from the goal of ending the war, and in many ways erodes support for the human rights struggle. The goals of that struggle remain the advocacy and protection of due process and equal protection rights and equal opportunity and economic justice for the dispossessed. These provided the framework for Dr. Martin Luther King's "Poor Peoples' Campaign" and they can do the same for a new anti-war or anti-dispossession movement. This essay seeks to explain why and how war is waged and offers a defense and offense against it. The strategy involves attacking stereotypes and the process of dehumanization and confronting and ending dispossession. Most important, reformers must engage in the advocacy of rational drug policies and humane legal alternatives. Government forfeits its moral authority to tell its citizens to stop killing when it has a policy of killing. It cannot command citizens to "stop the violence" and respect human life when it engages in a violent war that does not respect human life. The "war on drugs" is a failure for many reasons. Reformers must focus their efforts and energies on encouraging a new generation of anti-war activists armed with a compelling argument for ending the war. In turn, these activists must educate and mobilize on the ravages of war. Although religion is not a substitute for curing dispossession, reformers ought to encourage involvement from the religious community. When mainstream groups become supportive of the anti-war effort, it becomes easier for elected officials to support policies that some may view as "liberal," "radical" or whatever pejorative label the drug warriors attempt to place on opposition to the war. No effort for social change starts in the mainstream. It starts with a few people who attempt to draw a crowd. The crowd gives the politician the will to act.

Waging war

One in three young black men in the United States is under criminal justice control at a cost of $6 billion every year. One in 15 black men is incarcerated. 683,200 black men are behind bars, compared with 674,400 white men. Blacks make up 12% of the U.S. population, 13% of drug users, but 55% of convictions for drug possession. It takes five grams of crack to get five years in federal prison versus 500 grams of cocaine. In 1992, 89.7% of all those in state prison on drug possession charges were black or Hispanic. 94% of crack defendants in federal courts in 1994 were black. Because addicts often share dirty needles, AIDS is now the leading cause of death for black men and women ages 25 to 44. For black injecting drug users, the risk of getting AIDS is seven times the risk of dying from an overdose.[11]

Whenever government wages war on something, more often than not that something turns out to be people. The government's drug war targets black people. Countless anecdotal examples exist on the insidiousness of the war. A case encountered while researching this essay describes the pervasiveness of the war. The story involves a black man in his early forties named Delane from a rural county in South Carolina. Delane is a carpenter by trade. He repairs mobile homes, puts up sheet rock, paints, and does other building-related jobs. He does not make much money, and would be considered in the lower middle-income level. Society commonly labels him working class. Before accepting an invitation to his friend's cookout (which turned out to be a "stakeout"), he had avoided being a convicted drug felon. Delane tells the story of being invited to a weekend cookout by a co-worker named Melvin. He went to the cookout and, upon arriving, asked for Melvin, the friend who invited him. A man, who was later revealed to be an undercover police officer, told Delane, "Melvin is gone to get beer." Delane told the person to tell Melvin he came by. As he turned to leave, three undercover agents grabbed him and threw him to the ground. His friends in the car, thinking that they robbing him, got out of the car to help him. They arrested them too. Delane and his friends were taken inside the host's house and ordered to sit on the floor in handcuffs. When Delane went into the house, he found himself with several other people, many of whom he knew, sitting on the floor in handcuffs. One person, Al, resisted and "got some knots up side his head." Police promptly arrested all who stopped by and asked for the cookout's host. They arrested and formally charged about thirty persons were with intent to buy crack-cocaine, including Melvin, the cookout's host. We should note that no physical evidence — crack-cocaine — was found or presented in court. Asking for the host qualified as grounds for arrest. Upon being taken to the county jail, defendants were not allowed to call family or legal counsel for at least twenty-four hours. Delane had just gotten his paycheck cashed and the police "confiscated every dime in [my] pocket." After spending the weekend in jail, they released him on a $2,500 bond. A year passed and they called up Delane's case on the docket. Unlike the other defendants, he at first chose to plead not guilty. Yet nervous because his court-appointed attorney was absent, Delane changed his plea to guilty. The judge, skeptical of Delane's decision, raised his bond and ordered him back to jail "to give him some time to think" about accepting the "deal" the police gave the other defendants. The deal was a felony drug charge — intent to buy — although no physical evidence was presented; 240 hours of community service — which consisted of washing police cars, doing repairs around the jail and picking up paper on the highways; one year probation — suspended upon completion of community service; twelve months' suspension of drivers' license; and loss of voting rights. The latter can be returned upon completion of state supervision. Although it seems that Delane accepted the deal out of expedience, he claims that he felt powerless and isolated and had to take it. Delane's final comment reflects the growing concern of black voter disenfranchisement due to the war. He stated, "The bad thing about what happened was that it was right before elections. And they had van loads of us going to jail that weekend."

One cannot have war without an enemy. The first act of the drug warriors was to claim that they were protecting citizens from an evil enemy — illicit drugs. One cannot wage war against a substance, so the drug warriors' attention predictably shifted to identifying a living breathing enemy. An enemy that society deems to have less value than whites — blacks. After identifying the enemy, war supporters peppered the air with cries of national unity and war metaphors. The metaphors helped create a militaristic environment. Criminologists Peter B. Kraska and Victor E. Kappeler write:

> Metaphors play a central role in the construction of and reaction to social problems: they act to organize our thoughts, shape our discourse, and clarify our values (Ibarra and Kitsuse 1993; Spector and Kitsuse 1987). Sociologists have documented the spread of the medical metaphor — defining social problems as "illnesses" to be treated by medical professionals — as an important trend in twentieth-century social control (Conrad and Schneider 1992; Conrad 1992)... The ideological filter encased within the war metaphor is "militarism," defined as a set of beliefs and values that stress the use of force and domination as appropriate means to solve problems and gain political power, while glorifying the tools to accomplish this — military power, hardware, and technology (Berghahn 1982; Eide and Thee 1980; Kraska 1993).[12]

When the enemy is a targeted group of people, they face immediate dehumanization. Martin Luther King, Jr. often called dehumanization as *thingafication*. Public acceptance of the growing incarceration rate is due in large part to the continuing *thingafication* of blacks. Rather than picturing the black and Latino fathers, mothers, brothers and sisters that are being jailed, politicians and demagogues dismiss them as criminals — the "enemy." The obvious consequence of dehumanization is an erosion of respect for human rights and the constitutional protection of those rights.

Additionally, because of where they are conducting the war, historical racism, and so on, the war and crime link to race politics. Race politics are a form of "wedge politics." Wedge politics is designed to separate — to drive a wedge through a group's connection to the whole of society and, to drive a wedge through group cohesiveness. It intends to dismiss the political significance of a group. Nixon's use of crime to attack blacks is the most often cited example of using wedge politics. Wedge politics in a racial context is analogous to race-baiting. There is an abundance of examples of contemporary race-baiting. The image of the black man behind bars remains a staple of crime and race politics. Race politics is evident in George H.W. Bush's 1988 Willie Horton "political ad" and Bill Clinton's Stone Mountain "photo-op" (posing in front of a phalanx of black, Georgia prison inmates during the 1992 Presidential election). It is a cornerstone of United States politics to exploit people's legitimate fear of crime. Political posturing on crime cultivates racial animosity and prejudice that neutralize citizen opposition to the war.

Dehumanization has a variety of elements; nonetheless, in the drug war racism is the most obvious. The war's propaganda reinforces the notion that the enemy possesses an inherent or genetic predisposition to violence. This validates disproportionate state action and control. Since the objects of scorn have no humanity, they are not worthy of justice or even of life. During World War II, the Japanese were labeled "Japs" and assigned a variety of stereotypes. This made the decision to drop atomic bombs on them seem less barbaric. During the Vietnam War, the North Vietnamese became "Charlie" or "gooks," which partly explains why the United States could not envision losing a war to a group of 'pajama clad commies." When whites enslaved Africans for their labor and they exterminated North American aborigines for land, they respectively called them "dumb savages" and "noble savages." In the war, black men labeled are "predatory," in an attempt to reinforce dehumanization. Labeling black youth as "predatory" arose from attacks against foreign tourists in Florida in the early '90s. It was also used (along with the term "wilding") to describe incorrigible youth in New York City. In 1993, during the heat of the crime debate, news programs, such as *NBC's Meet the Press*, revived and popularized the D.W. Griffith *Birth of a Nation* stereotype of the black male "predator."[13] Naturally, all crimes are predatory in nature. Milwaukee serial killer and cannibal Jeffrey Dahmer was surely predatory; however, he was not a black or a teen when he committed his crimes. Furthermore, neither Dahmer nor Colin Ferguson —the Long Island Train killer— had any arrests prior to their murderous acts. To apply the term *predatory* based on age reinforces the perception of the youthful offender as more violent than the adult offenders. To add race simply implies that black youth offenders are more violent than all others.

Society and culture also seduce the targets of the war into believing the negative things said or written about them. Slogans, such as "black-on-black crime," when used by black leaders, insinuate that black inter-racial crime is more insidious than black intra-racial crime. It implies that black criminals should spare their brothers (that is, a criminal should choose their victims on the basis of race). In contrast, pundits and politicians seldom referred to crimes committed by whites against other whites as "white-on-white crimes." Criminologists commonly know that whites commit crimes against other whites and blacks commit crimes against other blacks at roughly the same rate of occurrence. Most crimes are neighborhood crimes. Moreover, victims and perpetrators are generally known to one another. To categorize neighborhood crime as differing racially is an attempt to portray black crime as more insidious and violent. Moreover, the notion of the black perpetrator preying on whites is deliberately used to stir the fears and passions of whites. Political scientists James Lynch and William Sabol assert that the black underclass poses less of a threat to whites than the white underclass because it (the black underclass) is segregated residentially and therefore is less proximate to the working and middle classes than is the white underclass.[14]

Many black politicians and community leaders have been manipulated into adopting racist arguments and stereotypes that support the lie that blacks are more violent than whites. The seduction has taken place partly because many white liberals have changed their positions and beliefs about social justice. Liberalism was in vogue during the '60s and '70s. White officials then exhibited a greater willingness to look at the causes of crime. Liberalism involved believing that doing something about the human condition was part of the solution. Today it seems that liberals have apparently abandoned this mode of thinking for a mind set supporting inherent racial pathologies. Taking their cues from the white liberals, along with a lack of consistent focus on cause, often puts black leadership at odds with itself. Case in point: calling drug laws' racist but telling kids "to turn those suspected of dealing into the authorities." Such a request is fraught with obvious contradictions. It says that although the system is unjust, some are unworthy of justice. Black leadership has been unable to find a cogent vision, language and message to strike at dispossession created by white supremacy. So they have followed the liberal lead and capitulated to the dominant [i.e. conservative] ideology of the time. Consequently, they often promote the vision, language and message of the forces that society has historically arrayed against them.

In 1994 civil rights activist Jesse Jackson made an "off the record" comment that media widely reported during the crime debates. Jackson stated: "There is nothing more painful to me at this stage in my life than to walk down the street and hear footsteps and start thinking about robbery and then see somebody white and feel relieved."[15] Jackson traditionally criticizes stereotypical characterizations. Nonetheless, that comment provided succor to those harboring racist attitudes and beliefs. Perhaps it was "painful" to Jackson because he realized that the stereotypes of war had seduced him too. No matter the reason, the message in effect tells whites that he can understand and does not blame them for being racist because he too is relieved that the person walking behind him is not black! This suggests that any white person is justified in fearing black people. Some insist that we cannot fault Jackson for his fear of the stranger behind him because making a risk assessment for the likelihood of being victimized by crime is reasonable for people. Still, Jackson made his comments in the crime debate. Several things come to mind when one considers Jackson's public pronouncement of fear. Jackson often mentions the 319 death threats he received during his bids for the presidency.[16] It would be revealing to know the number of blacks issuing threats. The answer would no doubt prove his fear misplaced. Jackson is a public figure. The civil rights leaders made his comments in the middle of a policy debate and observers can assume that he was addressing public policy. His comments were supportive of policies that result in discriminatory treatment for those other than "somebody white." Such statements often justify curfews, random searches and similar policies. There appeared to be no risk assessment of personal danger, only a political assessment. Jackson, it seemed, wished to remain politically visible by not appearing soft on crime. The effect of the comment was that it gave Jackson "credibility" in the prevailing conservative political order. (In fairness to Jackson, as the consequences and pressures on the black community due to the drug war increased, he sought to mobilize the black church community around the increased incarceration rate. Jackson encouraged ministers to set up bail funds for non-violent drug offenders as well as church-based mentoring programs. He also criticized the government's focus on the building of prisons at a rate twice that of public housing or school construction. Jackson also condemned the sentencing disparity and was openly critical black ministers' support of the 1994 Crime Bill with its sixty-two death penalty provisions.)

Before war supporters fully inserted troops into a war zone, the enemy's resistance must be broken down to a manageable level. Many of the tools and techniques to crush resistance are reminiscent of both slavery and Reconstruction. Enslaved Africans needed a traveling pass or a specific reason to be anyplace, and their masters imposed curfews from dusk to dawn. It was during Reconstruction that loitering and vagrancy laws were first imposed to maintain order and control of blacks. The Black Codes made it unlawful for more than two blacks to congregate simultaneously in the same area. Columbia, South Carolina offers an example of a modern day Black Code. In the 1980s the city council passed an ordinance that allows police to determine if a bystander is "aimlessly" loitering.

In addition, the "victim's rights" movement produced a concomitant erosion of human rights protection. This erosion of rights involved not only criminal defendants and prisoners but all those suspected of being involved in illegal activities. The Founding Fathers established the criminal justice system to settle disputes between parties, not direct arbitration and restitution. Instead of duels, private tribunals, vigilantism, and such, an "impartial" criminal justice system was set up. Both the alleged perpetrator and the victim surrendered the right of private settlement to the courts. The premise of justice was that defendants were innocent until proven guilty and, protection of the innocent was paramount. The first was a protection against false or fraudulent charges; the latter led to the establishment of the writ of *habeas corpus* to insure the protection of the innocent.

Battle cries by victims' rights advocates that "criminals have too many rights," undermined the foundational premise of the criminal justice system. Now many blacks view the justice system with suspicion and mistrust. In the cities, 80 to 90 per cent of the criminal defendants are black men.[17] In the current environment criminal defendants are guilty until proven not guilty. Passing regressive laws that aim to punish and exclude rather than rehabilitate and include is easier when the perception exists that criminals have too many rights.

"Truth in sentencing" — the crack-cocaine racial sentencing disparity[18] aside — became a euphemism for sending the convicted to jail in record numbers for longer periods. As the war progressed, state and federal 'three-strikes" legislation passed with little opposition from elected officials or the public in spite of objections from judges, criminologists and civil libertarians. Reagan era[19] drug policy inspired the resurgence of boot camps and chain gangs, the removal of exercise equipment from prisons, and the end of conjugal visits. With press restrictions on contacts with inmates and limits on other types of visits (friends, for example), inmates face an increased disconnection from family and community. Many friends and family members would rather avoid the dehumanizing experience of being strip searched or having their children, even babies' in diapers, patted down for contraband. One would assume that the more contact with the outside world, the easier the transition would be for the inmate returning to his or her community. Unfortunately, it seems that prison officials are more concerned with making sure the outside world remains ignorant of conditions inside jails than with what type of individual emerges from their facilities. This insures that a human face is not placed on the "enemy" and they get just what they deserve — punishment or elimination.

Once society identifies, dehumanizes, and strips the enemy of his or her rights, it sends the troops into the war zone. Supporters give the troops overwhelming resources and power to accomplish their mission. In the war the police are the troops and undercover agents are the spies. Often the task of the spy is deception. Ascribing a single description to the drug informant is difficult. They can range from the sheer opportunist to those concerned about solving a crime problem. Resources include money and equipment. The number of troops deployed or the caliber and newness of their weapons do not measure power. The lack of personal liberties measures police power. The more liberties restricted, the more power granted to the soldier/ police. At best, the hope is that the police will act responsibly and in "good faith." At worse society does not care about police conduct because it believes that the police are ridding society of criminals. In any case, when police deploy into a neighborhood and the balance of power tilts toward them, abuses may occur. This is particularly true in an environment described using war metaphors. In a militaristic environment the widely popular community-based policing becomes a means of gathering covert information for the war effort and a public relations device to gain acquiescence to the war. The coercive nature of militarism encourages tyranny and abuse that citizens are often powerless to combat Any charges of abuse are met with disbelief, scorn or a "they deserved it" attitude by the public-at-large. Police abuse is frequently answered with claims of ignorance, negligence or the oft used "acting in good faith" excuse.[20]*

The rise in the number of SWAT teams is also a dangerous trend in the militaristic environment. SWAT stands for Special Weapons and Tactics. Police researcher Peter Kraska conducted a survey of 600 law enforcement agencies serving cities with populations of 50,000 or more and found that 90 per cent have active SWAT teams. In SWAT units formed since 1980, their use has increased by 538 per cent. He also found that two out of three rural departments have active paramilitary units. Kraska calls this "militarizing Mayberry," and states that the mission of the SWAT unit has expanded from highly specialized actions to drug-related "dynamic entries" and gang suppression. Seventy-five per cent of their mission is devoted to serving high-risk warrants, mostly through drug raids. The teams often move through neighborhoods in armored or special vehicles with an assortment of weapons and equipment such as battering rams, chemical agents (tear gas and pepper spray), assault rifles, and 9mm, fully automatic machine guns. [21]

The drug warriors target the enemy by use of a profile. The profile allows police to make cursory assumptions about who they suspect is apt to engage in criminal activities. How one fits the profile can depend on many things. It can be something as obvious as gender, race and age. Profiling can encompass the area one drives through or lives in. It can be the time of day one drives down a highway or the fact that one drives on a certain road at all. Profiling takes into account one's car and its "gold" accessories. Those driving with tinted car windows, any type of neon light and chopped or hydraulic suspensions are always suspect. It can be a haircut: dreads locks (hairstyle associated with Rastafarians) mean reefer smoker. One style of dress — baggy pants and oversized jacket — means gangbanger. In addition, "colors" are some dead giveaways. It can be "eye balling" a police officer or looking away. To travel with a crowd or to travel alone can be reasons for detention by police. Profiling can entail anything, everything and nothing. The most often used profile is that of being a young black man. Consequently, the number of these "profiled" individuals from targeted areas going to jail is on the rise.. To this extent the drug warriors' battle plan is a success. The data presented in Figures 5-2 show the rapid and disparate increases in drug arrest of blacks and black youth under 17 from 1965 to 1992. Figure 5-3 shows the likelihood of arrest of black and white drug users for possession, in 1993. Figure 5-3: blacks over 18 were seven times more likely to be arrested for drugs than whites.[22]

While young black men are the most targeted group in the war, Reagan-era drug policy has also snared a disproportionate number of black women in its web. The group with the greatest increase in correctional supervision during the past decade has been black women. Between 1989 and 1991 the rate of correctional supervision for black women rose 78 per cent due to drug-related arrests[23] and criminal prosecution of pregnant drug users.[24]

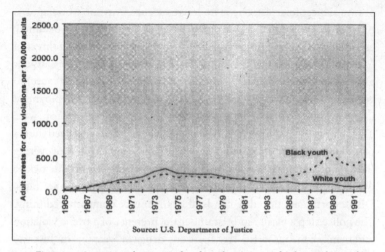

Figure 5-2. Among youth age 17 and under, , the arrest rate for drug violations for
blacks has been growing while the arrest rate for whites, rose in the 1970s and then
fell, 1965-1992

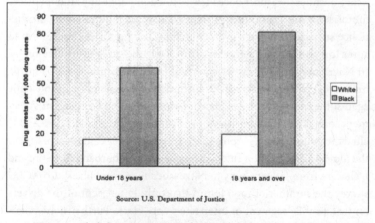

Figure 5-3. Black drug users were much more likely than white drug users to be
arrested for drug possession, 1983

Some raise the question, "What about those in the black community
who are begging for police protection?" In the war zone everyone of color
"fits the profile," including those begging for police to 'protect' them.
Every resident of the area becomes subject to arrest and search. If one is

115

always subject to arrest, one is no longer secure. Anyone who happens to be black faces an increased threat of being dehumanized, detained, escorted, arrested and imprisoned, despite class or status. The threat of "dynamic entry" increases because police can create probable cause or assert "reasonable suspicion" (a standard lower than probable cause) to go into any house or apartment. The police claim that their deployment into neighborhoods of color represents a "crisis," "emergency," or "war." This state of affairs makes "DWB" (driving while black)[25] and even the act of walking down the street grounds for reasonable suspicion. Uncovering the economic impact created by the disparate issuance of traffic tickets would be interesting since violations have an impact on insurance rates. Disproportionate ticketing can lead to insurance company redlining. The police stop a black motorist under the pretense of a traffic violation and then ask the motorist, "Are there any drugs or weapons in the car?" They ask to search and most motorists acquiesce. If they find drugs, in come the troops. If they do not find contraband, issuance of the "nigger ticket" justifies the stop. Police view as uncooperative any attempt by the motorist to assert his rights. A rights-conscious motorist often arouses police suspicion, perhaps even contempt. If a motorist chooses not to agree to an officer's request, more than likely the car is searched anyway. In November 1996, the American Civil Liberties Union (ACLU) filed a motion in Federal Court in Baltimore asking for a contempt of court fine against the Maryland State Police for violating a 1994 settlement agreement to make highway drug stops without regard to race. The ACLU cited the police agency's reports showing that 73 per cent (600 of 823) of the motorists stopped on Interstate 95 between suburban Baltimore and Delaware from January 1995 to November 1996 were black. An ACLU survey the summer of 1996 found that only 17 per cent of the drivers on that 44-mile segment of Interstate 95 are black. Furthermore, police found nothing in 70 per cent of those searches.[26]

Profiling and targeting of individuals using race and color as a determinant ultimately reaches all economic classes within a racial group because class is not as readily apparent a social marker as is skin tone. The war expands the black underclass and extends into the black middle class. Lynch and Sabol found that for blacks who were not in the underclass - that is, for blacks with connections to labor markets and mainstream institutions - the increase in drug incarceration rates between 1986 and 1991 was the largest increase of any group. They argue that since blacks are segregated residentially and underclass blacks are proximate to non-underclass blacks, or more so than whites — the law enforcement targeting strategies may be unable to distinguish class differences as easily as for whites. Consequently, strategies targeted at the underclass may have large spillover effects into the non-underclass.[27]

This is a polite way to say that all blacks and Hispanics generally look the same to police. Law enforcement officials also employ the widespread use of "John Doe" warrants for mass round-ups of suspects. The John Doe warrant contains a vague description of a suspect, an age range and the estimated weight of the unnamed, unknown, alleged suspect. Thus police can make anyone they wish (provided they are of the same race) fit the warrant. Where the John Doe warrant leaves off, some localities have passed "loitering with intent to distribute" laws. These ordinances target individuals who hang out or pass through areas designated by police to be high drug areas. Moreover, local ordinances make anyone and everyone within "reasonable proximity" of an unclaimed stash of drugs culpable for possession of the stash. The war also uses the tactic of punishing people who might not have committed a crime, but who lived in the same home as a "suspect" or knew of the suspect's activities.[28] This breeds abuse, not only by the police, but by neighbors hoping to protect themselves, their family members, or their friends from prosecution or investigation. Often groundless accusations from anonymous informants, often paid, create "reasonable suspicion" that becomes probable cause for arrest.

Opponents of the war in Southeast Asia rallied and sang songs of protest, and argued that it had accomplished absolutely nothing. If efforts to curb illicit drug usage were a measure of the war's success or failure, then our country's current domestic war is also a failure. It too has accomplished absolutely nothing for scores of blacks. The total quantity of cocaine consumption remains at historically high levels. In addition, hard-core crack users are just as addicted as ever. Revealing true intent without possessing the power to read minds is impossible.

The hidden intent may be ideology, racism, profit or political gain. War has had the effect of increased incarceration of scores of young black women and men. (The increase in incarceration rates is even more sinister if there is validity to the charge that the crack-cocaine epidemic was promoted in the black community by agencies and agents of the United States government to provide financing for the Contra war.) If increased incarceration of these people is the goal, then the war is a success. The Sentencing Project reported that from 1980 to 1984, crime fell steadily, by a total of 15 per cent. Then, from 1984 to 1989, crime rates rose by a total of 14 per cent. Thus, in a decade, prison population increased and crime went down. Prison population then continued to increase and crime increased; therefore, the cause-and-effect relationship far from certain.[29] Increased incarceration rates beget an increase in the criminal underclass.

Data exist to confirm the growth of the underclass along with the growing income gap between the rich and poor. The average offender is a high school dropout who goes to jail poor and returns to the street poorer. With cutbacks in educational programs, the education received by most inmates is a real crime. After inmates serve their time, they return to where the drug warriors harvested them. Inmates who feel that society unjustly imprisoned them are not usually a more well adjusted or rehabilitated citizen. Because of conditions in many jails and prisons, a more violent person may emerge after incarceration. Most people emerge from jail disconnected from society and stigmatized. This can make finding legitimate employment difficult. Also, many ex-offenders lose their right to vote. According to The Sentencing Project, approximately 1.4 million African-American men are currently or permanently disenfranchised from voting because of a drug-related conviction.[30] Thus they have no economic or political power and no economic or political future.

Many in American society have adopted the arguments and stereotypes that support the lie that blacks are more violent than whites. The stereotype of the "violent" and "predatory" black male is central to the justification of the war. "They sell drugs because they are lazy and don't want to work!" "They shoot and kill one another because they are more violent than everyone else!" These sentiments are common among those supportive of tyrannical and oppressive social policies. The reality is that one *is* working when one sells drugs. One reason those drug sales proliferated in minority communities is the lack of entry level employment for the young. Communities of color have also experienced a general lack of capital development. For many of those engaged in drug sales, pushing is the most dependable source of employment in their neighborhoods. Drug dealers are capitalists, entrepreneurs who sell drugs to satisfy their material needs, real and imagined. For black men in the 18-24 age group, their reported unemployment rates in the mainstream economy have remained consistently high over the past decade. In 1991 the official government unemployment rate for African-American male teenagers was 36.5 per cent. Reported unemployment among black women in the same age group for the same period was at 36.1 per cent. The National Urban League estimated the unofficial or "hidden" unemployment rate for black men *and* black women in this age group at 56.9 per cent.[31] Thus employment in drug trading fills the void created by surplus labor and a lack of economic opportunity.

Next is the issue as to whether drug dealing is more violent than other occupations. Illicit drugs, a valued commodity more costly than gold, require the same type of physical protection as does gold. Valued commodities usually require armed protection. Those protecting gold and those protecting illicit drugs use force appropriate to protect their products. Both will, and do, use violence when thought necessary. Because certain drugs are illegal, violence is the only method the drug dealer has to protect his investment. Moreover, the use of violence is the only measure that a drug dealer has to select and appraise his employees. Consequently, the young dealer engages in violence to build a "rep" or to protect his "spot." This is the same kind of protectionism that the United States engaged in the battle for oil in the Persian Gulf War(s).

The war seems to rest on the notion that leaders, whatever their political affiliation, ideology, or race, always seek to act in the best interest of society. Citizens hope that their leaders will place their own interest second, and that they are fair-minded and just. However, neither the legacy of Ronald Reagan and George H.W. Bush nor the promise of

Bill Clinton and Al Gore constitutes a successful campaign against drug abuse in the United States. Instead, they have promoted and maintained a war that erodes the rights of all citizens, but selectively targets those who lack the financial ability to defend their way through the justice system. Ninety-five per cent of all African-Americans detained by this system have to rely on an overstressed, underfunded public defender system.[32] Moreover, cutbacks in treatment programs and educational and training opportunities for inmates make it apparent that the war is not concerned with enabling ex-addicts to become productive members of society. If protection of rights and humane treatment of addicts had been goals, Reagan-era policy would be considered a failure. Instead, drug warriors fill the prisons beyond capacity and prison building is a growth industry. For those who seek rehabilitation as a goal, the policy has offered tyranny, violence, dehumanization, further dispossession and hopeless entrapment of those in the ever-expanding underclass. These are some of the factors that contribute to the need to self-medicate.

The war paints with a broad brush, coloring everyone in the black community as potential lawbreakers in one stroke. Reform lies in confronting the myths, scapegoating and stereotyping that are inherent in the war, drawing a line between fact and fiction. Exposing myths entails critical analysis of the popular culture and the environment in which stereotyping and war supporters perpetuate racial myths. Stereotypes perpetuate ignorance that breeds fear and hostility. Thus reformers should expose and reject those who use stereotypes. Speaking "truth to power" involves recognizing and challenging war hawks, no matter their political party affiliation or race.

Those cultivated to be the criminal underclass must lead the anti-war struggle. The war ensures their continued subjugation. Wars create prisoners of war, and drug war POW's serve as convenient props for ambitious politicians. The politicization of the victims of war is a significant step in organizing opposition to the war. (There appears to be a growing awareness by inmates of their POW status as evidenced by the 1996 uprisings by black inmates in federal and state prisons over the crack and cocaine sentencing disparity.) Organizing and mobilizing the families, friends and relatives of those incarcerated is crucial to resistance. In addition, opponents of the war must make it clear to society-at-large that oppressive social policies have dire consequences: destabilization of communities and the eventual destabilization of civil society. Communities with an ever expanding, stigmatized criminal underclass face a violent future and an ever growing war. Reform must seek an end to a violent present and avoid a more violent future.

Few leaders and organizations are standing up for the rights of the poor. Inmates and criminal defendant have even less support. Fewer still are the leaders who have the long term vision to recognize the ultimate impact on everyone's rights should the war continue. The notion exists that there is conflict between "prisoners' rights" and "victims' rights." Obviously, the victims' rights movement has more public support. Often, when the public imagines prisoners' rights, they think about inmates having access to cable television and weight lifting equipment, not habeas corpus or fair treatment while incarcerated. Traditional institutions and groups, churches and fraternal organizations, civic and civil rights groups must take steps to provide political support for the incarcerated and their families.

The task of reformers is to learn, understand, and expose the strategies and tactics employed to maintain the many false assumptions of the war. To reverse the "success" achieved by the drug warriors, reformers must debunk their assumptions. Those assumptions are that increased incarceration rates suggest success in obtaining safety and security, that is, threat reduction; citizens should be willing to surrender certain rights for threat reduction; an increase in the criminal class is good for society; certain groups and people are sufficiently more dangerous than others that they require control and containment; police are fair and always follow the rules; those claiming concerns about solving the problem of crime place society's interest before their own. A variety of contradictions are evident when these assumptions are examined. Ultimately, the public at large must understand clearly that ending the war — changing drug policy — is a progressive step toward more secure communities. Therefore, success is obtaining safe communities through humane policies. Reform must advance economic solutions over militarism. It must maintain a harm reduction and health focus over dehumanization and criminalization. Reformers must also confront the racism, stereotyping and scapegoating, whenever they appear.

The tough job for policy reformers is overcoming the taboo associated with advocating drug legalization as a rational alternative to the war. Legalization is a means of ending the violence associated with the drug war. Drug sales employment will continue until government and business fills the economic void in the affected communities. Many argue that legalization will increase access, thus increasing usage and the number of those addicted to drugs. Right now, the drug addict has unimpeded access to illicit drugs, inside and outside of jail. Why a person has a particular addiction is best left for another essay. However, the war puts drugs on the *black* market instead of the open market. This encourages high prices and high profits for the suppliers. Because profits are so high, suppliers are encouraged to expand their territory and use whatever means necessary to protect that territory. This is what has created the phenomenon of the pusher or "slinger." Legalization drives down the price of illicit drugs. Not many addicts will pay a corner pusher an inflated price for medication of questionable quality if they can be purchase it cheaper at the corner drug store.

Also, reformers must address the health questions. Poverty is miserable and depressing. Not to validate or condone crack use, crack is the poor person's antidepressant medication. The poor do not go to the public mental health clinic or a psychiatrist's office to get a prescription to ease the pain of poverty. The poor rarely have the income to afford professional psychiatric treatment. They most often seek out the corner pusher. The rich simply get a doctor to write a prescription for their problems of depression. Use of drugs by the middle class and rich to cope is not only legal, but considered a rational response to their particular malady. Another health concern is AIDS. The main reason there is an AIDS crisis among addicts is that they share needles. Allowing addicts to purchase clean needles reduces short- and long-term health care cost because it reduces the spread of the HIV virus.

As for the violence of the war, although competition between corner drug stores is often fierce, there have yet to be any reports of gunfire between local pharmacists. Moreover, the police are not kicking in doors

at corner drug stores. Just as the shooting stopped when alcohol prohibition ended, the same will occur when drug prohibition ends. The
problem of addiction is a legitimate concern. Still, an increase in police
power and the building of more jails and prisons has not provided a
solution. In the black community a root cause of the substance abuse
problem lies in dispossession. Thus, to solve systemic and structural
problems, any vision of change involves a focus on dispossession.

Dispossession

Dispossession is denial of justice, past and present. In economic
terms it is the injustice caused by denial of capital and access to capital
which underlies the racial disparity in poverty, accumulated wealth
and business capital. The term *dispossession* more accurately describes
the economic problems facing blacks than more common descriptions
such as *poverty* or *disenfranchisement*. Economists define poverty as
substandard consumption and disenfranchisement as *substandard political power*. Both are due to the lingering effects of dispossession which
is substandard ownership of capital. In this regard, slavery and racial
discrimination are viewed in terms of devalued or stolen labor, and institutional denial of access to capital. The result is economic marginality.[33]
Persistent racial disparity in educational and employment opportunities is symptomatic of dispossession. In human rights and civil liberties' terms it is the injustice caused by the denial of due process, equal
protection, and equal opportunity rights. As an instrument of white
supremacy and white male hegemony, dispossession maintains social
order and control.

Dispossession and racism are interwoven. Both are about political
and economic power used to maintain a privileged position seen as an
entitlement by many whites. The war, as a tool of dispossession, is a manifestation of oppressive social order and control measures over an economically marginal group. Consequently, the war has been enormously
successful in maintaining control of a population that has historically
faced economic marginality and lacks the socio-political means to fight
deleterious policy.[34] Legalization of drugs is merely a tactical response

that aims at an effect of dispossession. It provides a respite from the violence of the drug war but it does not solve the fundamental problem of dispossession. Members of the marginalized group may opt for other illicit occupations if drug sales employment ends and legitimate opportunities are limited or non-existent.

Dispossession is difficult to cure for many obvious reasons. First, the cure involves dispelling the notion of white entitlement to privilege and changing the nature of institutions that protect such privilege. This would change the social order. A change in what is considered common is painful because it challenges history and a majority culture's sense of itself. Some whites fear that they would have to give up material wealth and status with a change in social order. Accordingly, they feel that they have a personal stake in maintaining the current social, political and economic structure. The backlash against multiculturalism in education, diversity in the workplace and in electoral representation exposes the fight to preserve supremacy and hegemony. The notion of the "angry white male" or constant media and pundit focus on the relative strength, attitudes and importance of white male voters is also a reflection of a backlash against attacks on white male hegemony. Curing dispossession requires recognition of an economic injustice and payment of restitution. While some charge that affirmative action attempts to right a wrong with a wrong, others see affirmative action policy as recognition of injustice and an attempt to redress it. Yet, affirmative action such as race-based preference in hiring, government contracting, and school admissions, only deals with the symptoms of dispossession; it could never provide a cure. This is why many economists, activists and scholars call it conservative, restitution-avoidance policy. Nonetheless, even if society or government acknowledges a debt, the ongoing difficulty in addressing dispossession from a practical perspective is the size of the debt and/or the form of restitution.

Both conservative and liberal social policy maintain the condition of dispossession. The "conservatism" of the Reagan era attacked poor people on three fronts. First, conservative policies cut and restricted access to benefit programs. This intensified the vulnerability of those citizens whose economic dependency on government had been seeded by "liberal" welfare-state policies of the '60s. The vulnerability was further exacerbated by an increase in the number of people struggling at the bottom for unskilled jobs while the labor demand was for high-end technological jobs. "Liberal" welfare-state policies cultivated a permanent underclass by promoting social programs whose economic gains for the poor were limited to consumption rather than production. Little emphasis was placed on the capital accumulation necessary for full participation in a capitalist economy. This channeled many poor into illicit drug employment. Second, conservative budget cuts limited the ability of poor people to challenge the erosion of substantive constitutional rights by cutting back on funding for legal services and, in essence, denying them attorneys. Third, conservative courts curtailed constitutional protection against unlawful search and seizure in acquiescence to a Republican administration's execution of its domestic wars, the "war on drugs" and the "war on crime," both of which were financed by a Democratic Congress.

An anti-war movement must be a restitution movement. The movement must resist what passes as ideology in the current social, political, economic and cultural context. White supremacy, as an ideology, is the belief and practice that all that is good, human, valuable, worthwhile, civilized and right is European-based or white. Defenders of the status quo see it as establishing a universal standard. When countering the status quo ideology of white supremacy, reformers must present rational alternatives to fill the resulting voids. For activists and reformers from communities of color, positive structural alternatives are not just diversions, such as the promotion of pseudo-nationalism, separatism and racial chauvinism. One cannot right a wrong with a wrong. One must right the wrong. Diversions usually benefit those who support dispossession. The goal of reform is economic, social and political inclusion and expansion. Reform should also seek a reverse in the trend of the growing permanent underclass. Ultimately, solving the problem of dispossession requires justice. In economic terms, abolitionists, activists, and many economist see justice as restitution. Many across the United States, from religious groups to political leaders, call for racial "reconciliation," "repentance," and "redemption." However, achieving any of the three without restitution will be difficult. In a religious sense, acts of faith or contrition grant redemption. In a political or legal sense, if one is aggrieved, injured or harmed by another, the person or persons committing the injustice are liable for damages. Justice means restitution — paying the debt. No justice, no peace!

The Profiteers

The profiteers generally fit into one of the following categories: (1) those who have an inherent interest in maintaining the status quo — including ideologues and politicians seeking power within the prevailing social order; (2) those claiming an entitlement to privilege — for them the war represents "threat reduction" and the protection of material wealth, the notion of threat reduction may be viewed as false by opponents of the war, but those seeking to maintain status quo see the threat as real; (3) those seduced, co-opted, and manipulated by ideologues, politicians, and private interests, including those who are considered members of the war's targeted group; (4) those with private interests (this group claims a "legitimate" profit motive), including (but not limited to) those involved in correctional privatization efforts and other participants in the security industry; (5) the drug elite — the kingpins who control the manufacturing, supply and distribution of illicit drugs; and (6) those who earn a living from the war's delivery system, including the police (to include the various state and federal law enforcement agencies), military organizations, courts, lawyers, and all other prison-industrial complex employees.

Politicians have historically used the issue of crime for political profit. It has become a ritual for politicians to take photos with police and swear their allegiance to the "war on crime" or the "war on drugs." In 1992 Bill Clinton promised a national police force and 100,000 additional police on the street to fight the war. During the 1996 presidential campaign, Republican candidate Bob Dole of Kansas accused Clinton of being responsible for increased drug use among teens. Predictably, he used a gathering of law enforcement personnel to make his charge. Dole then promised, if elected, to escalate the war. He concluded by proclaiming,

"Just don't do it," a parroting of Nancy Reagan's "Just say no" slogan-eering. However, Clinton provides the best example of maintaining the racial status quo using co-optation and manipulation with his use of the image of Martin Luther King, Jr. If one wished to co-opt an influential black leader, King is the person one would choose for several reasons. King is the most revered of black leaders. Moreover, he cannot respond to a misappropriation of his message and philosophy. Therefore, Clinton's attempts to co-opt the message of King was somewhat successful. The co-optation influences black public opinion on the issue of crime and expands the war with the support of those most negatively affected by that expansion. Building on his 'new Democrat,' 'law and order' image, Clinton linked crime to blacks when he went into Memphis to speak before the predominately black Eighty-Eighth Annual Holy Convocation of the Church of God in Christ (COGIC) in November 1993. In the Mason Temple pulpit where King last preached, Clinton cast off the Cold War, revised King's philosophy, and supplanted the domestic war focus in a patronizing tone. He presumed to speak for King, stating:

> How would we explain it to Martin Luther King if he showed up here today and said, "Yes we won the Cold War. Yes without regard to race, if you play by the rules, you can get into a service academy or a good college. How would we justify the things we permit that no other country in the world would, explain that we gave people the freedom to succeed and we created conditions in which millions abuse that freedom to destroy the things that make life worth living, and life itself? We can not."

Clinton continued:

> If King were to reappear by my side today... he would say, "I did not live and die to see young people destroy their own lives with drugs and then build fortunes destroying the lives of others... This is not what I died for."[35]

Clinton, by misappropriating and revising King's message in a black venue, painted crime black and played to race politics. Mainstream media affirm the revisionism by not comparing what Clinton says against King's actual philosophy on crime, poverty and dispossession and government's role in curing the problems, and by not challenging the misappropriation.

Political leaders, professional athletes, celebrities, and other well known figures from within dispossessed communities are often seduced, co-opted, and then manipulated into giving "credibility" to the war. This allows the leadership of the majority to advance whatever punitive, regressive, or oppressive measures they wish to use. Some members of the dispossessed community profit because the status quo rewards them with privileges not extended to other members of their group. Society and its functionaries often seduce and manipulate many dispossessed without their knowing it has been done. At times seduction and co-optation occur out of ignorance or naiveté. At other times the manipulated person seeks out seduction or co-optation, believing them to be a way of gaining recognition by the status quo. Jesse Jackson cited an example of seduction at an April 1997 gathering of ministers in Memphis, Tennessee to mark the assassination of Martin Luther King, Jr.. Jackson scolded a group of "influential" black ministers who had accepted an invitation to meet with Bill Clinton before enactment of the 1994 Crime Bill. Apparently Clinton persuaded the Christian clergymen to accept the sixty-two additional death penalty provisions in the bill in return for such "crime reduction" programs as "Midnight Basketball." Jackson referred to the nonfunded recreation program as "fluff." Later, Congresspersons Charles Rangel of New York and Maxine Waters of California met with Clinton to discuss the additional death penalty statutes and the draconian nature of the crime bill. In response to the lawmakers' concerns, Clinton allegedly praised the black ministers for endorsing the bill. According to Jackson, Rangel was crestfallen. Jackson charged that the Congressional Black Caucus opposed the 1994 Crime Bill; however, the ministers undercut their elected representatives by endorsing the bill without first meeting with them. The ministers got a photo-op with the President. In exchange, the chief executive gained support for an expansion in the use of the death penalty.[36]

Seduction and co-optation lie on both the left and right sides of the political spectrum. We can also see it in the liaisons between sides. C. Delores Tucker of the National Political Congress of Black Women entered an "anti-rap" liaison with conservative William Bennett, former Secretary of Education. Tucker became an agent of both conservatives and liberals. She not only supported the war, but also advocated the restriction of rights within the dispossessed community. Tucker proposed the restrictions as a solution to the problem of cultural misogyny and urban "violence." She frequently blasted the culture of the underclass as immoral and abnormal. This generalization reinforces dehumanization and ignores the degrading environment and consequences of dispossession. Tucker's liaison gave conservatives a cover to continue their suppression of the underclass and liberals cover to continue their control of it. The control takes the form of calls for suspension of free speech, support for government-mandated school prayer, the suggestion of martial law using federal and state troops, and a proposed network of police informants. Such tyranny falls under the guise of addressing crime and "immorality" in minority communities. The conservative political agenda shifts the public focus to guns, drugs, music, movies, television, video games, crime and violence — everything but the real cause of the problem, the institutional, government-sanctioned, economic violence waged against the black community, and the dispossession created by that violence.

Blacks, Latinos, and the poor are the raw material for the prison-industrial complex. Private and public entrepreneurs not only profit financially from housing incarcerated citizens, but they are also able to select laborers for a variety of profit-producing tasks. Prisoners are now doing jobs from road and infrastructure repair to manufacturing furniture. Prison labor is used for "marking up" or converting the Library of Congress' Archive holdings for use on the Internet. Inmates manufacture blue jeans and package computers. High prison occupancy means high profits. The criminal justice industry, like most exploitative capitalist ventures, produces wealth for a few. Many companies with familiar names profit from the $30 billion dollar a year[37] prison-industrial complex. Goldman, Sachs and Company, Prudential Insurance of America, Smith Barney Shearson, Inc., Merrill Lynch and Company, Westinghouse Electric Corporation, and Corrections Corporation of America[38] — all have an interest in maintaining the war. Corporate support of the war effort is grounded in profit, not rehabilitation or solving the abuse problem. They have little concern about group dispossession — unless solving the problem will lead to greater profits.

Next in line are the media conglomerates such as BMG/Arista, Sony and Time/Warner. These companies make huge profits exploiting the high unemployment, consumer-obsessive behavior, sexual and racial stereotypes, and the need for recognition of those trapped in the "hood." Often, they try to shield themselves from public criticism by subcontracting their rap music interest to "independent" labels and using arm's length distribution entities. For instance, Interscope Records and Universal Music Group, which owns half of Interscope (Universal was formally known as MCA Music Entertainment Group), serves as the distribution company for "independent" label Death Row Records, which was the home to murdered rapper Tupac Shakur. Interscope's parent company is Seagram's (the liquor company). Death Row is the west coast gangsta rap music rival to the east coast's Bad Boy Entertainment. Bad Boy was home to murdered rapper Christopher Wallace, also known as The Notorious B.I.G. Other "independents," such as Lynch Mob Records, have company names that exploit stereotypes and artists who are encouraged to "keep it real." In the cases of Shakur and Wallace, both were victims of the so-called "East Coast/West Coast Rivalry." Their last albums suggest the dehumanizing and hopeless focus of their industry. Shakur's last recording was *If I Die Tonite*, and Wallace's contributions to the rap world include his first album *Ready to Die* and his last album *Life After Death*. Both artists' final work made millions for their record companies.[39] While many artists come from middle-class suburbia, those "ballers," "bangers," and "slingers" from the hood who do "make it," generally have their pain and anger exploited for short term perks. Those perks include living in a rented home and the ability to drive a luxury, leased car.[1] Many fail to receive fair compensation for their work and are discarded after record company promoters harvest new and hungrier voices. Raising the issue of gangsta rap music with its purveyors and exploiters is not to stifle the pain, misery, or debauchery emanating from the music. Nor is it a challenge to their free speech rights. The music will change when society changes the way it views and treats the poor.

Television programs such as *Real Stories of the Highway Patrol*, *America's Most Wanted* (and its many local spawns), and *COPS* are now a staple of the entertainment industry. Not surprising, this manifestation of "trash TV" appeals to the very people who end up in the back of police cars. Network television offers up *NYPD Blue*, *New York Undercover*, *Law and Order*, and a host of prime-time cop shows. These programs reinforce the war mentality and provide a numbing effect on citizens to the abuses of law enforcement. The illusion cast by these programs is that the police will conduct themselves as if a television camera is always following them around. The Rodney King video, of course, shows us what racist police will do when they think no one is looking. The connection between the cop show and the officer on the street is apparent. Cop shows support the drug warriors. Producers of the "reality" shows want excitement. Challenging unregulated police power is irrelevant to shows buoyed by the exercise of power. The result is a steady broadcast of shoot outs, chases, dynamic entries, stings and the like. Plus, when all is said and done, the officer on the screen gives the pitch for needing more men, money, and equipment. They prod citizens with the often used refrain, "There are more criminals than police and the bad guys have better arms."

The war produces an ever-increasing profit margin for members of the privileged drug elite. The elites are those who manufacture illicit drugs and control the lucrative drug distribution networks. Most illegal drugs are produced and initially distributed by an elite group of unscrupulous "businessmen" who rely on the government's war to protect their cartel from price competition in the marketplace by eliminating their competitors, at taxpayer expense, thereby guaranteeing outrageously high profit margins. The government's war also immunizes the drug elite from product liability. The police hunt down the victims of debilitating and dangerously misrepresented drugs as criminals. The drug warriors in that way deny victims the right to sue producers or distributors in the courtroom. Despite printed warning labels, smokers and government — both state and federal — now go to civil courtrooms and sue companies that manufacture cigarettes from government-subsidized tobacco crops. States are also suing the tobacco companies for their share of health care cost. However, they permit users of crack-cocaine to see the inside of courtrooms only as criminal defendants on their way to government-operated prisons where the illegal drug traffic rivals that on the streets.

Escape from product liability allows the drug elite to invest more money into protecting their product. When governments buy bigger and better weapons, the cartels can purchase better weapons. Also, when drug warriors threaten profits, the drug elite purchases governments and government officials, such as in Mexico and Panama, just to name a few.

"Kingpins," "Czars," and CEOs come and go with the flow of business. Although the drug elite make lots of money, no one group or identifiable figure is making or controlling it all. To attack the elite on their own soil takes the cooperation of governments and their citizens. Any attack on them, especially in their own countries, could expand the war in the classic military sense. A military expansion of the war would pit poor people from one country against poor people in another country. Also, in the drug producing countries where the cartels rule, leadership changes. When governments jail or kill a publicly identified kingpin, another person steps in to take the risk and reap the profits. There are no identifiable United States or foreign drug kingpins or Mafia bosses that society can focus its anger on, although the drug elite has a highly organized and efficiently operated drug distribution structure. Additionally, the use of the term *kingpin* evokes skepticism: law enforcement frequently applies the term to the street-level slinger all the way up to the head of a cartel.

For law enforcement agencies, local and national, the war is a boon. War supporters divert government funds not only from social programs but also from the economic growth and development normally stimulated by peacetime investment. The diverted funds purchase equipment, weapons, SWAT teams, and build and maintain prisons and other institutions characteristic of society at war. In the war, the suspension of civil liberties increases police powers. This suspension of rights is the most significant profit for law enforcement. In a material sense, property and money seized by police agencies provide secondary financing for many of those same agencies. Not surprisingly, property forfeiture by law enforcement has led to abuse. In Jefferson Davis and Cameron parishes in southwestern Louisiana along Interstate 10, out-of-state travelers, particularly minorities, were stopped without cause, arrested, and had their property seized without evidence of drugs in their cars. Under state law, to sue for a return of their seized assets, uncharged citizens must pay the highest bond in the nation — 10 per cent of the property's value or $2,500, whichever is greater. The burden of proving innocence is on the accused citizen. In Louisiana, 60 per cent of seizure proceeds goes to the law enforcement agency that seized the property, 20 per cent goes to the district attorney, and 20 per cent goes to the state judges' judicial expense fund.[41] Obviously, seizure laws represent a conflict of interest that encourages law enforcement officials to abuse their power.

A specific group that has gained employment in the prison-industrial complex prompts particular attention — those blacks who join police agencies. In the past, civil rights organizations had to sue municipalities to increase the number of blacks on police forces across the country. Having a proportional number of minority officers and a minority police chief is now commonplace for a city with a significant minority population. Who better to preside over a system that incarcerates an ever-increasing number of minorities? In the past, when police agencies were headed by a preponderance of white men, at the first word of police abuse a minority community would investigate and mobilize if warranted. Many blacks are now supportive of their black police chiefs, whatever the abuses that take place under their watch. Blacks worry that if they are critical of their black chief, his replacement might be a white person. Some black chiefs and officers, however, act like the stereotypical white racist cop. Moreover, when they abuse a black or minority citizen, black and white citizens grant them immunity from charges of racism because of their color. They grant this immunity although they are often carrying out the mandate of a racist system.

The military has also profited from the war. In 1993 South Carolina deployed National Guard units to so-called high crime areas. In the summer of 1996 National Guard troops conducted weekend training in targeted neighborhoods in Washington D. C. Trying to curb drug crime, guard units posted troops in military vehicles on street corners where suspected drug trafficking was taking place. These areas were exclusively black. Needless to say, many residents did not see military deployment as an effective method of dealing with the drug problem. Use of the military is solely a police-state response that ignores the causes of poverty and crime. Military occupation did not affect suppliers and manufactors, only increased the jail time for young black pushers and users. National Association for the Advancement of Colored People (NAACP) officials in South Carolina noted that military personnel arrested several citizens. Still, no change occurred in economic conditions or the drug abuse problem in the targeted communities. The drug dealers simply shifted their activities to another location. Meanwhile, war supporters still compelled residents to surrender their privacy rights as troops shone lights in windows at night and everyone became a suspect. For state military organizations, looking for a new role in a post-Cold War society, a domestic war provided the opportunity to find relevance, a new role and new enemies to conquer.

When a politician uses the war to gain office and power, the profit is in winning the office that he or she seeks. For those who support that politician, the profit is in maintaining an ideology and social order that keeps them on top or on the job. Legitimate corporations profit from the war because citizens have perceived their actions as providing a needed service. Most citizens have no idea or do not care about corporate expansion in the prison-industrial complex — unless that expansion directly affects them. The "legitimate" profiteers receive a handsome return on their investment, yet this is apt to change the cost of war to the taxpayers continues to escalate without an end in sight. The anti-war goal is to persuade the executives and corporations to take an "enlightened self-interest" view toward investing in poor and dispossessed communities.

Plenty of everyday people profit from the war as it gives them employment and the means to care for their families. In addition, the jobs give them a sense of identity and self-worth. The insidiousness of the war lies in the fact that so many individuals and organizations gain identity and function in maintaining the war effort. Without the war many unemployed people would fight for jobs — including many middle-class black people who believe that they have made some small foothold through affirmative action. The fear may be that if attention shifts from crime and prisons, a huge economic void would result. Because so many people profit in so many ways, attention must be directed to the system itself. The war on drugs is a by-product of the system and ideology of white supremacy. It is the perpetuation of this system that has caused so much · pain in the black community.

The United States spends $44 billion a year on police, prisons, judges, probation officers and parole officers. Yet, with the increase in spending, drug use remains unabated in this country. With only 5 per cent of the world's population, the United States still consumes over 50% of the world's drugs. Furthermore, this nation incarcerates black males at a rate nearly five times greater than for black males in South Africa. The United States imprisons more people per capita than any other country in the world. Also, this country spends an estimated annual expenditure of $35,000 (per prisoner) to feed, house, and care for inmates locked in our prisons.[42] Reversing such trends is not a goal of trash television. In addition, more police with better guns have not abated illicit drug use. As for those behind bars, in some states inmates are charged room and board. This creates the possibility that, after years of incarceration ex-offenders may return to the streets in financial debt to the state. This type of scheme only perpetuates and increases the inter-generational nature of dispossession.

The war has its profiteers. However, contrary to popular opinion, they are not those bejeweled and bedecked, Tommy Hilfiger-wearing, gold-accented Lexus cruisers. Nor are they the poor, young blacks and Latinos occupying the jails and prisons. The cruisers are engaged in pure, dead-end consumption. They are not investing in anything because everything they have is at risk of confiscation.

Finally, Clinton was correct regarding King's disappointment over the economic status of blacks and the violence dispossession produces. Nonetheless, King would have denounced the racist innuendo that the black community was inherently more criminal than the white community. King believed that poverty and ignorance breed crime, whatever the racial group. He was explicit about the government's culpability and responsibility for the ongoing economic violence against the poor and blacks.[43] King challenged the lack of economic justice, citing urban decay as a symptom of dispossession. Whenever asked who he thought was responsible for inner city crime and blight, King often quoted Victor Hugo: "If a soul is left in the darkness, sins will be committed. The guilty one is not he who commits the sins, but he who causes the darkness."[44] King's last speech was a call for economic boycotts against banks that redlined and industries which refused to hire blacks. King was killed in Memphis while leading garbage workers fighting for labor rights and calling for an end of the Vietnam War. He said that the war took away resources from the dispossessed. King died trying to change the status quo and fighting against economic dispossession. Therefore, the idea of King supporting the war, totalitarian-style crime bills, and the racist hysteria that replaced meaningful public discourse is hard to conceive. Casting crime in a race context reinforces group dispossession; it provides the illusion of safety and security to those claiming an entitlement to privilege. The solution rests with a focus on ending dispossession. Minority business ownership and self-determination, rather than food stamps and economic dependency, erode dispossession. The economic power of the marketplace, not the police power of government, reverses those factors that perpetuate conditions of poverty. The conditions of poverty breed the contempt for human life and the disregard for property rights that are the roots of drug abuse and crime in the United States.

Peace and Justice

> It is not enough for the Negro to declare that color-prejudice is the sole cause for their social conditions, or for the white South to reply that their social condition is the main cause of prejudice. They but act as reciprocal cause and effect, and a change in neither alone will bring the desired effect. Both must change, or neither can improve to any great extent. The Negro can not stand the present reactionary tendencies and unreasoning drawing of the color-line indefinitely without discouragement and retrogression. And the condition of the Negro is ever the excuse for further discrimination. Only by a union of intelligence and sympathy across the color-line in the critical period of the Republic shall justice and right triumph.—W.E.B. Dubois[45]

The way to peace is through justice. In advancing the anti-war effort, the dispossessed, facing the most oppressive conditions, must seize the offensive through direct and political action. They must show a renewed understanding and assertion of their human rights. The role of the reformer is to offer humane solutions for dealing with symptoms of dispossession. Ending drug prohibition would at the least make drug producers more accountable for the health care cost associated with addiction. At best, it would relieve the violence associated with the industry and end the state of house arrest and the resulting dehumanization that exist in many communities of color. A social movement with drug legalization as a tactic, along with the reinstitution of individual human rights, strikes a blow at the elite within the drug distribution structure.

Should the erosion of rights continue to occur, individual and organizational efforts will predictably become more demonstrative. Society will witness an increase in emphasis on the delegitimization of institutions associated with the drug war. It is just as predictable that the initial focus of delegitimization will be law enforcement agencies and the criminal justice system. If the politicization of the poor, blacks, and other minorities intensifies, more violent social disorder will spark more extreme police-state measures. Thus an end to drug prohibition, or legalization, while intended to lessen inhuman treatment of addicts and violations of human rights, is a preventative measure to avoid an increase in social disorder and greater restrictions on rights.

In war, tactical diversion — for instance, bait and switch or divide and conquer — keeps those opposed to the war fighting skirmishes instead of the main battle. A diversion is easy to recognize because those who practice it can rarely provide a rational explanation as to where certain policies lead. Often their responses are full of hyperbole and emotionalism, or merely parroting existing policies and policy statements. Society manipulates many dispossessed defectors into leading the diversionary charge, not just conservative talk radio hosts or the black conservative Republican legislators. A defector can be anyone who feels that they profit from diversion for maintenance of the status quo. Diversions can come from paternalistic liberal or religious leaders. Consequently, minority communities should reject diversion from all quarters, and demand a positive and productive strategy to end the economic dispossession and violence in their community. Drug warriors and those seduced by them should be identified and their message confronted by the war's opponents.

However, this is not a primary focus of the anti-war effort. The anti-war effort should be proactive in its attack on tyrannical politics. Achieving reform is about challenging irrational policies not merely attacking personalities. Further, reformists ought to not merely hold the line until traditional, recognized, and institutional leadership comes to the front of the battle. Anti-war activists must show the way by example. Education, mobilization and resistance are key ingredients in countering regressive social policies. Therefore, reformers must build grassroots participation in organizations that promote drug policy reform and attempt to address dispossession. Linkage between new and traditional structures, such as Families Against Mandatory Minimums (FAMM) and the National Association for the Advancement of Colored People (NAACP) is vital.

Reformists must also create new grassroots structures dedicated solely to the structural problems of, and a structural remedy for, dispossession. All must engage in mobilization and direct action to coerce politicians into changing the tone and substance of the drug debate and to support politicians seeking progressive reform. Group cohesiveness and the ability to mobilize a politically focused constituency is critical to policy reform. The communities punitively affected by Reagan-era drug policy do not have resources equal to those seeking to maintain the status quo; thus their human capital is their greatest resource. Thomas "Tip" O'Neill of Massachusetts once said, "All politics are local." Local structures influence national politics and shift the tone of the debate from one centered on criminal justice remedies to debate that regards drug abuse as a health care concern. The substantive effect of a change in tone would also strike at the rapid growth of the prison-industrial complex. Instead of waiting for media or politicians to decide the saliency of the issue, reformers should go to the churches to meet with ministers, and speak to groups within the community and local elected officials. The most obvious and compelling ammunition for ending the war is the disproportionate spending on the construction of jails and prisons as opposed to the construction of schools and even public housing. In the '90s jail has become the new form of public housing and has the potential to further resegregate American society. Only by attacking dispossession can reformists reverse this trend.

Proponents of war always ask the citizenry to give up some of their liberties during the conduct of war. Proponents of the war on drugs ask the citizenry to give up some rights to fight crime and drug abuse. However, their request erodes the foundation of "innocent until proven guilty," the cornerstone of jurisprudence for any free society. From the very beginning, the Founding Fathers defined rights as limits on democratic power. The American Revolution occurred in the wake of the experience of living under a police-state. British soldiers conducted house-to-house searches to enforce harsh tax laws and seize literature hostile to the Crown. Those searches were feared then as drug dealers and burglars are feared today. The architects of the Constitution sought to prevent the much-feared recurrence of injustices suffered at the hands of the standing army in colonial America — injustices such as the imprisonment and detention of citizens without a judicial officer's determination of the existence of "probable cause" to believe that the individual had committed a crime. The Second, Third and Fourth Amendments along with the writ of habeas corpus protect those rights. They insure that military and police power remain subservient to private citizens with the means to defend their liberty. Those inside and outside of the war zone must ask themselves the following questions. How many additional rights should be surrendered to agencies such as the Bureau of Alcohol, Tobacco and Firearms (BATF), Drug Enforcement Administration (DEA), Federal Bureau of Investigation (FBI) and the Central Intelligence Agency (CIA). Do citizens want these organizations operating with impunity in their neighborhoods? Do they want their children to grow up in an environment where the acronyms for these agencies are everyday expressions? A right is a limitation on the power and authority of government. The purpose of the Bill of Rights is to protect against the tyranny of the majority and excessive government power. Thus anti-war activists must be steadfast in their support of these protections and they must teach the meaning of rights.

Citizens must not allow the war mentality to prevail. They must challenge and reject war metaphors, which breed other war metaphors, as illustrated in this text. If reformers fail, the current environment of racism, dehumanization, and dispossession will worsen. As the number of blacks, Latino and poor people locked away in prisons continues to grow, than, to quote Malcolm X, "the chickens will come home to roost." To put an end to the genocidal implications of the war, those who proclaim their commitment to law and order founded on the Constitution and the Bill of Rights must join a new, domestic, anti-war movement. That movement must restore and safeguard the protection of life, liberty, and property here at home. If reformers are successful in ending the "war on drugs," and attacking dispossession, the nation will be well on its way to a more secure future.

Here is one last story that is a sign of encouragement. In rural America, a pickup truck is often a person's most prized possession. One morning, as I was riding down the road (in my truck), I noticed a big, red Ford "dually," a 4 x 4 pickup with a sticker on its chrome-plated bumper. This four-door truck had all the extras — tinted windows, custom striping, CB and mobile phone antennas, the works. Pulling besides the truck I noticed a bumper sticker that read, "This Vehicle <u>Not</u> Purchased With Drug Money!" I followed the truck until its driver turned into a fast food restaurant so that I could interview him. The driver was a black man in his mid to late fifties named Jesse. I asked him why he had the bumper sticker and his reply was an obvious one: "When I first bought this truck, the police would see a black man in a nice vehicle and pull you over and want to search. I got tired of it. A friend of mine knew what I had been repeatedly going through and he gave me this sticker. Now when the police stop me, it is often to ask where I got the sticker. A lot of them think that it's funny and some have even called other officers to the scene to see it."

Policy reformers have many allies and supporters out there who need only to be encouraged to speak out against the war. They are the people such as Jesse, who are tired of being stereotyped. They are the working guys like Delane, who realize that a decision made for convenience can have long-lasting effects. They are the motorists like Tim, who is surrounded by six patrol cars and a paddy wagon, detained, searched, and given a ticket for a bad headlight. They are women like Cornelia Whitner, branded a bad mother and jailed because she has a addiction. The support base is the inmates and their families. For the anti-war activists, organizing will always start with a few. As Jesse Jackson puts it, "Rosa Parks did not start with a committee, she sat on the bus alone." An effort to change policy starts with a few. The drug war has had such a profound and devastating effect on blacks that a change in policy and direction can no longer be avoided by the community. Social abuses have piled up to the point that they can no longer be ignored. The dispossessed must reject the basic assumptions of the drug war and replace them with new ones.[46] At the very least, legalization will create a more humane and less violent society.

The consequences of the current drug war have been painful. It is time that we learn from the pain and move on to a policy that will decrease incarceration and focus on treatment for those addicts who need help. Perhaps it is an overused cliché — nonetheless, when dealing with dispossession and its diversions, such as the "war on drugs," activists and reformers must "keep their eyes on the prize." Ending dispossession is the prize. The human rights community must end its retreat from dealing with the tyrannical and counterproductive laws now in place in society. It must move to reverse bad public policy. Policy can change with effort. Slavery was public policy. Jim Crowism was public policy. Separate but equal was public policy. It will take a new anti-war effort to end the bad policy known as the "war on drugs."

References

Ani, Marimba. *Yurugu: An African-centered Critique of European Cultural Thought and Behavior* (Trenton: African World Press) 1994.

Boehlert, Eric. "'Suge' Knight is sentenced to nine years in prison." *Rolling Stone*. Issue 758, April 17, 1997.

Day, Dawn. "Drug Arrest: Are Blacks Being Targeted?" (Princeton: Dogwood Center) 1995..

Dubois, W.E.B. *The Souls of Black Folk*. (New York: Bantam Books) 1903.

Waiting for Lightning to Strike

Elden, Jennifer. "Drug Sentencing Frenzy." *The Progressive*. Vol. 59, No. 4, April 1995.

FBI Uniform Crime Report. "Age-Specific Arrest Rates and Race-Specific Arrest for Selected Offenses, 1965-1992." (Washington: U.S. Department of Justice) 1993.

FBI Uniform Crime Report. "Crime in the United States 1993." (Washington: U.S. Department of Justice) 1994.

Fineman, Howard. "An Older, Grimmer Jesse." *Newsweek*. Vol. 123, Issue 2, January 10, 1994.

Fish, Jefferson. "Discontinuous Change and the War on Drugs." *The Humanist*. Vol. 54, No. 5, September/October 1994.

Garland, Greg. "I-10 drug searches." *Baton Rouge Advocate*, February 9, 1997.

Hatch, Roger D. *Beyond Opportunity: Jesse Jackson's Vision for America*. (Philadelphia: Fortress Press) 1988.

Hendrickson, Matt. "Notorious B.I.G., 1973-1997: The hip-hop community mourns as another rap star is gunned down." *Rolling Stone*. Issue 758, April 17, 1997.

Holmes, Steven A. "The Boom in Jails is Locking Up Lots of Loot." *The New York Times*. November 6, 1994.

Kellner, Douglas. *Media Culture: Cultural studies, identity and politics between the modern and the postmodern*. (London: Routledge) 1995.

King, Martin Luther, Jr.. *Stride Toward Freedom*. (San Francisco: Harper and Row, Publishers, Inc.) 1958.

Kraska, Peter B. and Victor E. Kappeler. "Militarizing American Police: The Rise and Normalization of Paramilitary Units." *Social Problems*. Vol. 44, No. 1, February 1997.

Lynch, James P. and William J. Sabol. "The Use of Coercive Social Control in the Race and Class Composition of U.S. Prison Population." Paper presented at the meetings of the American Society of Criminology, Miami, Fl, November 9, 1994.

Marriott, Rob. "All That Glitters." *Vibe*. Vol. 5, No. 4, May 1997.

Mauer, Marc. "Lock 'Em Up and Throw Away the Key: African-American Males and the Criminal Justice System," in *The African-American Male: A Second Emancipation*. (Washington: National Urban League) 1993.

Mauer, Marc. "Politics, Crime Control and Baseball." *Criminal Justice*. Vol. 9, No. 1, Fall 1994.

Mauer, Marc and Tracy Huling. *Young Black Americans and the Criminal Justice System: Five Years Later*. (Washington: The Sentencing Project) 1995.

Mauer, Marc. "Intended and Unintended Consequences: State Racial Disparities in Imprisonment." The Sentencing Project. January 1997.

National Drug Strategy Networks. "HUD Announces One-Strike Rules for Public Housing Tenants." *NewsBriefs*. Vol. VII, No. 5, May 1996.

National Drug Strategy Networks. "Maryland State Police Still Targeting Black Motorists." *NewsBriefs*. Vol. VII, No. 12, December 1996.

National Household Survey on Drug Abuse: Population Estimates 1993. (Washington: U.S. Department of Health and Human Services) 1994.

Perry, Bruce. *Malcolm X: The Last Speeches*. (New York: Pathfinder Press) 1989.

· Scott, Robert E. "Trade: A Strategy for the 21st Century." in *Reclaiming Prosperity*. Economic Policy Institute. (Armonk: M.E. Sharpe) 1996.

Smith, Deann. "Foster to review drug forfeiture laws." *Baton Rouge Advocate*, January 5, 1997.,

Tidwell, Billy. *The State of Black America, 1993*. (New York: National Urban League, Inc.) 1993.

Thomas, Paulette. "Making Crime Pay: Triangle of Interests Creates Infrastructure to Fight Lawlessness." *The Wall Street Journal*. May 12, 1994.

Thomas, Paulette. "Rural Regions Look to Prisons for Prosperity." *The Wall Street Journal*. July 11, 1994.

Washington, James Melvin. *A Testament of Hope: The Essential Writings and Speeches of Martin Luther King. Jr.* (San Francisco: Harper Collins Publishers) 1986.

Webb, Gary. "Dark Alliance: America's 'Crack' Plague has roots in Nicaraguan War." *San Jose Mercury News,* August 18, 1996.

Weikel, Dan. "War on Crack Targets Minorities Over Whites," *The Los Angeles Times,* May 21, 1995.

Whitner v. South Carolina. Opinion No. 24468, Filed July 15, 1996.

Wilhelm, Sidney M. *Who Needs the Negro.* (New York: Doubleday Anchor Books) 1970.

X, Malcolm. *By Any Means Necessary.* (New York: Pathfinder Press) 1970.

Endnotes

1. Bruce Perry, *Malcolm X: The Last Speeches* (New York: Pathfinder) 1989: p.160.
2. Rob Marriott, "All That Glitters," *Vibe*, Vol. 5, No. 4, May 1997: pp.54-56.
3. Douglas Kellner, *Media Culture; cultural studies, identity and politics between the modern and the postmodern* (London: Routledge) 1995: pp.111-112. Kellner's revision of deconstruction is useful as a simple Marxian take on "false consciousness."
4. Marimba Ani, *Yurugu: An African-centered Critique of European Cultural Thought and Behavior* (Trenton: African World Press) 1994: p.xxi. *Maafa* is a Swahili term which means disaster, calamity, damage, injustice, misfortune, or catastrophe. Ani refers to it as "'The Great Suffering' of our people at the hands of Europeans in the Western hemisphere." Africentrics used the word to depict what is considered as the "African *Holocaust*" — "the great crime" — which was the enslavement of Africans, the slave trade and the violence and death both produced.
5. Dan Weikel, "War on Drugs Targets Minorities Over Whites," *The Los Angeles Times*, May 21, 1995: p.1. "Records show that federal officials prosecute nonwhites..., Virtually all white crack offenders have been prosecuted in state courts where sentences are far less. The difference can be up to eight years for the same offense."
6. Robert E. Scott, "Trade: A Strategy for the 21st Century," in *Reclaiming Prosperity*. Economic Policy Institute (Armonk: M.E. Sharpe) 1996: pp. 245-246. "Between 1980 and 1994, the U.S. current account balance, the broadest measure of income from trade in goods and services (including investment income) went from a surplus of $2.3 billion to a deficit of $151.2 billion...

When the U.S. imports more than it exports..., there is downward pressure on wages and an undermining of bargaining power of U.S. workers..."

7. Steven A. Holmes, "The Boom in Jails is Locking Up Lots of Loot," *The New York Times*, November 6, 1994: p.E3.

8. Paulette Thomas, "Rural Regions Look to Prisons for Prosperity," *The Wall Street Journal*, July 11, 1994: p.B1.

9. U.S. Department of Justice, "Age-Specific Arrest Rates and Race-Specific Arrest Rates for Selected Offenses, 1965-1992": p.206-207 and, U.S. Department of Health and Human Services, "National Household Survey on Drug Abuse: Population Estimates 1993": p.18f, cited in Dawn Day, "Drug Arrest: Are Blacks Being Targeted?" *NewsBriefs*, April 1995: p.22-27. Reproductions of the article are available through The Sentencing Project, Washington, D.C.

Although arrest per 100,000 for persons of all races for drug violations grew from a low of 26.7 in 1965 to 452.4 in 1993, the patterns for blacks and whites show distinctly different patterns. In 1993, about 12 per cent of both blacks and whites reported using illicit drugs. Yet in 1993, there were 136 arrest of blacks for drug violations per every 1000 users versus 31 arrest of whites per 1000 users. This suggest that blacks are arrested at a ratio of 4-to-1 when compared to white drug users.

10. Gary Webb, "America's 'crack' plague has roots in Nicaragua war," *San Jose Mercury News*, August 18, 1996: p.A1. A three-part series on how Nicaraguan Contras in the eighties — aided by the CIA — provided a direct pipeline to a Los Angeles cocaine dealer who spread 'crack' throughout Los Angeles, supplied rival gangs (the Crips and the Bloods), and shipped crack across the country.

11. Marc Mauer and Tracy Huling, *Young Black Americans and the Criminal Justice System: Five Years Later* (Washington: The Sentencing Project) October 1995.

12. Peter B. Kraska and Victor E. Kappeler, "Militarizing American Police: The Rise and Normalization of Paramilitary Units," *Social Problems*, Vol. 44, No. 1, February 1997: p.1.

13. *NBC News, Meet the Press*, October 3, 1993. Host Tim Russert interviews columnist William Raspberry. Russert asks Raspberry to "speak to America," and to the "predatory youth." On October 17, 1993, Russert posits the same characterization of youth to Jesse Jackson. However, it is noted that the term "predatory" was commonly used during the 1993-94 public crime debates by columnist such as Raspberry of *The Washington Post*, Richard Cohen of *The New York Times*, and others.

14. James P. Lynch and William J. Sabol, "The Use of Coercive Social Control and Changes in the Race and Class Composition of U.S. Prison Population," paper presented at the meeting of the American Society of Criminology, Miami, Florida, November 9,1994: p.23.

15. Howard Fineman, "An Older, Grimmer Jesse," *Newsweek*, Vol. 123, Issue 2, January 10, 1994: p.24.

16. Roger D. Hatch, *Beyond Opportunity: Jesse Jackson's Vision for America* (Philadelphia: Fortress Press) 1988: p. 109.

17. Mauer and Huling, *NewsBriefs*: p.11.

18. The Anti-Drug Abuse Act of 1988. The sentences for possession and distribution of cocaine base (crack) are 100 times greater than for powdered cocaine. This is commonly referred to as a "100-to-1" quantity ratio. 'Crack' is the street term for cocaine base. Crack is manufactured by heating cocaine hydrochloride (powdered cocaine) and baking soda or some other cutting (diluting) additive. Five grams of crack cocaine carries the same penalty as 500 grams of powder cocaine. Congress passed these laws in 1986 and 1988. Opponents on the sentencing disparity claim that the law is arbitrary and irrational because it assigns such disproportionate penalties to two forms of the same substance. They argue that the law discriminates against African-Americans since the majority of those charged with crimes involving crack are black (92.6 per cent of those convicted in 1992 for violations involving crack were black, 4.7 per cent were white), whereas, powder cocaine users are predominately white.

19. The [Ronald] Reagan era is defined as that period from 1978 continuing through the term of William "Bill" Jefferson Clinton. Reagan era policies are deemed as those which are derived from a fundamentalist, nationalistic and "conservative" political agenda. However, the contemporary roots of the "war on crime" extends back to the Richard Nixon administration where the "get tough" movement was initiated within the context of the Civil Rights Movement, the urban riots of the sixties, and the social division created by the Vietnam War. Nixon's campaigning focused on a "return to normalcy." This spawned the contemporary 'law and order' movement. Still, it was Ronald Reagan who forced Democratic politicians to adjust their positions on crime to gain electoral support from a white, suburban political base.

20. *The classic example of police tyranny can be gleaned by the actions and attitudes of the Los Angeles Police Department prior to the Rodney King beating being captured on videotape. Before the nation witnessed the brutality of the police on film, complaints by affected citizens were ignored or dismissed by most whites. Gangsta rap was emerging as a means of alternative reporting. Artists, such as Los Angeles-based Ice-T (Tracy Marrow) and Tupac Shakur, told tales of urban combat between the police and the black community. The theme of police abuse was common in the music of young people. Marrow's reporting on police violence and urban warfare/retaliation, on his album "Cop Killer," met with attack, denial and reprisal by mainstream institutions. His record contract was canceled as police organizations and politicians (including then-President George H.W. Bush) across the country condemned Marrow and his work. Then, the King video became public. After the King incident, it was revealed that there were over 45,000 unresolved complaints of police abuse languishing at the United States Department of Justice. Still, as evidenced by the first trial of the officers involved, an all-white jury freed the officers based on the stereotyping of King as an "animal" who somehow got what he deserved. Talk of the "thin blue line" separating "them from us" enabled jurors to suspend their knowledge that the officers' actions were inappropriately violent. Police practices in Los Angeles and other cities did not change after the King incident nor did practices change after the rebellion following the first trial verdict. Moreover, recent cases of police abuse have been uncovered in Washington, New Orleans, Philadelphia, New York, Miami, Detroit, Pittsburgh and other police departments across the country.

21. William Booth, "Exploding Number of SWAT Teams Sets Off Alarms," The Washington Post, June 17, 1997: pp.A1, A10.

22. Dawn Day, "Drug Arrest: Are Blacks Being Targeted?" *NewsBriefs*, April 1995: p.22-27.

23. Marc Mauer and Tracy Huling, *Young Black Americans and the Criminal Justice System: Five Years Later* (Washington: The Sentencing Project) October 1995, cited in "Prisons," National Drug Strategy Network, *NewsBriefs*, Vol. VI, No. 9, December 1995: p.11.

24. See Whitner v. South Carolina, Opinion No. 24468. Filed July 15, 1996. In a 3-2 decision, the South Carolina Supreme Court ruled that a woman could be held criminally liable for actions taken during pregnancy that might affect her viable fetus. In February 1992, Cornelia Whitner gave birth to a healthy baby who tested positive for cocaine. Two months later, Whitner pleaded guilty to and was convicted of criminal child neglect and was sentenced to 8 years in prison. Whitner filed a motion for post-conviction relief in May 1993 arguing that she was wrongly charged and convicted and, that she was given ineffective assistance of counsel. The conviction was overturned in state appeals court, however, the appeals' ruling was overturned by the S.C. Supreme Court thus upholding the original conviction.

25. Paul W. Valentine, "Maryland State Police Still Target Black Motorist, ACLU Says," *The Washington Post*, November 15, 1996: p.A1, cited in National Drug Strategy Network, *NewsBriefs*, Vol. VII, No. 12, December 1996.

26. Ibid.: p.A1.

27. Lynch and Sabol: pp. 29,30.

28. National Drug Strategy Network, "HUD Announces 'One-Strike' Rule for Public Housing Tenants," *NewsBriefs*, Vol. VII, No. 5, May 1995: p.9. On March 28, 1996, HUD introduced a "zero-tolerance" policy designed to screen and evict tenants involved in drug or other criminal activity (59 Crl 1047). Referred to as "One Strike and You're Out."

29. Mauer and Huling, *Young Black Americans...*,: p.58.

30. Marc Mauer, "Intended and Unintended Consequences: State Racial Disparities in Imprisonment," The Sentencing Project, January 1997: p.26.

31. Billy J. Tidwell, ed., *The State of Black America, 1993* (Washington: National Urban League, Inc.)1993: p.259.

32. Mauer and Huling, *NewsBriefs*: p.11.

33. Lynch and Sabol: p.3.

34. Ibid.: p.7.

35. Doug Jehl, "Clinton declares emotional appeal on stopping crime," *The New York Times*, November 14, 1993: p.A1.

36. Author attended Jackson's regional Rainbow/PUSH Coalition meeting in Memphis, Tennessee April 3-4, 1997 to commemorate the assassination of Martin Luther King, Jr.

37. Paulette Thomas, "Making Crime Pay: Triangle of Interest Creates Infrastructure to Fight Lawlessness," *The Wall Street Journal*, May 12, 1994: A8.

38. Ibid.: p.A1.

39. Eric Boehlert, "'Suge' Knight is sentenced to nine years in prison," *Rolling Stone*, Issue 758, April 17, 1997: p.30. Also, Matt Henderson, "Notorious B.I.G., 1973-1997: The hip-hop community mourns as another rap star is gunned down,": p.30.

40. Rob Marriott, "All That Glitters,": p.59.

41. Deann Smith, Foster to review drug forfeiture laws," Baton Rouge Advocate, January 5, 1997: p. B1, and Greg Garland, "I-10 drug searches," Baton Rouge Advocate, February 9, 1997: p. A1, cited in NewsBriefs, Vol. VII, No. 5, May 1996.

42. Marc Mauer, "Lock' Em Up and Throw Away the Key: African-American Males and the Criminal Justice System" in *The African-American Male: A Second Emancipation* (Washington: National Urban League) 1993: p.57.

43. Martin Luther King, Jr., *Stride Toward Freedom* (San Francisco: HarperCollins Publishers) 1986: p.194.

44. Martin Luther King, Jr., "Next Stop: The North," in *A Testament of Hope: The Essential Writings and Speeches of Martin Luther King, Jr.* edited by James M. Washington (San Francisco: HarperCollins Publishers) 1986: p.192.

45. W.E.B. Dubois, *The Souls of Black Folk* (New York: Bantam Books) 1903: pp.131-132.

46. Jefferson Fish, Discontinuous Change and the War on Drugs?" *The Humanist*, Vol. 54, No. 5, September/October 1994.

Big Daddy and the Plantation

GREW UP IN A *NATIONAL ENQUIRER* HOUSE. MY MOTHER READS IT weekly and my brother works in the plant that prints them. There is something cosmic about Reverend Jesse Jackson, for whom I used to work, being in the same rag that regularly reports on space aliens. Now, every time I think of Reverend, Diana Ross' "Love Child" plays in my head. And I have gotten enough email cartoons. The one with Reverend's head (with a ponytail) on a little girl's body was low down — as low down as the state of black and progressive politics. And that should be our real concern.

Some defend Reverend as a prophet while others condemn him as a profiteer. As far as Reverend being a prophet I can only suggest counseling for the believers. In this case, the difference between prophet and profit resembles the difference between praying and preying.

Recently, Reverend was cheered when he attended a Chicago area basketball tourney. Every church he has attended since the baby story broke has forgiven him. Often when a black leader faces attack or criticism by the powers that be, many blacks take the position that if white folk are giving a "brother" hell then he must be doing something right even when the person benefiting from support is screwing them royally. This is the present day's version of racial solidarity. Ironically, Bill Clinton benefits from this rule. Lani Guinier and Jocelyn Elders did not. And for all the love that folk like Toni 'the closest we will ever come to a black president' Morrison shower on Clinton, more black men went to jail under NAACP Image Award winner Clinton than under Ronald Reagan. I guess it's "hate the game" don't hate the "playa." In ghetto slang Reverend and Clinton are "playa playas." [Translation — They are so good they can play the playas themselves; so good they can con the cons.]

The age-old stereotype is that blacks care little about Reverend's sexual behavior because of their "inherent immorality." We hear the same thing whenever Bill "Cotton comes to Harlem" Clinton and black people are mentioned in the same sentence. A more useful idea-that black people practice that rarest of all Christian maneuvers, hating the sin not the sinner, understanding that Saturday night is followed by Sunday morning, not the other way around. But this is never suggested, possibly because in the "true" white American Christianity, such tolerance and forgiveness do not exist. (Ask Ashcroft.)

For most of those doing the evaluating, the logic is far simpler: Clinton apparently likes to fuck so he's black. Jackson is unquestionably black, so we ought to expect him to fuck.

But the problem with Reverend Jesse Jackson isn't that he fathered a child with a woman he didn't marry. The problem is that Reverend has used a movement predicated on protecting rights of the many with gaining privilege for a few. Our movement is anti-privilege. Now, Reverend's privilege and privileges are being challenged. Who's to say that's a bad thing?

I once believed that Clinton and Reverend really didn't like each other. For instance, I was with Jackson and Tom Harkin in South Carolina when Clinton called Reverend a backstabber. Reverend certainly didn't respond to the remark by joking "Hey, it's just my homey Bill jonesing a little on a brother." I was at the Rainbow meeting in Washington when Clinton trashed Sistah Souljah. It took Reverend a little bit to realize that Clinton had once again kicked him in the ass but when he figured it out he was pissed. (For some reason the expression "Arkansas cracker" comes to mind.) Truth be told, how could Jesse Jackson and Bill Clinton not like each other? They are like peas in a pod or, anyway, at least a boss and a straw boss. When Reverend was counseling Clinton I had two thoughts: It's going to blow up in his face and they're comparing notes. So maybe it was inevitable that Clinton and Reverend would become cut buddies, each vying to be the cash and carry Negro leader.

The new "morality" questions, as well as past financial problems at Operation Breadbasket that led to his split with Martin Luther King's Southern Christian Leadership Conference, are now regular fodder for the Sunday morning talk shows. The pundits' assessment — Reverend is not now and has never been accountable to anybody. *Washington Post* columnist David Broder gave Reverend's refusal to run for mayor of DC as evidence of his fear of accountability. Columnist Clarence Page, the only black guy on a news show on a regular basis, said the stories and financial questions were old news. Both fretted over Reverend's troubles but neither counted him completely out. Still, maybe his days as a national leader were numbered. (Maybe?)

But the problem isn't that Reverend is a has-been. It's worse: he's become an insider. That's what makes my desire to see Reverend either change or be gone from the scene different from Broder's and Page's. To them, Reverend is becoming ineffective as the "designated Negro."

There are also those waiting for the day when Vice President Dick Cheney has the big one (or a big enough one) so that Colin Powell becomes vice president. Understanding racial solidarity, they believe that African-Americans will predictably rally around the first black vice president. This group doesn't want Reverend to affect that dynamic. So, they beat up on him now in hopes of getting him out of the way. Things they ignored in the past make the *Enquirer*'s cover. They have no desire to see Al Sharpton elevated to "national Negro leader" but they know that Powell trumps Sharpton or anyone else for that matter. Powell as vice president would be the death of black politics, and you could be sure that his personal Operation Breadbasket, his participation in the attempted cover-up of the My Lai massacre, would never come back to haunt him.

This is the new dilemma for Reverend and others who make their money by manipulating the masses. How could they overcome what could be the ultimate manipulation?

The baby's mama drama is a symptom of something else. Reverend isn't the first, only or last man to have his brain in the wrong head. That's how he got here. Give him credit for claiming his child? It was from Reverend that I first heard that you don't get points for doing the right thing. But the woman is no "that man used me" victim. She's a thirty-something Ph.D. breast cancer survivor. She wanted his seed. Initially, she said it wasn't Reverend's baby. She lied to her mama to protect him, and in the part of the nation that reads the *Enquirer* that's a lot more extreme than lying to the FBI.

Workplace sex will always be around. No doubt, on the job there is sexual harassment and conniving plotters of both sexes. The problem with Reverend isn't workplace sex (except maybe to his wife Jackie and those who believe a minister and married man should act a certain way). Jesse Jackson and the Rainbow Coalition's problems are patronage and bossism.

The Rainbow "organization" is not committed to any movement — past or future (unless we are foolish enough to believe in a "Wall Street movement"). Jessephiles have no particular political goals, agenda or ideology beyond cutting the deal and protecting their privileges as part of the black bourgeoisie. It's always been about big daddyism, a concept from back in the day that covers it all: sexual harassment, nepotism, exploitation, plotting, foolishness, favoritism and all kinds of other isms, schisms and confusion. A "big daddy" is a straw boss thinking he is the boss, or putting up the front that he believes it, as part of doing the boss's business. Tupac called it thug life.

Most — not all, but most-Jessephiles want to be close, accepted, recognized or loved by big daddy. They want big poppa's favor. Big daddy's on the inside, with the status quo, the in-crowd.

To the Jessephiles, the Rainbow Coalition's biggest accomplishment was to become Rainbow/PUSH, but that's nonsense. The Rainbow Coalition was supposed to be about politics and organizing. PUSH is about "getting the gold." The "gold" comes with being silent about the exploitation and unfair practices of the corporate givers. To know whose doing the buying one needs only to read the magazines or newsletters of any black organization. In return for silence some "big daddy" gets some stock, a seat on a board, a job or a check. Reverend isn't even the master of this game; that would be Vernon Jordan.

Much of Reverend and his crew's present good fortune comes from the lawsuits or threats of lawsuits by grassroots groups whose primary concern is that their constituents receive fair treatment. Grassroots groups sued merging banks (such as Bank of America for gobbling NationsBank, which used to be Citizens and Southern/Sovran) over adherence to the community reinvestment act. The outcome was that Reverend and the Jessephiles got the gold. The price was the abandonment of attempting to enforce the community reinvestment act. "Big daddys" often stifle grassroots protest, threats of economic actions or boycotts because there is an existing deal with the company or a deal waiting to be made. Reverend often says, "The only bad deals are the ones you are not in the room for." A watered down CRA was passed last year with little public comment. Why? Because the banks and the feds now sidestep grassroots groups and cut the deal with the big daddies, who have become their straw bosses in the matter.

The powerful have learned that it is easier and cheaper to buy black leaders than to bust them. The real money is in busting street niggers in bulk. That's what racial profiling is all about. And Reverend isn't the only one bought and paid for. Past NAACP director Ben Chavis and ex-chair Doc Bill Gibson were part of the demise of grassroots' effectiveness in maintaining a remote semblance of accountability by predatory banks. The only thing that the late Khalid Muhammed ever got right was what he said about Ben Chavis. Condemning Chavis for stealing from the people, he called him counterrevolutionary. But, that's what all the big daddies do. It's what Ben Chavis was taught, and taught by experts. Look at the King family's exploitation of all things Martin, right down to pimping footage of his speech from the March on Washington as a product advertisement.

Today many civil rights organizations work counter to black empowerment. Promotion of individuals, symbols and organizations, all living on someone else's past glories, replace movements of the poor and disenfranchised. The NAACP and the Urban League have their fair share or economic development programs. The black churches and preachers take the money with no demand on the system except maybe a bank loan to build a bigger church. Every big daddy gets as much money as they can from wherever or whomever they can get it. COINTELPRO was never so effective at turning politics in the black community to shit.

The movement business is good to Reverend and his kids. One son is an alcohol distributor in Chicago, a second is an investment banker and Jesse Junior is a Congressman. But in spite of the fact that one son is a "legal" dealer, Reverend is hypocritical on the issue of drug legalization and on the wrong side in the war on drugs. What he should do is demand that the POWs be set free. Start protesting at the prisons. Call for active resistance against the drug war. Those are things that need saying and doing. The drug war is now spawning the next wave of black voter disenfranchisement. The background checks by the Florida Republicans were possible because of that state's disenfranchisement of ex-felons for 15 years after their term of imprisonment. That's why the Republicans were able to run criminal background checks, falsely report the results, and prevent balloting by thousands of black voters. The same tactics are going on in South Carolina and across the South. The only way to stop this is to oppose drug criminalization.

Cash checking services, cash advance lending, predatory mortgage practices, property rights, land loss and decreasing home ownership are just some of the pressing the economic issues affecting blacks. In cities such as Washington, DC, Charlotte, Atlanta and many others, inner city blacks are dealing with redevelopment, gentrification and eroding voting districts. So why aren't the Rainbow, Urban League, NAACP or the SCLC dealing with these problems?

A recession in the country as a whole and it's a depression in the black community. The latest unemployment statistics, officially edging towards 10 per cent, bear out worsening conditions in black households. How does Reverend's Wall Street Project help black Americans forced into the secondary lending markets during hard times or at any time? The high interest charges blacks pay is what makes the investment bankers on Wall Street billionaires; it's where the funding for the Wall Street Project comes from, too, and Reverend and the other big daddies know it, which is why they don't challenge it.

Ask the average person what the Rainbow stands for and if they say anything it will be "it's Jesse Jackson's organization." But what has Reverend and his organization produced? What can that person on the street see, feel and touch? No one can call the organization on the phone for help. They can't get a question answered or a problem solved. They see no action. They feel nothing. They see nothing. That's because there is nothing-for them.

Reverend's legacy is that he ran for president, twice. He's been out the movement for a long, long time. He's been in the movement prevention business just as long. Any chance of movement building died when he dismantled the Rainbow to suit Clinton and Ron Brown in 1988. After that Reverend truly became "Jesse Jackson Inc." The tradeoff for scattering the troublemakers the 1984 and 88 campaigns brought into the political tent was job as head overseer on the Democratic Party plantation. Now Reverend holds the franchise on black votes. If he has a fear, it's losing the franchise.

Many of those at the center of the Jackson campaigns, like Jack O'Dell who worked with Martin Luther King, Frank Watkins who worked with Reverend for more than 20 years, Ron Daniels, Nancy Ware, Steve Cobble and a host of others including me — wanted to connect to the people, build an organization and create a movement. They were not chumps. They put the larger than life photos of Reverend at the headquarters in Chicago in historical prospective. But big daddyism got the best of them. They moved on and the Rainbow's potential to really change and challenge America went with them.

As an institution, the Rainbow will fade away completely. Then maybe we will build organizations capable of responding to the people's needs. Maybe if we stop depending on the straw boss we can take protest back to the streets and begin tearing down those institutions and ideas that need to crumble. Since the glory days of 1988, we have been poor stewards of the goals of a progressive/black movement. The success of that movement is the salvation of this country; its failure is its damnation.

The goals were set at the founding of this country. Black politics is the counter to anti-black politics. It's the demand for equal opportunity, equal treatment and protection, due process and economic justice for the descendants of enslaved Africans, which is the only way those things can be ensured for everyone else.

Soul Brother?
Bill Clinton and Black America

[Clinton] has always wanted our love and wanted to share his love with us. It is not about the skin. It is about the spirit and the soul of this soul brother.— Former Transportation Secretary Rodney Slater

I WAS MILDLY AMUSED, A BIT DISGUSTED BUT NOT SURPRISED WHEN former President Bill Clinton was named to the Arkansas Black Hall of Fame. Unfortunately, there is no shortage of gullibility when it comes to the relationship between blacks and the man from Hope. Towards the end of his term, he was viewed favorably by a staggering 83 per cent of African-Americans. Now Clinton has been named honorary chairman of the $37 million national Museum of African-American History in Charleston.

Besides just having a big name draw to raise money, it should be obvious what's going on. Clinton is reworking his image by creating a phony civil rights legacy. Forced to resign because of Watergate, Richard Nixon attempted to reshape his image into that of a foreign policy expert before his death. Jimmy Carter left office a failure with hostages in Iran and an economy in crisis. He was still able to remake himself into a statesman and international peace advocate. Should Clinton get his way, memories of his real race record will fade as he transmogrifies himself into a racial healer. And he is getting plenty of help, from black people.

Charles King, the hall of fame's executive director, said the former president deserved induction "to show him our appreciation not only for what he did as president but for his lifelong association with us. He came to us. We were responsible for him being governor, and president. He held on to that. And we held on to that."

Clinton is now the only white person among the hall's 62 members, who include poet Maya Angelou, John Johnson, founder of *Jet* and

Ebony magazines, and former Clinton administration Surgeon General Joycelyn Elders. Remember Elders? Clinton fired her because she said it wasn't a bad idea to talk about masturbation in sex education classes.

The evening of the induction Clinton shared the dais with soul-turned-gospel singer/preacher Al Green. The two have so much in common that it's a wonder Clinton hasn't had a pot of hot grits flung at him. Their commonalty has more to do with them being doggish, busted males than with some twisted sense of racial or cultural empathy.

Since leaving office, Clinton has been working his "ghetto pass" overtime. When complaints arose about the cost of his office space in Midtown Manhattan, what did he do? He moved to 125th Street in Harlem, historically the intellectual capital of black America. The community that nurtured Malcolm X, Langston Hughes, Claude McKay, Jessie Fauset, W.E.B. Du Bois, Zora Neale Hurston, Adam Powell and a host of others ate it up. Harlem was Clinton's second choice and for that he got a hero's welcome.

At present, the only national political figure the Democratic Party has black or white that blacks identify with is Clinton. In 1998 the party's get-out-the-black-vote effort consisted of mailing out postcards with Clinton posing beside black families. In the 2002 elections black households once again got their postcards with Clinton's picture followed up an automated phone message from their good buddy Bill.

No other president in United States history has managed to get so much black support for giving so little. But what makes Clinton's race act so successful is that black America never asked him to do much to begin with. In the 1980s, Clinton was the first white candidate for governor to reach out to Arkansas's black voters, to eat on their porches, pray in their churches, invite them into the governor's office. For 12 years before Clinton, Ronald Reagan and George Bush insulted and ignored black people. Consequently, when Clinton wooed African-Americans, most were just happy someone was finally paying attention. To some degree, black support of Clinton is also acknowledgement of the black community's need for white acceptance.

Some argue that Clinton deserves support because his economic policies were a boon for African-Americans. During his administration median income reached an all-time high, and poverty among blacks dipped thanks in large part to his increases in the minimum wage and the Earned Income Tax Credit. But on the other side of the economic coin the black-white wealth disparity remained fixed and the gap between the rich and poor expanded under his administration.

Others point to the record number of African-Americans in the Clinton cabinet and the picture of racial diversity it projected. At times Clinton talked the social justice talk, lavishly invoking the name of Martin Luther King. While touring Africa he even gave a half-hearted apology for America's part in European colonization and enslavement. A black man, Vernon Jordan, was his best friend. A black woman, Betty Currie, was his personal secretary. It's debatable whether the blacks around Clinton had any real power, but real or not, his mostly symbolic gestures were much more than black people had ever seen from a white person in power. And those gestures have carried Clinton a long way.

The joke that refuses to go away has Clinton as America's first black president a sentiment enthusiastically affirmed by black celebrities, elites and quasi-intellectuals. In his routine, comedian Chris Rock used Clinton's "persecution over a $300 haircut" to support the claim. Former Southern Christian Leadership Conference head Joseph Lowery said that blacks like Clinton because "he plays the saxophone." Harvard professor Alvin Poussaint joked, Clinton "must have black ancestry." Back in 1998 during the height of the Monica Lewinsky scandal, writer Toni Morrison said, "black skin notwithstanding: this is our first black President" citing his dysfunctional upbringing as commonality with black males. But the joke's an insult. The punch line is that Clinton is decadent and promiscuous, got rhythm, got caught and got over — so he's black!

The notion of Clinton as a great friend of the black community or defender of civil rights is just as crazy. Clinton co-opted civil rights themes and figures and distorted their meaning for his political advancement and survival. Whether it's his telling blacks how disappointed "Dr. King would be [in them] if he were alive today", because of black-on-black crime or his attorney comparing him to Abraham Lincoln during the impeachment hearings, Clinton was an expert at playing the race card. All the while, his policies and attitude on due process, equal protection and equal treatment, or civil rights (rights guaranteed to all), were horrible. A couple of examples of his racial hypocrisy come to mind. One was his initiative requiring citizens, mostly black, in public housing to surrender their Fourth Amendment or privacy rights. Another was the "one strike and you're out" policy under which public housing residents convicted of a crime, along with anyone who lives with them, are evicted without consideration of their due process rights. But while the Rehnquist Court upheld these assaults on the rights of the poor, Jeb Bush (via his daughter Nicole) and Clinton (still on the public dole) all remain exempt from the laws they promote.

Southern politician Clinton has always played the race-crime game to perfection. In his first presidential race Governor Clinton ran for office supporting the death penalty at a time when the country was split almost down the middle on the issue. Then for good measure, he rushed back to Arkansas to oversee the execution of convicted killer Ricky Ray Rector, a brain-damaged black man. For years after his first election, I kept a picture of Clinton and Georgia Senator Sam Nunn posing in front of a phalanx of black inmates in white prison suits taken at Stone Mountain, Georgia. Historians generally give Pulaski, Tennessee, the dubious honor as the birthplace of the Ku Klux Klan. But Stone Mountain is hailed as the Klan's second home. The picture appeared in newspapers all across the south the day of the southern primaries in 1992. That picture is what Clinton has always represented to me.

So, the fact that Clinton left behind a larger mostly black prison population than when he took office should come as no surprise. Black incarceration rates during the Clinton years surpassed Ronald Reagan's eight years. The incarceration rates for blacks increased from around 3,000 per 100,000 to 3,620 per 100,000 people during his administration. That he did nothing about mandatory minimum sentences was no surprise. That he did nothing to change the sentencing disparity between crack and powder cocaine that disproportionately affects African-Americans was no surprise. That he successfully stumped for "three strikes and you're out" in the crime bill, for restrictions on the right of habeas corpus and expansion of the federal death penalty was no surprise. When he came into office one in four black men were in the toils of the criminal justice system in some way; when he left it was one in three. In many states ex-felons are denied the right to vote, a factor that had a direct impact on the 2000 presidential vote in Florida. Again, no surprise.

Shortly after leaving office, Clinton published a piece, "Erasing America's Color Lines", in *The New York Times*. He wrote that "America was now at a point where we can write a new preamble to the 21st century, in which color differences are not the problem, but the promise, of America." He outlined a path that would allow the Bush administration to reduce systemic racism. The list included a ban on racial profiling, an examination of mandatory minimum sentencing and a presidential commission on voter reform.

But Clinton's suggestions were another bit of hypocrisy given that he refused to implement them while he had the chance. And his knowledge that George W. Bush would never take any of his suggestions made the whole exercise just another piece of grotesque symbolism. The commentary was a perfect postscript to Clinton's marriage with black America, a relationship that is characterized by the James Brown song "Talking Loud and Saying Nothing".

On the night Clinton was inducted into the Arkansas hall of fame, Charles King must have lost his memory. He forgot that, as Governor, his guest of honor refused to sign a civil rights bill. In Charleston, the people behind the civil rights museum forgot that Clinton dumped his friend Lani Guinier from consideration for the Justice Department's office of civil rights over her advocacy of cumulative voting the next frontier for civil rights, which would break down voting by race and party.

Maybe Clinton's name and service on the board in Charleston will help lure the money needed to make the project a reality. Maybe now blacks will get to use him and maybe get something in return for a change. But he shouldn't be allowed simply to fundraise himself into a legacy or assume a legacy he doesn't deserve. A legacy should be more that just showing up. As for being a soul brother? He's got a very, very long way to go.

The Legacy of Strom Thurmond

I GREW UP NEXT TO THE TRACKS IN A BLACK NEIGHBORHOOD CALLED Freyline in what was then rural Spartanburg, South Carolina. Some called it "Niggerline." There was (and still is) one road in, one road out. A main Southern railway line and Mr. Jack Dobson's cow pastures and cornfields locked us in. Dobson lived at the top of the hill in the traditional white big house complete with those huge white columns on the big porch that rung the house. The house sat framed by centuries-old pecan, magnolia, and weeping willow trees that kept it cool in the summer.

As a youngster I cut both black and white folks' grass to make school money. Saturday was generally white folks' day. I had my regulars and was usually hired for the whole day for a variety of chores. And although change was in the air, I was their boy back in the day when most white folk still had at least one, usually named Leroy, Charlie, or Bo (as in short for boy). And if your name wasn't Leroy, Charlie, or Bo, it was by the end of the day. Straight up rednecks called you boy right off the bat.

Labor was cheap and many moderate-income white families also had a black maid. Polite whites referred to their "colored" housekeepers as "domestics." The others called them girls. The younger women made the daily early morning one-to-three mile walk to their employers' neighborhoods or to the bus stop, but some of the more benevolent white wives would pick up "Mama," as older workers were often called, around the time the morning school bus ran. At the end of the day, after the floors were mopped, the clothes were hung on the line and the kids fed, about a half hour or so before the sun went down, white women in their shiny cars would make the regular trip back to "Niggerline" or "Niggertown" to their workers' home. Almost always, the black housekeeper would sit in the back seat of the car. I remember wanting to hurl a rock but Mrs. Alberteen or someone else I knew was also in the car.

One of my Saturday customers was someone we all knew to be in the Ku Klux Klan. Word had it he was a Great Titan, Giant, or Exalted Cyclops. Whatever his title, he was the local leader. He was a redneck when a redneck was someone to avoid. This particular fellow stayed just off the main road at the entrance to our neighborhood. Looking back he was a pretty stereotypical Southern cracker, complete with that chewing tobacco lump in his lower lip. He wore his white shirt tucked into his blue khaki work pants, sleeves rolled up. Most memorable was that bad smelling, stomach turning Brylcreem grease in his always-wet hair, the small black clip comb in his shirt pocket, and his hands, ever wet from constant preening. I did my best to keep a safe distance between us and I was always prepared to bolt, leaving my lawn mower if necessary.

He may have been a cotton mill supervisor although I don't really know for sure. In the class of white people to work for it was always better to get a teacher, preacher, or some type of professional than a mill supervisor whom we regarded as low class but with power to misuse. Polite whites did not constantly remind you of their power; it was clearly understood.

Yet knowing the boss man was Klan didn't stop us from dealing with him. And although he probably burned the cross in the cornfield in front of our house, he still umpired the integrated little league baseball games and his son played catcher for our team. I cut his and his father-in-law's grass. After integration I went to school with his kid. My uncle's wife was his maid. My first cousin is his daughter.

That's how the South was when I was growing up in the sixties and early seventies. The white man burning crosses and ranting about race-mixing would also buy all the little black boys sodas after the game and still have enough hypocrisy left to screw the black housekeeper and dare her to tell. Whether it was a young James Strom Thurmond or the neighborhood Klansmen, rape and race-mixing have always been a part of the story of the South. Thurmond's contradictions only mirrored those of South Carolina and the nation.

The Reverend Joseph Lowery, former head of the Southern Christian Leadership Conference, called Thurmond "a racist by day and a hypocrite by night" when it was revealed that, at age twenty-two, he had fathered a child, Essie Mae Butler (Washington-Williams), by Carrie Butler, his family's sixteen-year-old maid. But many black South Carolinians saw Thurmond as a life-long hypocrite because they saw him through the race, sex, and power prism.

South Carolina activist Modjeska Simkins, who died in 1992 at the age of ninety-two, kept the "Essie" (as she called her) story alive through her years on earth. Simkins, a feisty woman not afraid to poke her finger in a raw sore, was an NAACP organizer during the years Thurmond was governor. She often told of the "bi-racial baby born to a teenage domestic in the Thurmond home, a girl so poor that her neighbors had to help feed and clothe the child."

Still, knowing about Thurmond's black daughter may have actually softened black feelings towards him even though blacks knew it was no coincidence or mystery that Butler and her six-month-old child, left, fled, or were relocated to a northern state. As Nadine Cohodas, author of the biography *Strom Thurmond and the Politics of Southern Changes,* said after hearing confirmation of Washington-Williams's paternity, "The black teenage servant must have figured that if she spoke out, she might not be believed and might put herself in extreme danger." It is also not surprising that Butler died shortly after her baby's birth, as a young girl carrying a secret child may not have sought or had access to much medical care.

Washington was following custom when she returned to be educated at South Carolina State College, the state's public black college. Throughout the South, many of the "colored" offspring of patrician white males were educated at state-supported black colleges and received "loans" from white "patrons". As John Wrighten, who attended South Carolina State Law School with Julius Washington, who later married Essie Mae Washington, said, "There were so many half-white children at South Carolina State College when I was there; there were five or six girls you couldn't distinguish from white girls." He said Washington was in that group.

Many interracial sexual trysts, long-term relationships, or accommodations were seemingly consensual. That is unless you were the unlucky black guy caught having consensual sex with a white gal. Even if the women didn't holler "rape" (which was usually how the scene played out), she may as well, or someone did it for her. Still, on the southern social ladder, being "high-yellow" (light-skinned) often meant a ticket to the black middle and upper class, a better job, house, college, and a different kind of treatment by whites. And there were those who may have naively hoped that having sexual relations with a black woman might lead a white man to treat black people better.

Since Washington-Williams's announcement, some people have speculated that perhaps Butler intentionally became pregnant with a conscious plan to have a child who would have a better life than her own. This helps Thurmond apologists avoid the subject of rape. But rape, like racism, is about power. Carrie Butler was fifteen years old when Thurmond impregnated her. And although at the time, the age of statutory rape in South Carolina was fourteen, Butler still had no power in the relationship — only a vagina. The relationship, if one wishes to call it that, seems more akin to that of master and sex tool or toy. For even as Jim Crow was eroding, the ultimate expression of white male power was the ability to do to a black woman anything, anytime, anyway they wanted to with absolutely no guilt and no fear of consequence or responsibility. It was common for a young white boy, such as Thurmond, to "learn about sex on the colored side of town." Some "did right" by the children they sired while many others did not even acknowledge their black offsprings' existence. Yet, even if Thurmond was not a deadbeat dad, Washington-Williams's revelation of her long held "secret" and her expression of affection for her biological father were more like the delusional yearnings of a neglected child lost in the hope that one day her cruel parent would see what a wonderful offspring he had produced and embrace her. And this pretty much explains the psychosis afflicting African-Americans in their relationship with white America.

Those attempting to put a positive face on Thurmond's legacy ignore the issue of the strong possibility of rape in the Butler story because it not only clashes with their contrived heroic image of the lawmaker but it also gives Butler rights she did not possess during the Jim Crow period of American history. Their refusal to recognize Butler as more than a necessary detail in this story is their refusal to recognize black humanity. And that refusal is rooted in an unwavering belief in white supremacy that goes far beyond bare-boned race hatred. As a white Southerner once told me, "That's the mistake people make about Southerners. The masters never hated the slaves. Whites, in particular powerful white men, during Jim Crow didn't hate blacks. That would have been like hating your mule or your dog."

Miscegenation was one of the first big words I learned as a youth. From white lips it was a sinister thing. Blacks saw it as the white man's greatest fear and weakness. Obviously, the hypocrisy of it all was and is evident in the faces of all the high yellow and light brown kids running around. And while the anti-miscegenators fretted over white racial purity and advocated — and committed — murder as punishment for black men and white women having sex, most mixed-raced kids were a result of race mixing between white men and black women. Not only was the sexual contact an expression of white male power; it was also a psychological response to the stereotypical fear of the black man as hyper-sexed beast: Mandingo.

The Mandingo myth originated in the Old South where white slave owners believed that the Mandinkas were the fiercest warriors of Africa. After a Caribbean slave revolt in the 1800s, John C. Calhoun of South Carolina, the leading intellectual of the Southern gentry, invoked the specter of Mandingo slaughtering white masters as justification for their enslavement. Black male sexual prowess was also a big part of the myth. The often used colloquialism, "once you go black you never go back," is the myth of the big, black, well-endowed buck, Mandingo.

In the 1970s, the myth became the movie *Mandingo* in which one-time heavyweight champ Ken Norton played a noble slave who burns down the white man's plantation and escapes to freedom with the blonde Southern belle in his arms. My mother took us kids to see the "controversial" movie when it was shown at the local drive-in theater. And at the top of her stack of romance novels was a book whose cover displayed a muscular, caramel-colored black man caressing a buxom, blonde lass, her ample white breast barely covered by the straps of her torn hoop dress, her long blonde ringlets cascading over her shoulder, with the title *Mandingo* emblazoned across the cover.

The Mandingo stereotype entraps black males to this day as evidenced by the pop culture embrace of the pimp, gangsta rappers along with a host of psycho-sexual-social illusions. The myth fuels denial over homosexuality and feeds rampant homophobia in the black community. As black gay and bisexual men practice a dangerous sexual secrecy, the AIDS crisis in the black community worsens. As a friend told me, "One of the worst things to be is a gay black man in the South. The preacher wants you to lead the choir, and maybe even give him a blowjob every now and again, while condemning, denying, or damning your very existence from the pulpit."

As for white women, during slavery, a white woman marrying or consensually having a child by a black man usually found herself in legally sanctioned bondage. "Defilement" or being spoiled during the Jim Crow era most often meant being banished — stripped of being "white" for one's "nigger-loving" ways. White men used "protecting white womanhood," the first plank in the Klan platform, as a pretext for controlling white women, but in some respects it trapped the men in a psychotic effort to prove their own sexual dominance.

In Thurmond's youth and political prime, lynching and the fear of it was the primary weapon to discourage black men from even looking the "wrong way" at white women let alone having sexual relations with them. And lynching was accepted at all levels of white society as a means of controlling race mixing. Even in the late seventies, my first organizing job, with the Southern Christian Leadership Conference back when Ralph Abernathy was the head, was over the death of a black man, Mickey McClendon, murdered for dating a white woman. McClendon, from Chester, South Carolina, was shot, tied behind a pick-up truck, set on fire, and dragged down a road, much the way James Byrd, Jr. was in Jasper, Texas, in 1998. Today, whether it's Kobe Bryant in Colorado or high school football star Marcus Dixon in Georgia, whenever a black man is accused of the rape of a white woman, black Americans view the alleged crime in the context of history.

Sex is the prevailing theme of Thurmond's life. While he was alive and after death, the local press gleefully retold the story of a young Strom "sneaking out his upstairs bedroom for a romantic tryst with unnamed women." Thurmond's "virility," his marrying a twenty-two-year-old, Nancy Moore, at age sixty-six, having four children even as an old man, and his "secret" black child were all a testimony to Southern white male power.

Thurmond's initiation into the "customs and traditions" of segregation, sex, and white supremacy began with his political mentor Benjamin Ryan Tillman. "Pitchfork" Ben Tillman, a virulent white supremacist, also from Edgefield, Thurmond's home county, constitutionally (and otherwise) reinstituted white rule after Reconstruction. Pitchfork Ben was proud to have driven blacks demanding rights out of the state at gunpoint. He and his Sweetwater Sabre Club members wore white shirts stained in red to represent the blood of black men. When Tillman came to power as governor in 1890, blacks were the majority in the state. Today, blacks represent a third of the population. The decrease is directly due to Tillman's political legacy. Tillman's assault on black rights was immediate. He quickly revised the state constitution to ensure legal segregation of the races, stripping blacks of all political and economic power. As a United States senator, Tillman declared, "We of the South have never recognized the right of the Negro to govern white men, and we never will."

Thurmond's father, J. William, himself a state legislator, once served as Tillman's campaign manager. Tillman later rewarded J. William by naming him U.S. attorney (a job that was also held by Strom's son — Strom Jr.) in a new South Carolina district even though Thurmond had killed a man in an argument over Tillman's politics. Tillman was a frequent visitor to the Thurmond home, a "symbolic part of the family," according to Cohodas, and a godfather of sorts to the Thurmond children. But to blacks, Pitchfork Ben was the prime purveyor of Negrophobia. And wrapped around Tillmanism was the ideal of the "pure, defenseless, southern white woman." "There is only one crime that warrants lynching," he said, "and governor as I am, I would lead a mob to lynch the Negro who ravishes a white woman." During Tillman's first term there had been five lynchings, in his second term there were thirteen.

Still, black South Carolinians were initially optimistic about Thurmond, who began his career as a Democrat. As a South Carolina state senator in 1938, despite the Tillman influence, he publicly opposed lynching and declared that the Ku Klux Klan stood for "the most abominable type of lawlessness." Thurmond called himself a "progressive" and upon election as governor in 1946 he declared, "We need a progressive outlook, a progressive program, a progressive leadership." He spoke of improving black schools, revising the Tillman Constitution of 1895, and abolishing the Tillman poll tax that was used to keep blacks from voting. He supported "equal rights for women in every respect," saying, "women should serve on boards, commissions, and other positions of importance in state government." He also called for "equal pay for equal work for women."

At his inaugural Thurmond said, "more attention should be given to Negro education. The low standing of South Carolina educationally is due primarily to the high illiteracy and lack of education among our Negroes. If we provide better educational facilities for them, not only will much be accomplished in human values, but we shall raise our per capita income as well as the educational standing of the state." But Thurmond was not calling for an end to segregation, he was hoping for a new and improved "separate but equal." It would take the federal courts to strike down "separate but equal" and to force desegregation, or "integration," as the Thurmond forces would define it.

Thurmond stood squarely with Tillman on race mixing — he was against it and let stand the constitutional prohibition against it. It took 103 years before South Carolina finally voted to remove a ban on interracial marriage from the state constitution. Although it was not actively enforced, Tillman added the clause to the state's constitution in 1895 prohibiting "marriage of a white person with a Negro or mulatto or a person who shall have one-eighth or more of Negro blood." Up until 1997, state legislators refused to allow voters to decide whether to remove the ban. A constitutional amendment, passed in 1998, finally deleted the line.

Still, at the start of his career blacks gave Thurmond high marks for his handling of the Willie Earle lynching, which stamped his administration as "liberal without being radical" by whites outside the South. On February 16, 1947, a young black man from Pickens County was arrested and charged with the murder of Thomas Brown, a white Greenville taxicab driver. The next day a mob broke into the Pickens County jail, took Earle, shot him, stabbed him, and then beat him to death on the outskirts of town. The FBI and state officials investigated the crime at the behest of Thurmond, who also called for the prosecution of those accused of lynching. But after a highly public trial, the jury acquitted the accused men.

However, when President Harry Truman desegregated the armed forces and announced his broad civil rights program in 1948, Thurmond could not tolerate the challenge thus posed to the "customs and traditions" that defined his deepest beliefs. Thurmond ran for president that year as the "Dixiecrat" States' Rights candidate, admonishing the faithful that holding power boiled down to one thing — race and he would make sure that only white men held it. As Northern Democrats pushed for civil rights, Thurmond and his fellow Southern Democratic governors cried "states' rights just as their ancestors did to justify African enslavement. As author Karl Frederickson wrote, Thurmond and other Dixiecrat governors appealed to racist "conservative white men suffering from a self-diagnosed case of political impotency."

Thurmond as Tillman's political heir was the icon of the new "anti-miscegenation" movement. In his acceptance speech as the Birmingham meeting announcing his presidential bid he speechified, "All the bayonets in the Army cannot force the 'Negrah' into our home, our schools, our churches, and our places of recreation."

Candidate Thurmond's platform stood for segregation and against race-mixing. When the votes were counted Thurmond had 1.1 million votes, won four states and garnered thirty-eight electoral votes. 1.1 million Americans voted in favor of segregation — it was not enough to defeat Truman, but the Democratic Party was never the same.

Eventually Thurmond was elected to the Senate as a write-in candidate in 1954, a post he would retain for a half century, until his retirement in January 2003. Throughout his congressional career, he opposed almost every major civil rights initiative. In 1956, he authored the infamous Southern Manifesto, a document signed by nineteen of the twenty-two Southern senators that urged the South to defy, as they put it, the Supreme Court's "clear abuse of judicial power" in outlawing segregation in public schools. In 1957, he executed the longest filibuster in history while trying to halt the first Civil Rights Act proposed in the Senate and backed by Eisenhower.

Lyndon Johnson's success in passing the Civil Rights Act of 1964 was the last straw for Thurmond. He left the Democratic Party and signed on with Republican Barry Goldwater. Upon leaving, Thurmond declared, "The party of our fathers is dead."

Thurmond's departure signaled a major shift in American politics. It was the birth of South Carolinian Lee Atwater, Jesse Helms, Newt Gingrich, and Trent Lott's Republican Party. The Thurmond defection prompted the GOP ("Grand Ole Party") appeal to white southern conservatives and foreshadowed Richard Nixon's race-inspired "Southern Strategy." This framework exists today. Race supremacy is the ideological glue that keeps white men in the South in the Republican Party. Today they are called the "Bubba vote" and NASCAR dads, but the appeal is build on Tillmanism, the Dixiecrat Movement, the Southern Manifesto. It's almost always couched in the language of "states' rights," but race and social control is the subtext.

Race politics explains Ronald Reagan beginning his 1980 campaign at the Neshoba County fair in Philadelphia, Mississippi, the place where civil rights workers Michael Schwerner, James Earl Chaney, and Andrew Goodman were murdered. His declaration then, "I believe in states' rights," sent the same message as George W. Bush's 2000 sojourn to the fundamentalist college Bob Jones University in Greenville, South Carolina. The school's founder has been often linked to the Klan and for years provided a Biblical sanction for racism. The school refused to admit blacks until 1971 and banned interracial dating until 2000.

In the seventies, as the country's racial attitudes changed, Thurmond did as the self-serving do to stay in office — he changed, at least cosmetically. With blacks representing a third of the voters in South Carolina he hired the first black man ever employed by a Southern senator and actively re-courted the black vote. Thomas Moss, a Korean War veteran and organizer with the meat packers union (in the "right to work state") in Orangeburg, South Carolina, headed the Voter Education Project, a program that encouraged blacks to register to vote. Working with Moss,

Thurmond began championing grants to black colleges, businesses, and municipalities. He voted in favor of extending the Voting Rights Act — a law that guaranteed the federal government's right to enforce a citizen's right to vote. He also voted in favor of the Fair Housing Act and the Martin Luther King federal holiday. His reward? During his 1978 re-election bid, ten of South Carolina's eleven black mayors endorsed him.

Back in 1996, I was organizing a national conference on the epidemic of church fires in the South. As it just so happened, South Carolina led the nation in the number of church fires and the National Council of Churches was sponsoring the conference being held in the state. An old friend and NAACP member Joann Watson of Detroit, made the trip down south. And as fate would have it, Joann and I were talking in the lobby of the Downtown Holiday Inn when who should stroll in? Strom in the flesh, looking kind of dazed but still moving, his aide not a step away. Joann immediately threw her two arms up in the air and like Moses appealing to pharaoh, cried in a strong but not loud voice, "Senator, let my people go!" Strom, leaning just a little, stopped, stuck out his hand to Joann, and said in a clear, twangy voice, "Go where? I love everybody. Everybody's my friend!"

Thurmond was the epitome of the classic pork-belly politi-cian. Graduate from high school and you'd probably get a letter from Thurmond. If a parent had trouble reaching a kid in the military, call Thurmond's office. Need help with the V.A.? Call ole Strom. The "rural myth" is that Strom shook the hand of almost every South Carolinian. His apologists want us to remember that Thurmond.

When black State Senator Kay Patterson of Columbia agreed to eulo-gize Thurmond, it was front-page news all across the state. Patterson said, "Strom's experience is on the road to Damascus. I supported him since he left his segregationist ways and became a real American citizen and tried to be the senator for all the people of the state." Patterson's atti-tude mirrored African-Americans' optimistic hope for Thurmond when he began his career.

But a new generation was reminded of Thurmond's legacy and iconic status at his 100th birthday party. Mississippi Senator Trent Lott praised Thurmond's 1948 campaign saying, "I want to say this about my state.

When Strom ran for president, we voted for him. We're proud of him. And if the rest of the country had followed our lead, we wouldn't have had all these problems over all these years, either." Although Lott fell on his sword and apologized all over himself, his signal was unmistakable. Had it not been for blacks getting rights and race-mixing, the world of white men with total power would be intact.

In the end, regardless of whatever changes Thurmond made later in life, his legacy can be described in two words — "Segregation Forever." Or maybe, "Segregation and Hypocrisy Forever!" Even if Essie Mae Washington-Williams's name is chiseled alongside the names of his other children onto the Strom Thurmond statue that stands facing the Confederate Women's Monument on the Statehouse grounds, his contradictions and hypocrisy will still be etched in stone. But maybe, in a way, the day they chisel that name will be the day white South Carolina finally begins to confront its own contradictions.

The Sun Never Sets: How Did We Become an Outlaw Nation?

> We must make clear to the Germans that the wrong for which their fallen leaders are on trial is not that they lost the war, but that they started it.... No grievances or policies will justify resort to aggressive war. It is utterly renounced and condemned as an instrument of policy. — Supreme Court Justice Robert L. Jackson, a U.S. representative to the International Conference on Military Trials at the close of World War II.

O F COURSE THE WAR ON IRAQ IS NOT JUST ABOUT OIL. IT'S ABOUT imperialism, capitalism, the spread of white supremacy and privilege and the extension of unchecked American power, directed by people who look or think like George Bush, Dick Cheney, John Ashcroft, Donald Rumsfeld, Paul Wolfowitz, Richard Perle, Bob Jones and their big business and religious fundamentalist buddies. But "no blood for imperialism, capitalism, white supremacy and the extension of unchecked American power" is too much for a bumper sticker. And it's harder still to get many white Americans (or people of color) to reject, let alone fight to dismantle such an unjust way of existence.

Whether the killing is inspired by the imperatives of "Manifest Destiny", "Divine Right", "God's chosen people", the "Master Race" or "the sun never sets", someone's land and resources end up being stolen and the people enslaved, oppressed or killed by their so-called "liberators". Bush can adorn his war with the nonsensical adjectives "pre-emptive" or "preventative"— a war to pre-empt war? — but the United States is clearly the aggressor nation. This is not a war of self-defense.

Now, I wouldn't want to live in Iraq, nor do I have any fondness for Saddam Hussein. But imagine Hussein is the most racist, unpleasant Klansman on an average American block. And people are scared of him, because they know what he's already done, and they think he could do just about anything. What would happen if, unprovoked except by their own fear, the black folks from another block decided to firebomb his home, killing him and his family—or maybe just his family, because he was at a meeting? They wouldn't have a legal leg to stand on. No prosecutor, no jury in the land would accept an argument of pre-emption, or prevention and a weasel apology, "Sorry about the kids, collateral damage." But this is exactly the argument Bush is demanding that Americans and the world accept.

There are far more reasons to be against Bush's war than for it. The biggest reason to oppose war is that it is an instrument of death. Even if the inspectors had found chemical weapons products in Iraq that does not give anyone the right to kill its children. Even if they had found elements for the production of nuclear bombs, that does not give anyone the right to kill its children. Because that's what war means. That's what the past twelve years of sanctions have meant — Iraqi children dying. To take the additional step of committing American young people to attack a nation of young people-because over 50% of Iraq's population is under 15 years of age-and to do this in the name of a plan for empire building hatched by Paul Wolfowitz twelve years ago: now that is criminal.

Bush and his backers hope for a quick war. First, they hope to seize the oil fields while waging a bombing campaign they have named "Shock and Awe," dropping 3,000 or more bombs in the first 48 hours of the attack. This is the so-called "Baghdad First" strategy. It has another name: terror bombing. As one Pentagon official said, "There won't be a safe place in Baghdad." One of the basic features of terrorism is that it makes anyone a target, civilian or military, guilty or innocent. Everyone is afraid, because no one is safe. Still, immediate surrender isn't a given. There could well be some bloody door-to-door urban fighting. And with all of this, let's remember, Baghdad is a city of 4 to 5 million people who aren't all named Saddam Hussein.

A few years ago, former U.N Ambassador Madeline Albright was asked what she thought about a report that sanctions had led to the death of 500,000 Iraqi children, from lack of medicine, food, clean water. "Is it worth it?" *CBS*'s Leslie Stahl asked her. Albright, after a considered pause, said, "Yes, we think the price is worth it." Now mix Albright's morbid calculus with the Bush Administration's casual approach to instigating a human catastrophe. (Once again the power grid, on which the water purification system depends, will be a target.) What we are faced with is something quite simple and easily understood: the cheapening of human life. But not any human life — Iraqi human life, foreign human life. Their life, their children, not ours. American, more often, white, life is priceless. American children are priceless, worth so much that only the idea that they might not be safe, that they might live in a world where everyone doesn't just love them, is used to justify threatening and snuffing out the lives of other children, lesser children, lesser people.

It is a fundamental moral precept that every human being is of equal value. If we in this country condone or ignore what this present administration is doing, we will be accomplices to mass murder.

As hard as Colin Powell and Condoleezza Rice tried to conjure one, there is no hardheaded geopolitical consideration of the normal kind precipitating war on Iraq. This time, Hussein hasn't gassed the Kurds or the Iranians — which when he did he was receiving military intelligence and biological and chemical weapons agents from the United States. The running joke in Washington is that "America knows Saddam has these weapons because it has the receipts."

This time, Iraq has invaded no one, seized no land, occupied no territory, committed no sudden international atrocity, nor put the lives of people in other countries in particular peril. Even Iran, Iraq's next-door neighbor and the country it gassed, opposes a U.S. invasion. And our next-door neighbor, Canada, opposes the war.

Vice President Dick Cheney calls Hussein a "mortal threat" but let's be real. The United States has a $400 billion Pentagon budget; Iraq's military budget is about $4 billion. America has thousands of nuclear weapons, many of which are produced right here in South Carolina at the Savannah River Plant; Iraq doesn't have one yet, or the means to deliver it. And although chemical weapons have been internationally banned, the U.S. still has 75% of its stockpile. Anniston, Alabama, alone has enough sarin, VX nerve agent, and mustard gas to kill or incapacitate millions. So, even if Iraq obtained one nuclear weapon or two, would that present a "mortal" danger to the United States? The United States has survived for four decades against two formidable foes — Russia and China — with thousands of nuclear weapons aimed at us. And when it comes to the proliferation of weapons of mass destruction, "We're number one!"

If Iraq is a "mortal threat", what about the 16 other countries in the world that have or might have nuclear weapons, the 25 countries that have or might have chemical weapons, the 19 other countries that have or might have biological weapons, and the 16 other countries that have or might have missile systems? Is the United States going to invade them too?

Ironically, an American invasion may actually increase the odds that Hussein will use chemical or biological weapons. Back in 1991, he had chemical or biological weapons loaded onto missiles. The elder Bush warned Hussein that if he used those weapons, he would face devastating retaliation. Everyone, including Hussein, understood that meant having a nuclear bomb dropped on his country. So he backed down. Today, Bush the son is talking "regime change". So Hussein has absolutely no incentive not to fire whatever chemical or biological weapons he might have hidden at U.S. troops, Israel, Turkey or Kuwait.

War on Iraq is not about enforcing U.N. Security Council Resolution 1441 or any other resolution. If that were the case, the U.S. would have to invade Israel, a country in violation of numerous resolutions (223, 242,267,271, 298, 446,452 and 465) and led by Ariel Sharon, a war criminal. Sharon has effectively transformed Gaza and towns in the West Bank into concentration camps, where people are under constant curfew, penned in by barbed wire, surrounded by tanks and soldiers and threatened constantly with homelessness by bulldozing. Israeli soldiers kill Palestinians every day. On March 16, 2002 they killed an American, crushed her under a bulldozer. The death of Rachel Corrie, a U.S. peace activist, was not a mistake; it was a warning that the Israeli government doesn't care who is opposed to its policies of oppression and occupation.

Bush can talk about the United States not being at war with Islam or the Muslim world, but after a while, as the brutality escalates or America tires of "nation building" and paying to rebuild what it has destroyed, many in that world will find the argument insulting. Sooner or later the "chickens will come home to roost", with a greater likelihood of suicide bombers striking here in America. Already the run-up to war has inflamed Muslim fundamentalists, who had previously despised Saddam Hussein as an infidel. Even the government reports it has been a boon for al Qaeda's recruiters. Hard to see how that is in the interests of the United States.

As a civil libertarian, I believe an invasion of Iraq is unconstitutional. Article 1, Section 8, of the U.S. Constitution gives the right to Congress and only to Congress to take the United States to war. But Congress has been silent and impotent from the start. It gave Bush a blank check use-of-force authorization after 9/11, with Representative Barbara Lee (D-Calif.) as the sole voice of dissent. Now the most passionate voice of opposition to an imperial presidency and war without Congressional declaration or even debate is an ex-Klansman, Senator Robert Byrd (D-W.Va). Byrd accused his colleagues of "sleepwalking through history" and hoped "that this great nation and its good and trusting citizens are not in for a rudest of awakenings."

Since just after World War II, presidents have usurped this power of Congress, and Congress has abdicated it. There has not been a Congressional declaration of war since December 1941, though there have been plenty of wars since then — Korea, Vietnam, Panama, Grenada, the Dominican Republic, and the Gulf War. There also have been numerous other nations the United States has assaulted directly or covertly over the last six decades.

In regards to Iraq, some argue that Bush has the authority to wage war by virtue of three Congressional actions. First, in 1991, Congress gave his father the authorization to wage war against Hussein (though technically it did not declare war). But was that authorization an open-ended go-ahead to wage war against Iraq forever, or anytime any president happened to feel like it? And did Congress grant the son the right to change the regime there now, more than a decade later?

The second Congressional act that Bush backers cite is the September 14, 2001, use-of-force authorization, which allows Bush to attack any person, group, or country that he believes was involved in the attack of

9/11. But while Powell, Rice and others (to include corporate media) have been doing their damnedest to lay some of the blame for the 9/11 attack on Hussein, there is no evidence connecting the two and no credible link has been established between Hussein and al Qaeda, or between Iraq and the anthrax-laced letters that killed several Americans.

Then, in October of that year, prior to offering 1441 to the U.N. Congress passed a resolution authorizing the use of force, if necessary, against Iraq. But none of these measures was ever a Congressional declaration of war.

Presidential candidates Rep. Dennis Kucinich and Al Sharpton have been the most critical of Bush's war, but other Democratic presidential candidates use anti-war sentiment to the extent that they can carve out votes. Sharpton is the only candidate challenging both the legitimacy of the war and the legitimacy of the Bush presidency. No one has dared utter the world impeachment, yet.

Most Democratic candidates have not challenged Bush's legitimacy to wage war because in their heart of hearts most want to join the I-can-make-war Club. One of the qualifications for being president, after all, is the willingness to use America's nuclear "deterrent"—that is, to threaten or commit mass murder in the name of national security.

Sen. John Kerry, the Democratic presidential front-runner claims to oppose war but said, "When the war begins, I support the troops and I support the United States of America winning as rapidly as possible. When the troops are in the field and fighting remembering what it's like to be those troops, I think they need a unified America that is prepared to win."

Presidential candidate Howard Dean, who calls Bush's foreign policy "ghastly" and "appalling," has been painted as the Democrats' most vocal opponent of a unilateral war against Iraq. But once war breaks out, he says, "Of course I'll support the troops."

The impulse to support the troops is understandable. They're our kids, cousins, sons, daughters, fathers, mothers, neighbors, friends and even grandparents. We want our soldiers—young people who risk too much for too little pay—to come home in one piece. Many don't want to be where they are. There is an economic draft in this country, and many are there because of it. But blindly supporting the troops while they're fighting an immoral and illegal war is misguided and wrong. Perhaps the best way to support the troops is to increase the effort to get them home. The government is spending a billion dollars a day to keep soldiers in foreign lands for this war; we should demand that the money be used to educate kids and give them options other than the military. We should also be encouraging kids not to join the military. It makes them the imperialists' apprentices. In the era of modern warfare especially, it forces them to be murderers and terrorists. And when the war is over, if it doesn't kill them — and a low rate of U.S. battlefield casualties is becoming common — it kicks them to the curb. More than 164,000 Gulf War veterans are officially disabled. High percentages of every city's homeless population are veterans. Somehow the money always runs out when it comes time really to support the troops.

There have been only lies and immorality in the drive to war. Sure, Hussein is a bad guy but it really isn't about him. It's about what the U.S. stands for. Bush and all his apologists must be called to account, including Rice and Powell. In the African-American community, the two should be granted the same pariah status as Clarence Thomas: Rice as the "devil's handmaiden" and Powell as a company man. At this point Rice is just a mouthpiece, but many portray Powell as a man of principle. Remember the Powell Doctrine? It states that the U.S. should only go to war after addressing the following concerns:

Is a vital national security interest threatened? Do we have a clear attainable objective? Have the risks and costs been fully and frankly analyzed? Have all other non-violent policy means been fully exhausted? Is there a plausible exit strategy to avoid endless entanglement? Have the consequences of our action been fully considered? Is the action supported by the American people? Do we have genuine broad international support?

By Powell's standard, war on Iraq is without foundation. His doctrine has been replaced with the Wolfowitz Doctrine, which claims America's right to war by virtue of its superpower status and the rest be damned. Yet Powell has gone along with it.

The Bush Administration is using 9/11 as an excuse to terrorize and brow beat the world while simultaneously stripping away our rights here at home. Under Bush, the government has instituted a foreign and domestic policy of revenge, pre-emptive killing, support of political assassination and torture and the creation of a class of individuals, groups and countries with absolutely no human, legal and civil rights. Once labeled a terrorist an individual, group or country has no rights that anyone is bound to respect. Sound familiar?

The terrorist label has been extended from those that fly planes into buildings to those who sell and buy weed on the street to those who oppose the Bush plan for world domination. While the faces on the anti-drug television ads that tie the drug trade to terrorism are white, the faces that go to jail are black. The war on drugs has already stripped countless black Americans of their rights, once branded terrorists they will be reduced to below nothing status.

While opinion polls show only 19.2 per cent African-Americans supporting Bush's war aims, black people have not attended anti-war rallies in huge numbers. Blacks don't have any special obligation or greater urgency to oppose this war than whites, although we have a greater, far more bitter familiarity with the way lives are unequally valued. African-Americans, because of our history, understand white supremacy and privilege. And those of us who understand the difference between movement and opposition know that confronting these demons by creating a peace alternative is the movement that must be built.

African-Americans must also be mindful that well over 30 per cent of those U.S. Army troops sent to fight Bush's war are black. And while Bush gives lip service to diversity, he attacks affirmative action. He condemns Trent Lott one day and places wreaths on Confederate soldiers' tombs the next. While he takes the country down an economic spiral, which affects blacks disproportionately, he is willing to run huge deficits to wage an illegal and immoral war. Bush may hoist Powell and Rice as the new black leader archetypes, but they are not acting in the best interests of black Americans, or any Americans for that matter.

Maybe things will go well, the smart bombs will hit only military targets, and U.S. soldiers will make short work of the war. But what about the peace? Even if the war is a success by its authors' standards, the question of winning the peace in a pursuit that is so very wrong from the beginning is hard to fathom. What this moment in history does, in a sense, is sharpen what should have been the task for the black movement, the labor movement, the progressive movement, all along. Martin Luther King defined the real "axis of evil" 36 years ago. He warned, "that the problem of racism, the problem of economic exploitation, and the problem of war are all tied together. These are the triple evils that are interrelated." As for America, King said, "A nation that will exploit economically will have foreign investments and everything else, and will have to use its military to protect them. All of these problems are tied together."

Those "triple evils" of racism, economic inequality and militarism King talked about didn't just come together during the Vietnam era and are now coming together again. They where together from the beginning, one feeding the other in a relentless loop. Some say that under Bill Clinton we had "peace and prosperity", but the number of poor people stayed about constant with what it was 30 years ago, and more bombs were dropped on Iraq ton-for-ton during his administration than during the entire Vietnam War.

There's always a war somewhere; there's always a military system sucking the life out of societies at home and abroad, just as there's always racism and economic inequality. War makes all of those things worse. But the reason to oppose it, other than to save the lives of innocents, is the same as the reason to struggle in this world at all: because the present set-up is not serving the people, is not serving humanity, is not just or equitable or enlivening. It's a death trip. "Life, liberty and the pursuit of happiness" sounds more radical every day.

In wartime we must not lay down and be quiet for the sake of "unity." We must take to the streets, to the steps of Congress and the White House. Locally, we must go to those government institutions that feed the war machine to make the peace presence known, our voices heard and our demands met. We must support any international call for sanctions against this government. And we must call for a full investigation, debate, or whatever you want to call it, on how George Bush made

183

America an international outlaw nation. We must resist the impulse and drive to try to control the world.

Let us remember as Dr. King said, "There is a creative force in this universe, working to pull down the gigantic mountains of evil, a power that is able to make a way out of no way and transform dark yesterdays into bright tomorrows. Let us realize the arc of the moral universe is long but it bends toward justice. Let us realize that William Cullen Bryant is right: Truth crushed to earth will rise again. Let us go out realizing that the Bible is right: Be not deceived, God is not mocked. Whatsoever a man soweth, that shall he also reap."

The Packaging of Obama

MY WIFE, SANDRA, WARNED ME, "DON'T BE HATING." NOW San (as we call her), who has worked in retail sales, selling ladies shoes, throughout her working life, is not an overtly political person. She is one of those old-timey, "salt of the earth" types. But when she doesn't like a person, there is usually something wrong with that person. For instance, before it became evident that Al Sharpton's effort in South Carolina was going nowhere fast, she coined the now-popular phrase "scampaign" to refer to the Reverend's run. I know it is ill-advised not to take heed of her warning.

With San's admonition in mind, I tried to table her (and my) Oprah-tainted, media-hyped preconception of Barack Obama so that I could read *The Audacity of Hope* with an open mind and with the same hopeful spirit as the title seeks to portray.

But the book is like those two solid yellow lines on a two-lane mountain road. They're just there in the middle and never-ending, with a stop sign as the only relief.

He offers no boldness. Dr. King set out to change the social, economic, and political structures of this country. He described the change as a 'third way' beyond capitalism and socialism. King's "third way" is far different than Bill Clinton's "third way," promoted by Obama and all those around Hillary, who tout the Clintons as the second and third coming of Camelot.

The Clinton "third way" is Republican Party politics in slow motion. Under Bill Clinton, U.S. troops weren't trapped in Iraq, but just as many, if not more, Iraqis died as a result of his policies. His destruction of the welfare system, his embrace of capital punishment and other punitive and discriminatory crime policies, his bowing to Wall Street all made him palatable to Republicans.

The hope in Obama's title is for a mixture of Kennedyism, Reaganism, and Clintonism packaged as the new face of multicultural America. At its core, this is what *The Audacity of Hope* promotes, instead of any fundamental progressive change.

Nonetheless, it comes as no surprise that *The Audacity of Hope* is a *New York Times* bestseller. The book arrives amidst the hype of an upcoming and wide-open presidential race, the collective angst over the country moving in the wrong direction, an economy that working people know isn't as good as they are being told it is, and a war that has washed away — at home and abroad — the country's preexisting false sense of moral superiority. As the line in Ethan and Joel Cohen's 2000 movie, *Oh Brother Where Art Thou*, goes, "Everybody's looking for answers."

Yet, does Obama's book provide any real answers? Is there anything in it that will help stimulate measurable change? Or, is it all just talk, posturing, and positioning for personal political goals? Is it an orchestrated, consciously plotted pretext to inoculate a politician from the perceived liabilities of race, lineage and inexperience?

The answers are no, no, yes, yes.

I can agree with Obama on the need for a new kind of politics. But he suggests that what's broken can be fixed versus being replaced altogether. He opines that if we would all just recognize our "shared understanding," "shared values," and "the notion of a common good" that life (or politics) in the United States would be better.

Take, for instance, his praise of Reagan, hedged as it is by criticism of Reagan's "John Wayne, *Father Knows Best* pose, his policy by anecdote, and his gratuitous assault on the poor." Writes Obama: "I understood his appeal. It was the same appeal that the military bases back in Hawaii always held for me as a young boy, with their tidy streets and well-oiled machinery, the crisp uniforms and crisper salutes. ... Reagan spoke to America's longing for order, our need to believe that we are not subject to blind, impersonal forces, but that we can shape our individual and collective destinies. So long as we rediscover the traditional values of hard work, patriotism, personal responsibility, optimism, and faith."

Obama gets a lot wrong from start to finish. While people may indeed have a shared reality — which means we witness the same things — we don't always feel, understand, process, or react to what we witness in the same way. The simplest example of not having a "shared understanding" is the difference in how blacks and whites view the police.

What is lacking here is devotion to principles, which Obama constantly sacrifices on the altar of "shared values." And of course the issue is not of shared values. It's how we rank our values. Many people value religion, but which religion has more value? In this country we all know the answer to that question. As proof that the United States government values Christians over Muslims, consider that the United States is at war with an Islamic country. Consider that Muslims in this country are subject to increased government scrutiny and racial, ethnic, and religious profiling. No one in their right mind could believe that the United States place a Muslim on an equal footing with a Christian or Jew. The daily body count dispels that notion.

At the top of Obama's shared values matrix is his Christian faith, his heterosexual family, the American flag, and the Democratic Party. "Shared values" and "the notion of a common good" pretty much amounts to the same thing in Obamaspeak. It all sounds pleasant, but it's surely not new. It's somewhat reminiscent of Jesse Jackson's "common ground" theme that he built his '88 campaign around. Clinton picked up the phrase, and it is now a standard part of the political lexicon.

But the use and meaning of Jackson's phrase has changed over the years since Clinton co-opted it. Jackson's "common ground" meant bringing together a coalition of workers, women, men, blacks, progressive whites, gays and lesbians, environmentalists, anti-apartheid activists, those opposed to Ronald Reagan's illegal war in Central America, farmers, Latinos, Arab-Americans and other traditionally underrepresented or unrepresented groups. With Jackson's phrase, all could demand a seat at the Democratic Party table.

By contrast, Clinton wanted the Democratic Party to renew its "common ground" with those who left the party with Strom Thurmond and the Dixiecrats and those who jumped ship when Ronald Reagan rose to power: white men. Clinton's "common ground" was with the Democratic Leadership Council. Clinton "common ground" pushed aside those whom Jackson brought to the party. And *The Audacity of*

Hope places Obama squarely in the DLC camp, even if he never applies for a membership card.

As a political tome, *The Audacity of Hope* is kind of a new and improved, better-written version of Clinton's long-winded speech at the 1988 Democratic Convention in book form. Obama touches all the hot button words like the "nuclear option," "strict constructionists," and the like but never really says anything deep or brave or new other than to remind us that the hot buttons are really hot.

Give Obama credit for copping to the fact that his "treatment of the issues is often partial and incomplete." Overall, the treatise reads like a very, very long speech of sound bites and clichés arranged by topic and issue and connected by conjunctions, pleasantries, and apologies. Pleasantries like wishing for a return to the days when Republicans and Democrats "met at night for dinner, hashing out a compromise over steaks and cigars." Or, leading with apologias to describe painful parts of United States history or softening a rightfully deserved blow as when he describes racist southern Senator Richard B. Russell as "erudite." Or accusing his mom of having an "incorrigible, sweet-natured romanticism" about the '60s and the civil rights era as he waxes romantically about Hubert Humphrey's Democratic Party. It's like he did not have a clue about the 1964 struggles of Fannie Lou Hamer and the Mississippi Freedom Democratic Party.

The shame of Obama's lack of depth is that Hamer's conflict over representation pretty much set the table for how the Democratic Party deals with blacks today. But of course he was only three years old and living in Hawaii when Lyndon Johnson went on national television to give a speech so that Hamer's image and the MFDP challenge would be off the airwaves. Hamer's fight was a precursor to the candidacy of Shirley Chisholm, the first black to seriously run for President in 1972 (if you exclude Dick Gregory's 1968 bid). Chisholm continued Hamer's fight for a greater black and female voice in politics and government.

Throughout, Obama proffers an unnaturally romantic view of the Democratic Party for a person of his age. His appreciation of the party seems as times deeper than his understanding of the civil rights movement, which comes across as antiseptic. And he goes out of his way to comfort whites with a critique of black Americans that could tumble out of the mouth of William Bennett. "Many of the social or cultural factors that negatively affect black people, for example, simply mirror in exaggerated form problems that afflict America as whole: too much television (the average black household has the television on more than eleven hours per day), too much consumption of poisons (blacks smoke more and eat more fast food), and a lack of emphasis on educational attainment," he writes. "Then there's the collapse of the two-parent black household, a phenomenon that ... reflects a casualness towards sex and child rearing among black men."

The book has no soul. That perhaps explains why some (with motives good and bad) in the black community complain that he "is not black enough," or "he has no respect or appreciation for the past," or "he is the amalgamation of everything white folk want a black man to be," or "he's a white boy being scripted by smart-ass white boys."

The book is surprisingly short on substance. Given all the policy disasters of the Bush Administration, what troubles Obama about the Bush era is not so much the policies Republicans championed but "the process" or lack of process "by which the White House and its Congressional allies disposed of opposing views." In the end, all he offers is the promise of a 'hope' that he will manage the process better than the other guy or gal.

So then, why write the book?

Obama's face is everywhere. And, there is no shortage of opinion about him, which makes it difficult to read his book and sort things out without atmospheric bias. But *The Audacity of Hope* plays on the creation of a Kennedy-like mystique. I've spoken to a couple of writer friends who attended an Obama event and in both conversations the comparison to John Kennedy was bandied about. On cue, Obama plays the Kennedy-card throughout his book, tossing in passages from *Profiles in Courage*.

Although we now know that John F. Kennedy did not write *Profiles in Courage*, the book is one you have on your shelf that you might look through on occasion and actually enjoy rereading. *Profiles in Courage* is a historical marker in a way *Audacity of Hope* will never be. Not that I am a fan in the slightest regard of the early John and Robert Kennedy.

There was much to dislike about them even before the days when they authorized FBI director J. Edgar Hoover to bug Dr. King, after which the top cop and closet cross dresser (no disrespect to cross dressers) in turn authorized his agents to try to prod King into killing himself.

Not everyone writes a book before running for the Presidency. But some do, and those books reveal things about the person and the time. Jesse Jackson's *Straight from the Heart*, of which many people contributed to, still holds up as a record of where progressives stood at a particular point and where many progressives stand today. Ross Perot's *United We Stand* at least tried to confront some familiar problems such as the federal debt. And he actually wrote of reforming the system of campaign finance, increasing electoral participation, and eliminating the Electoral College.

The title of a book usually tells the story. Sometimes it may take reading the entire book, down to the last page before you realize how telling or appropriate a title is. *The Audacity of Hope*. You can't chant it in a crowd like, well, *"Keep Hope Alive!"* Or *"Keep the Faith, Baby!"* or *"Power to the People!"* And while the book is technically well-written with aspirations to inspire, Obama falls far short of the mountaintop. In the end, the reader feels trapped in a valley of buzzwords, catch-phrases, and insider jargon with words like "halcyon" thrown in for good measure.

So, if you are searching Obama's book for hints or even the language of the kind of change that means something in a structural and systemic way, it's not there.

But I'm afraid people are going to discount Obama not for what he says, but for who he is. I was at the bank talking politics, among other things, with Maria, the head teller. As I spoke in my usual unrestrained and audible way, so as to let anyone hear me without having to eavesdrop, Obama's name came up. An older white gentleman standing next to me said, "Ya know his middle name is Hussein? This country will never elect a man named Hussein President!" To which I could only respond, "Well, the country elected a man that is insane!"

The Black Primary

Columbia, South Carolina

THE PRESS DOESN'T PLAINLY SAY IT, BUT SOUTH CAROLINA is the black primary. The more common expression is that the state "offers a glimpse into what's important to African-Americans…" It might, because a third of South Carolina's population, 1.3 million residents, is black. The majority of Democratic voters here are black, and in 2004 "non-whites" made up about 60 per cent of those who cast a ballot in the Democratic primary. Yet at this point in the accelerated Election 2008 story, after two debates in the state by candidates from both parties, there's been a bit of race baiting, or "kick a nigger" politics as it is called down South, an a whole lot of posing — talking or acting like a friend while either spouting rhetoric or stabbing you in the back. Who's the bad guy (or gal) in the sad state of affairs is measured only by degree. What it amounts to is, as James Brown put it, "talking loud and saying nothing."

From what's not being said it is simple to gauge whom the candidates and their staffs aren't talking to. Everyday conversation in the black community here reveals the toughest issues facing blacks nationwide. The education system is failing their kids. Many can't afford to buy or keep their homes. Communities are coded out of existence to make way for white urban pioneers. Minority business ownership is down. Bankruptcy is up. In overwhelming numbers their kids are locked up or otherwise under state supervision. Many are brutalized by the police or by each other. Somewhere between 30 to 50% of South Carolina black youth are unemployed. Half of all black mortgagors in the state losing their homes to foreclosure: this is a social catastrophe. On the political stage, it's as these baseline circumstances didn't exist.

But if the realities of black life are of small concern to the candidates, race is not. For Democrats South Carolina provides a place to do retail politics just enough to punch their card with the party's most loyal base. For Republicans, the state has typically helped candidates assert their conservative credentials, measured by how extreme they are on race.

As he did back in 2000, Arizona Senator John McCain hired State Representative Rick Quinn, once editor of *Southern Partisan*, a white "heritage" magazine, as his spokesman in the state. At the height of that primary Quinn's magazine ran a full-page photo of Abraham Lincoln with the words of his assassin, "*Sic Semper Tyrannis*," under the picture. McCain was outplayed for the white supremacist vote by George W. Bush that year, which may be why he has so far avoided the most race-baiting politics this time. Others have filled the void. Almost as soon as he came South, former New York Mayor Rudolph Giuliani let it be known he believes flying the Confederate flag on government property "is a matter of "states' rights." Colorado Congressman Tom Tancredo spoke at a barbecue sponsored by the South Carolina chapter of the League of the South, a neo-Confederate group that had the event catered by Maurice Bessinger, famous for flying the battle flag and selling books defending slavery at his restaurants. At the close of his speech reportedly sang "Dixie" with men in dressed in Confederate soldiers' uniforms.

That blacks' view the Republican Party with antipathy is no surprise. The surprise is that, beyond symbolism, the Republicans are not that much worse than the Democrats.

Illinois Senator Barack Obama touted by *Time* magazine for having the courage to tell "inconvenient truths," used one of the oldest racial stereotypes in a speech to black South Carolina state legislators. "In Chicago, sometimes when I talk to the black chambers of commerce," he said, "I say, 'You know what would be a good economic development plan for our community would be if we make sure folks weren't throwing their garbage out of their cars.'" Translation: black people are dirty and lazy.

Obama's defenders claim he is saying aloud what blacks say privately. But presidential candidates aren't campaigning for a place in the conversation on the neighborhood corner or in the cut. Those same black state legislators whom Obama addressed had earlier released data showing that only 3 out of 10 black males and 4 out of 10 black females graduate from the public high schools in South Carolina; that 85 per cent of youth prisoners and 70 per cent of adult prisoners are black, and many did not have a high school diploma and were unemployed before their arrest and incarceration. Such problems aren't limited to South Carolina but are at crisis level in Illinois, New York, Ohio and across the country. And Obama has nothing to offer as a solution.

Neither does Hillary Clinton. While campaigning in Selma, Alabama, the New York Senator confused speaking in ebonics — "Aww don't feel noways tired" — with "walking the walk and talking the talk." She did something similar at a luncheon at Al Sharpton's National Action Network conference in April. Her apparent aim on both occasions was to 'out-black' Obama. In a speech at Rutgers shortly after the Don Imus gaffe, she summoned the ghosts of Harriet Tubman, Frederick Douglass and Sojourner Truth. Her husband appropriated black icons like Martin Luther King, Jr. right before he came down strong with his 'pimp hand' telling blacks if King were alive "he'd be ashamed" of them. Hillary 'acting black' may have been intended to remind some that her young, rival Obama — often compared to the Kennedys, "isn't black enough."

In South Carolina there is no question that Hillary Clinton and the other Democrats have a master teacher. Back in '92, Jesse Jackson's wife Jackie told me Yasser Arafat remarked to her, "Where you sleep is where your politics lie." Literally or figuratively, most of the Democratic candidates sleep with the playbook of Bill Clinton. I tend to see Hillary as the Susan Stanton character in the movie *Primary Colors*. The 1998 film adaptation of former Clinton ally Joe Klein's book is about an "unknown Southern governor running for the presidency with his strong, savvy and equally ambitious wife…" At one point the Bill Clinton-like character, Jack Stanton, tells his staff, "I don't want to give the sonovabitch the chance to make me the sonovabitch." In street slang that's called "flipping the script." It's what Don Imus did after his "ho" comment, deflecting blame onto hip hop culture. Hillary may have flipped the script on Obama leaving him to talk about what's wrong with black people.

Bill's classic examples of race-baiting include his infamous 1992 public backhands of Sistah Souljah and Jesse Jackson — just to let folks know he wasn't indebted to blacks — and his decision to make a high-profile rush to Arkansas to preside over the execution of Rickey Ray Rector, a brain-damaged black man who didn't even know he was being killed — just to let folks know he wasn't soft on crime (*aka* blacks). Obama told the *New York Times*, "I'm not interested in engaging in a bunch of Sister Souljah moments just for the sake of it. If I do that, it's not for effect but because it's what I really believe." It's a toss-up which is worse: that Obama raised the spectre of dirty blacks to score a political point or that he really believes it.

Meanwhile, the Clinton legacy affects what's being said or not said today in more subtle ways. The joke that refuses to go away is that Bill Clinton was "America's first black president," even as his policies on due process, equal protection and equal treatment — in other words, civil rights — were horrible. No Democrat is challenging his initiative requiring citizens, mostly black, in public housing to surrender their Fourth Amendment or privacy rights; or his 'one strike and you're out' policy under which public housing residents convicted of a crime, along with anyone who lives with them, are evicted without due process.

So former Senator John Edwards of North Carolina used Hurricane Katrina as his entrance ticket to 2008 campaign, but at a substantive level he seems incapable of addressing "the right of return" for the 250,000 displaced residents relocated after the storm. A "right of return" would require somewhere to live and work upon return. Many of the displaced were renters before the flood. Many have the kind of credit rating that disqualifies them for most private housing and some types of government assistance. New Orleans had the highest poverty/crime rate in the region before the storm, and many of the now displaced were unemployed. A significant percentage of the 250,000 have criminal records, or someone in their immediate family does, thus disqualifying them from public housing under Clinton's one strike policy even if forces in New Orleans weren't intent on eliminating public housing. Would Edwards or any of the other candidates support the repeal of the one-strike policy? Would they support waiving or lowering credit requirements? Not one has come out for homesteading or granting people a home and a clean start.

Hurricane Katrina isn't something that happened "down there" for most black people. It reinforced what they witness close-up right now, in Columbia or in Cleveland. They know how people have to give up the car because even though they have a perfect driving record they're still charged a higher insurance rate because of where they live or their credit history. How they have to choose between paying for medicine and paying the bills. How if homeowners fall into bankruptcy the insurance companies can either refuse to sell them homeowners' insurance or raise the rate– which is what a homeowner needs the least. Many African-Americans know too well that the "po' pay mo'", burdened with extraordinarily high interest on just about any purchase. Their kids are stuck in awful, segregated schools. If those kids don't graduate from high school, particularly if they are male, chances are they are going to jail, most likely for selling drugs. One felony drug charge is economic suicide, as many employers will not hire ex-felons. If an ex-felon is lucky enough to get a job, it often doesn't cover the basics. A student loan is out of the question. So the kid ends up back in jail. Many blacks also know that the problem isn't solved with more police with drug dogs, social workers and piss tests. They know how tenuous existence is. Social instability due to unemployment or gentrification is one thing. Massive foreclosures in the new sub-prime housing developments — where 50% of new buyers are likely to lose their home within seven years, making the populations of those developments more or less transient — is the new other thing. An "affordable" development might have hundreds of houses, yet with the constant turnover, it's never a community in the truest sense.

So blacks have the choice of believing that the majority of people losing their homes are irresponsible deadbeats, or that sub-prime mortgages serve to enrich the builders, banks and developers and exploit working class buyers. They can believe they are dirty, lazy and just need to pick up the garbage or that there is redlining and a lack of economic development and equitable lending practices where they live. They can believe that the majority of black school-age kids are inherently, pathologically inferior, unable to learn (which translates into stupid, unappreciative of education and deserving of jail), or that the system stinks and needs restructuring.

The presidential aspirants mostly leave them alone to assign social, rather than merely personal, responsibility for those issues. At the Democrats' first debate in Orangeburg, South Carolina, only retired Alaska Senator and ex-cab driver Mike Gravel dared to say the "war on drugs" is a sham. Among the Republicans, only libertarian Ron Paul has called the drug war foolish, failed and an affront to liberty. In a practical sense ending it means taking on the hot potato issue of decriminalization. No top-tier, mid-tier or even fellow fringe candidate is stepping out on that one. And what of ending mass incarceration, sending inmates to prisons far away from their families, sometimes across state lines? Most Democratic candidates slam the Patriot Act; a few even call for its repeal. Yet who would call for a roll back on enhanced police powers like no-knock warrants and the erosion of probable cause which makes it easier to detain and search people, homes and cars? The deaths of Sean Bell, Amadou Diallo and Patrick Dorismond in New York, of 88-year-old Kathryn Johnston in Atlanta and a host of others elsewhere are a result of unchecked power derived from the "war on drugs." In the case of 6-year-old Desreè Watson of Florida, taken to jail in oversized hand-cuffs, charged with felonious battery on a school official, disruption of a school function and resisting a police officer — all for throwing a temper tantrum — we have the ultimate symbol of the criminalization of blacks. Over the years the age that kids are tried as adults has kept dropping. Once society adopts the mindset that childhood misbehavior is criminal behavior, anything goes.

It's an outgrowth of Rudy Giuliani's "zero tolerance" policing. There's not much chance that he or any Republican will get many black votes in the primary or general election. The question is whether any Democrat will return to South Carolina or any Southern state besides Florida after the primaries. Recent history suggests they won't, which makes the black primary even weightier. Although a majority of black Americans live in the South, the January 2008 primary here could be the only occasion that Democrats have to vie seriously for black votes — which under-scores that what we've seen so far is a pantomime of politics.

It is not that the issues being emphasized — war, global warming, health care and immigration — are irrelevant here. Most blacks opposed the war before it started and register protest via the plummeting numbers signing up for the military. They are environmentalists when it comes to environmental racism, but they are more concerned with home heating than global heating; if warmer winters mean lower fuel bills it's clear what will be the rational priority for most people. They support universal health care although being uninsured has never stopped them from going to an emergency room when push came to shove. And they are torn on immigration reform, especially as the mainstream has defined that as a Latino issue. Blacks don't live in the same neighborhoods with Latinos, don't speak the same language and often compete for the same jobs. A politics that linked the Global War on Terror with the war on drugs, that perceived the environment as the places people live, and health as the condition of their life — asking not so much Are they insured as Can they survive? Will their kids have a future? — that made the connections between racism, economic oppression and labor exploitation at home and abroad: such a politics might speak to people. Instead, we're offered the politics of symbolism: the black candidate, the woman, the Chicano, the "two Americas" man trailed by a few other white guys hoping somebody makes a mistake.

In a real sense, Jesse Jackson's 1984 and 1988 Rainbow campaigns were the last time blacks and progressives had a significant policy and institutional effect on American politics. The Rainbow 'movement' brought a diverse coalition together on an agenda predicated on universal human rights and peace. That coalition brought issues of race, gender and sexual orientation into an analysis of class and American power. It opposed the proliferation of nuclear weapons and demanded restrictions on nuclear energy. It supported the property rights of small family farmers and black farmers as well as the rights of migrant workers and workers' rights in general. It brought people into the political process and spurred a nationwide increase in black elected officials. Many of those newly appointed or elected officials carried a platform that opposed apartheid in South Africa, supported human rights for the Palestinian people and sought peaceful relations with Cuba and Central America.

The Rainbow challenge had an effect on both political parties. On the republican side it prompted a top down approach to race politics with the ascensions of Clarence Thomas, Colin Powell, Condoleezza Rice and others. It's inspired Bush's "faith-based" schemes. On democrat side, it lodged people at every level of the party and propelled the backlash Democratic Leadership Conference (DLC), dedicated to reversing the political aspiration of the Jackson's coalition. Among today's front-runners, Hillary Clinton is a DLC star, chair of its American Dream Initiative touting free markets, balanced budgets and middle-class know-how. Obama's political action committee, the Hope Fund, has raised money for ten DLC Senators, or half of the groups' presence in the Senate.

At a recent speech in Hampton, Virginia Obama mentioned the "simmering discontent" in the black community. He got that one right. Even with more black officials than at any time in history — most of them Democrats, many African-Americans feel that things have been moving in the wrong direction for a while now. From high infant mortality rates to low life spans, the black misery index is acute. The effect of the huge number of black citizens under the direct control of the state through the criminal justice system, so much so it has led to diminished voting rights and participation, cannot be overstated. African-Americans have gone from a "freedom movement" to the edge of no longer being free. And there is Obama, providing cover for those who blame the victims or prodding the victims to blame themselves. There is Hillary, promising a restoration, the flimflam of Clintonism as the blacks' best friend.

I've always believed liberation must be won outside the confines of party politics. But it would be unwise to ignore what candidates are saying or not saying, since they can affect how and if you live. It is elementary in politics to demand that those vying for black votes address "what's important to African-Americans" in a meaningful way. So far, the most blacks have got are race gestures and a blind eye.

Race, Class and Art:
Hustle and Flow

BY AND LARGE I COUNT MYSELF AMONG THOSE WHO BELIEVE that what is generally promoted as a race discussion usually ends up a waste of time. Now that we're past Black History Month, during which columnist Clarence Page suggested that his PBS *NewsHour* viewers might look to the 1852 *Uncle Tom's Cabin* for racial guidance, maybe we can also get past sepia-toned reminiscences of slavery and eulogies for Rosa Parks and Coretta Scott King to the real grainy Technicolor ways folk live today, or try to. It's an understatement that the ravishment of the Gulf Coast, destruction of a major American city and dispossession of its majority-black residents have set conditions for more than talk. But that ongoing catastrophe also demands that when we do speak, we better tell it like it is.

Whenever people say things like Hurricane Katrina "ripped the veil off racism and poverty" I am reminded of a line from a song in Craig Brewer's film *Hustle and Flow*: "It might be new to you but it's been like this for years." In fact, the film pricked my race/class sensibilities more than anything else in the midst of the latest round of race talk.

Shot in the working-class neighborhoods of Brewer's hometown, Memphis, Tennessee, *Hustle and Flow* is the story of DJay (played by Oscar nominee Terrence Howard), a pimp having a "midlife crisis." He's 35, the same age as his father when he died, and he fears his life will soon be over unless he changes course.

The film's look, feel and sound are all intimately familiar. From the dirt on the walls of a shotgun house to the hot, wet, sticky red clay-tinted heat of a Southern summer and the ever-present, almost useless dirty portable fan. From the train track separating the haves from the have-nots to the get-by job that gets you to the weekend to the juke joint where anything happens. From the sound of the blues — even in rap music — right down to the neighborhood, language and attitudes, Brewer puts a face on the people those such as Bill Cosby wish to be invisible. Some of them are even white.

Brewer's people could be among the 35 per cent of blacks currently living below the poverty line in the United States or the poorest 20 per cent or so of Louisiana residents. *Hustle and Flow* reveals what Katrina revealed: those who've been left to fend for themselves. In New Orleans almost 40 per cent of households, nearly all of them black, earned less than $20,000 a year.

I have lived in either a predominately black or all-black neighborhood for most of my forty-nine years. It is not an endorsement of segregation; it's just the way it is. Yet, there are a couple of things to appreciate about longstanding southern black neighborhoods. For one thing, different economic classes still live amongst one another. They intermix and interact. This social interaction is represented in the film by DJay's relationship with Key, played by Anthony Anderson. Key, an old school friend, has become a middle-class audio technician. In addition, many of us move up and down — on and off the economic ladder throughout our lives. And most demographic data not only bear out that class intermix but also the precariousness of paycheck-to-paycheck living. Moreover, the typical black family doesn't conform to the 2 parents, 2 kids model. Single women head 62% of black families and 67% of black children are born out of wedlock. Moreover, blacks more readily accept whites into those communities than vice versa, even poor whites, even gentrifying white "pioneers."

Although there has been racial progress in the United States, for many African-Americans life is like ice-skating up hill. According to the most recent American Housing Survey only 49 per cent of blacks are homeowners as compared with 76 per cent of whites. Even with comparable credit, blacks are 210 per cent more likely than whites to be rejected for a mortgage. When black borrowers are fortunate enough to get a non-government home loan, a little less than a third of them will have to bear high-interest sub-prime financing, which usually doesn't mesh well with a sub-prime car loan and/or the interest on a payday loan. No surprise, the national foreclosure rate for blacks sits right at 50 per cent, and half of all African-Americans live in unaffordable, inadequate or crowded housing. Among people living on the street or in their cars, 40 per cent are black.

Wealth, equity, control over property — these markers of the "American dream" are largely white privileges. At the onset of the last recession, between 1999 and 2001, the net worth of Hispanic and black households fell by 27 per cent. As of 2002, the Pew Hispanic Center reports, the median Hispanic household had a net worth of $7,932 and the median black family had $5,998, while the median white family had $88,651. And, almost a third of black households and more than a quarter of Hispanic ones had zero or negative net worth.

The meaning of the numbers is obvious: a sizable number of households and the individuals in them are barely getting by. And those in the middle class are seldom permanently middle class. That is not to say there are no recognizable class lines. Lots of black families lead economically stable lives and have decent credit.

Yet the majority of blacks live under conditions where any little bind affects their whole life. They are the people who lose their sub-prime loan homes, choose between car repair or insurance, gas or taxes, food or medicine, and frequently need an extension on the electric or phone bill. They rent the cheapest place they can find and try to hold on in traditional neighborhoods in the face of just about everything — from economic redlining to strict property code enforcement to urban pioneering to population disbursement or marginalization. They routinely face racial profiling and aggressive, if not brutal, law enforcement, jail and unemployability. A majority is in the South, where 54 per cent of blacks still live. Others are concentrated in the ghettos although many cities have driven poor people out of the core of metropolitan areas all across the country. And then there are those holdouts who occupied the waterfront — be it the bayous, the barrier islands, along a lake or river, because that's where their ancestors fled to — only to have that land taken by developers, or a storm, because it is waterfront.

That's why *Hustle and Flow* is such a notable picture. It is not just the story of a pimp in Memphis who needs to make music. It is the story of another city on the Mississippi delta. New Orleans was built on race dating back to the day when the first Africans fled out to the bayous to be free just as a runaway Jim in *Huck Finn* was attempting to do. It's that superficial sense of freedom and abandon that still draws tourists to a battered New Orleans, although the benefits of an economy based on the arts and nightlife never will trickle down to everyone. That is, unless you consider the four-man stand-up band that used to live in the Ninth Ward and is now playing and dancing in the street on a weekend night in the French Quarter for the money out-of-towners throw in the collection box as trickle down economics.

The film's climax has the police at DJay's doorstep after his encounter with rap mogul Skinny Black, played by rapper Ludacris. And, at the story's end DJay is behind bars. Neither situation is unfamiliar. DJay is from that big neighborhood where, according to the U.S. Justice Department, the 12 per cent of African-American men ages 20 to 34 who are in jail or prison live before and after their release; where lifespans on average are six years shorter than those of whites; where having the police at the door, going to court every now and then or having a family member in jail is not so uncommon.

My father's dad was married a number of times, legally and not. My pop had three brothers and a sister by his mom; one brother died young, and the other two served time on the chain gang, both for murder. One killed a woman, the other a man, both of them black. My father's sisters had four sons and four daughters. Three of the males and two of the females served time for offenses ranging from the ridiculous to the serious. My three brothers went to jail in their youth for non-violent offenses, and I have a few relatives in jail now. Maybe it's just the odds, because it almost went wrong for me many times, but I have never been in jail overnight, although I have been handcuffed more than a few times and clamped in leg irons once. But I have visited more chain gangs and work camps, jails, prisons and courtrooms than I care to remember. Whenever I see the 1967 film *Cool Hand Luke* it conjures memories of family visits to take cigars or a carton of cigarettes to one of my uncles in the camp, or spotting someone familiar on a road crew, or having a Sunday family picnic lunch under the pine trees while my incarcerated eldest brother had a conjugal visit with his girl.

This is not to cop to some inherent criminality in my family in particular or black people in general or to offer apologies, regrets, excuses or
blame. Sometimes getting caught up with the law is as simple as making
a bad choice. Others times bad programming gets the best of a person.
Or, when folk are raised in and around violence it should be no surprise when they commit or accept acts of violence. He or she might be at
the wrong place at the wrong time with the wrong people and just gets
caught up in it. And there are those times when an offense is an act of
rebellion against it all, a straight-out scream because regardless of how
racists view blacks or how defeatists view themselves, all the negative
indices of black life are too huge to be coincidental.

After Katrina, rapper Kanye West famously quipped, "George
Bush doesn't care about black people." Most black folk believed it, and
Princeton's professor Cornel West affirmed it, adding, "...you have to
distinguish between a racist intent and the racist consequences of his
policies."

But labeling Bush and placing the problem solely at his feet is far too
simple. Poor people of all hues are disregarded in both good and bad
weather. Though it was class more than race that determined who got
left behind in New Orleans, African-Americans also take it as a matter
of fact that the class structure of this country is built on race. Under the
"racist consequences" standard, Louisiana Governor Kathleen Blanco,
a Democrat who gave the "shoot to kill" order to a police department
with a violent history, and Ray Nagin, the black Democratic mayor who
before Katrina had not factored poor people into any of his political cal-
culations, would also make the list of failed leaders.

So would former president Bill Clinton, who typically polls in the
high 80 per cent approval ratings with blacks. Clinton's policies and atti-
tude on due process, equal protection and equal treatment — otherwise
known as civil rights — were horrible. One initiative required citizens,
mostly black, in public housing to surrender their Fourth Amendment
or privacy rights. Another was the "one strike and you're out" policy
under which public housing residents convicted of a crime, along with
anyone who lives with them, are now evicted without consideration of
their due process rights.

Black incarceration rates during the Clinton years surpassed Ronald Reagan's eight years. He stumped for "three strikes and you're out" in the federal crime bill, for restrictions on the right of habeas corpus and expansion of the federal death penalty, and he got them. When Clinton went into office one in four black men were involved in the criminal justice system in some way; when he left it was one in three. DJay represents the one in three.

So what does all this mean? Once again art provides a clue. *Hustle and Flow* depicts a society without leaders and how people cope.

Brewer likens the lead character DJay to Rocky Balboa. But I see DJay as more like Tom Joad in John Steinbeck's *The Grapes of Wrath*. Joad returns to his Oklahoma home after a stint in prison to find that his family is leaving to escape not only the drought but also a state and class system that is crushing them. As the 1940 movie adaptation of the novel begins, Henry Fonda stops in front of a country store named for its location, "Crossroads." DJay is at that same place, as is his woman Shug (played by Taraji Henson), pregnant by Lord knows who, tormented by dreams of giving birth to "dead dogs" and "nursing a big old catfish," worrying that her unborn child is doomed and sensing for the first time her own creative power.

Standing at the crossroads is the obvious metaphor for where America is today. There is a feeling across the country that we are headed in the wrong direction and need to choose a better path.

Washington Post columnist Eugene Robinson said the passing of Coretta Scott King marked the "end of a 'black leadership' era." I would mark its demise some thirty-odd years earlier. But often the good thing about the end of one thing is the start of something new. The idea that African-Americans and the poor must have someone who speaks for them is at the least annoying and at worst racist. Who speaks of white leaders? And the problem with most contenders for the role of national black leader — regardless of who they are — is that they don't necessarily rail against what exists. They usually speak from a privileged perspective and often wrangle over symbolism or shout over not having a bigger piece of the pie. But effective social change happens when people from the bottom, speak for themselves, put pressure on the middle and the top, promotes a set of values and enforces them. Rosa Parks' legacy isn't a solitary act. Parks, trained in non-violent activism at the Highlander Center in Tennessee, is part of a peoples' movement that included folk like Claudette Colvin, who at 15 was arrested for refusing to take her place on a Montgomery bus nine months before Parks. And it wasn't just Martin Luther King Jr. dreaming out loud. The kids who filled the jails, the "Freedom Riders" and the grassroots voter registrars were leaders.

African-American opposition to the Iraq war today is black leadership. All those families and individuals discouraging their kin from joining up to fight have resulted in a decrease in black recruitment and a crisis for the system. And it didn't take a leader (other than George Bush) to set them on course.

The issue of race in America is hard to face, but it is inseparable from class, which might be why so many African-Americans support the concept of reparations. But though black communities are hit the hardest, amid staggering wealth disparities and social insecurity rampant in the land, they are not alone in need of repairing. W.E.B. Dubois in a 1960 speech at the University of Wisconsin, when presented with the question "What then is the next step?" called for "the stopping of a government of wealth for wealth, and by wealth, and a returning of governmental power to the individual voter, with all the freedom of action which can be preserved, along with an industry carefully organized for the good of the masses of people and not for the manufacture of millionaires." Seven years later King, pushed by black discontent in the cities and mass dissent from the war, called for "a restructuring of the whole of society." That was his Crossroads.

Some complained he was taking a radical path, but it was the only realistic one for society, as is plain today. The path for government now should be made clear: make the unwhole whole, not just Katrina victims in Louisiana and Mississippi but also the victims of life-changing storms over the past four years from Florida to North Carolina and the millions of structurally poor Americans of whatever race for whatever reason. Now is the time to demand serious public investment, full employment, debt forgiveness and a national housing policy in which homesteading is a significant part the plan.

Of course, grassroots advocacy for a new plan begins with Gulf Coast victims. For the renters and homeowners who lost everything the demand is simple: Homes. That is not to suggest that those who were well below sea level for reasons of history should be encouraged to rebuild in an unsafe area. New Orleans has the opportunity to rebuild an economically and racially integrated city if America has the will. That is, rebuild it in a new, more equitable way. As for the Gulf Coast rebuilding effort, citizens should insist that federal, state and local officials take the profit out of public works and put the money in the pockets of those who need it most instead of making rebuilding efforts into another welfare program for millionaires.

Finally, while promoting *Hustle and Flow* on *The Late Show with David Letterman* last year, Terrence Howard commented that the Hurricane Katrina victims in that city were "waiting on someone to give them something, instead of doing for themselves." If he was referring to those trapped on roofs, in attics and at overcrowded shelters, he was way off base. If he was referring to the need for poor people to organize, make a demand and speak and represent themselves, he's right.

Richard Pryor's Mirror on America

RICHARD PRYOR WAS APPEARING AT GEORGIA TECH ALONG with Earth, Wind and Fire the night before my 1974 high school graduation. I was sixteen and not of age to defy my father who like Richard's old man, often warned, "Have your ass home by 11." Still, I jumped into my soon to be sister-in-law's brown '72 Ford Pinto with a girl I was sweet on, and away the three of us went to Atlanta some 200 miles away.

I returned home the next morning just in time to change clothes and load up in the family Pontiac to go to graduation. Needless to say, my dad, as Richard's old man would have done, went upside my head as I eased into the car. I would have been disappointed if he had not given me that open hand slap to the back of the head. It was the cost of finding out what happens after 11:30.

A friend recently gave me the box set of Pryor's work although I already had every single album from the day they hit the street. Many of us have tried to mimic various Mudbone's lines like "Miss Rudolph, Miss Rudolph can you do something about the monkey?" or preach from the "Book of Wonder, Chapter Innervisions." Those who have listened to Pryor generally have a favorite bit or character that they'll try to do. But whenever I think of him it's in Georgia accepting a joint from someone in the crowd, taking a couple of puffs and walking across stage to pass it on. Then on to his impression of "Tricky Dick" in jail. Pryor, with his ass pointed up in the air as to get the business, informing the world what could happen to Richard Nixon if he ended up in a real jail. Of course the punch line is Nixon's own words, "Let me make this perfectly clear."

NBC's Dick Ebersol upon hearing of Pryor's death said that the comedian was "fearless and he had a conscience." I agree with the conscience or conscious part of that characterization but I don't see Richard as particularly fearless. He had all kinds of fears that he openly shared with us.

His comedy was rooted in his and our fears. And, he dealt with those fears in some screwed up ways just like the rest of us. To confront fear isn't fearlessness, it's courage.

Richard could separate the bullshit from what is real and true. Consciousness, not to be confused with "false consciousness," is seeing things in the proper context or confronting the pretext of a situation or condition. False consciousness is what society erects to keep us in line. Pryor's comedy confronted false consciousness or as the old folk used to call it, "taking the thorn out your eye."

Pryor, wittingly or not, challenged some of the stereotypes and taboos that accompanied "black consciousness." Back in the day as the societal desegregation we see today was first emerging, marrying a white woman was a very scandalous thing on both the black and white sides of the street. It's still kind of taboo although politically incorrect to express out loud. Richard crossed the line and then proceeded to tell us what was different and not so different about black and white women. And the lesson Richard left us with after taking us through his various relationships was that women were not mindless possessions totally under the control of men. In Pryor's world men were usually not in control.

Richard made it okay for black men to admit to having oral sex and not all having big dicks. And, if you didn't know what it felt like to be high or that drugs would screw your life up, Richard talked about his addiction.

Richard was a mirror. And at the end of most of his stories was the lesson that most often the stereotypes we define ourselves by are usually both wrong and contrived to allow someone or something to keep their boot on your neck or to protect someone's interest other than yours.

Bill Cosby quipped, "I wish that every new and young comedian would understand what Richard was about and not confuse his genius with his language usage." Cosby is wrong. Richard's genius *was* his use of language. Pryor was the anti-Cosby. Where Cosby used language to sugar coat reality and to lull people into unconditional, unconscious acceptance, Richard painted reality as it is — hard, messy, crazy, hot, sick, good, bad. A wino can be a repulsive, beautiful being. He could be pissy. He could be your dad or uncle. He could be beat down or just not give a fuck and that wine gave him the cover to say whatever the fuck he wanted to say. And sometimes you let the drunk ass wino say some shit for you. That's what Mudbone did for us. He said shit we were afraid to say.

Pryor changed on his use of the word "nigger" but it did not erase his role in leading the charge to sap the hurting power from the word. And what is wrong with taking away the power of a word to make you do something stupid or to give an asshole power over you? Or, giving blacks the power to use something that's off limits to whites—to where they now have to refer to it as "the N-word?"

Richard might have tried to put the genie back in the bottle but it is no coincidence that he would have an album entitled "That Nigger's Crazy." The crazy nigger could say things that would get a sane person killed. We called it "playing crazy." On the other hand, every so often a crazy nigger would emerge that had to be killed. At first the white folk might try to blunt the truth of what a truth teller was saying by warning the locals, "Don't listen to that boy, he's crazy." Other times it was the black folk trying to protect a truth teller calming the man with, "don't pay him no mind, that nigga boy is crazy."

There maybe an heir to Pryor out there, but nobody has been crowned yet. Dave Chappell is the closest contemporary comedian to Pryor stylistically but his "Black Bush" doesn't even come close to Pryor helping to image what some would consider justice—Nixon getting fucked. (Remember the poster "Dick Nixon before he dicks you!"). For my sensibilities "Black Bush" trying to pass off pound cake as "yellow cake" doesn't have the bite as, say, painting a picture of George Bush, Dick Cheney, Condi Rice and the rest of that evil crew attempting to negotiate their way through a prison system with the torture regimens that they put in place.

Richard Pryor made a lot of things clear for us. We cheered when he told the world what most blacks already knew—that the 'justice' in the American justice system — was "just us." It still is "just us."

Pryor's mark is far greater than simply giving life and voice to winos, prostitutes, pimps and other assorted characters. Pryor reminded us that the only difference between the whores on Park Avenue and those on any other avenue is location. And, more often than not, there is no line between the sacred and profane or between beauty and ugliness.

We love you brother. Now go "rub a little sunshine on your face."

The Soul Will Find a Way

I F MEMORY SERVES ME RIGHT, I MET JAMES BROWN ABOUT FIVE OR six times. I first met Brown when I was 4 years old in 1961 (through his music) after my father moved my mom Geneva, my three older brothers, my younger sister and me from Boston to rural Spartanburg County in upstate South Carolina after my granddad Andrew's death. My father Paul had fled the south in the 1940s by enlisting in the Navy. Twenty years later he returned to an inheritance of eleven shotgun houses and a juke joint at the foot of a hill in a tiny segregated, one way in / one way out community called Freyline. The 500-or-so person community was named after Jacob Frey, a white man who sold off a little better than 11 acres of his farmland to my grandfather. It was a small enough place where you knew the names of every person living there and almost every detail of their lives. Freyline sat astride the corn and bean fields and cow pastures of 3 large white-owned farms with the old Southern Crescent railroad line to lock us in. There was 'up the road,' 'down the hill,' and 'on the circle.' We had two tar and gravel roads; Frey Road and Frey Circle, which looped off Frey Road and back into it.

The sign up over the front door between the two round, red Coca Cola logos said Gray's Grocery but everyone called the gathering spot 'the store.' The little faux brick tar-sided, rusty tin roofed tinderbox had it all, including an old man named 'Pop' Hardy who ran the place during the day and wore a battered, sweat-stained, dirty grey wool fedora year round. Pop, his wife Ma, and their large family lived in one of my father's houses on the hill directly behind the store. Gray's Grocery was where all the maids, janitors, textile mill workers, field laborers, wannabe slicksters, young and old, sinners and saints met on weekends to dance, drink, gamble, talk, cuss, have an occasional scuffle, fist, gun or knife fight and generally let it all hang out.

The building was just a smallish wood barn with a floor. The hours were pretty regular. 10 to 11 on weekdays and a little past midnight on Thursdays to cash the mill workers' paychecks. On Friday and Saturday nights the store was open til the wee hours of the morning. Sunday was iffy. If someone came by the house before church needing something for Sunday dinner like flour, lard or whatever, one of us kids would go down the road and open the store for them. Often my dad would open after church. At night a neon Colt 45 sign in one of the barred windows and a yellow light over the front door were lit up. We not only had a front door — we had a back one as well. There were juke joints that nailed or boarded their back door because it's the first way a crook will try to break in. If something went down in a one way out joint you could be trapped inside. Our back door had ready access to the coal and bottle shed in the back of the building and served as an escape route when a fight broke out or we had to quickly get rid of illegal contraband such as liquor or gambling items. It had a wood and metal bar across it. On the parking side of the building was a large tin Pabst Blue Ribbon sign that primarily served to keep the weather out. This side was also reserved for dice and horseshoe games. The other side was where folks generally relieved themselves. It was always pissy smelling, even on the driest day, and not a place to go in the rain. The two front windows were barred. There was a small window on each side — high up and boarded up to keep out burglars. Still, every now and then, someone, even sometimes my older brothers, would manage to break in. Either by prying the boards off the pissy side window or going under the store — which sat on brick piers — and up through the floor. Or prying the locks off the front or kicking in the back door, even with the metal bar.

Inside the store was tight, no matter the number of patrons present. There were about 3 or 4 bar stools along the L-shaped counter with just enough room for two small tables. The tables weren't a regular fixture through the years because of space. They were probably a reminder to my dad of his time in the service and of real bars in faraway places. At the far end of the long counter close to the exit was a glass bread case. The pot-bellied stove sat in the corner tucked dangerously close to the main counter and a long, lacquered, wooden church bench that ran down the wall to the juke box. While we had more than our share of drunken winos and out-of control scufflers, they always managed to avoid falling on the stove while it was hot. The glass on the bread case was another matter. It was replaced more times than I can remember. In the winter we'd nail cardboard to the walls for insulation. Whenever the stove was blazin' we constantly had to go outside to make sure the crumbling, leaning, brick chimney didn't cause the building to catch fire. The chimney's inefficiency was worsened by us kids constantly tossing beer cans and mud clogs up into it as a kind of game.

The main or short counter faced out towards the front door. On it sat one of those cash registers with a handle that you pulled after you punched in the cost of an item. Cases of sodas were stacked underneath the counter. Tucked in the bottles on the top case of sodas was my pop's .32 pistol and a raggedy, loaded single-barrel shotgun with the stock held together by black, cloth electrical tape. The shotgun was pretty much for show, as everyone knew that if it were ever used it would probably backfire and kill the user. To the right of the register, and built up slightly higher, was the candy counter with big jars of pickled everything on top. Eggs and dill pickles, pigs' feet and knuckles, beef tripe and tongues and red hot sausages. And lots of jars filled with 1 cent, 2-for-a penny and 5-for-a penny cookies and those big peppermint sticks. Under the counter in a glass-enclosed case was any kind of candy a kid could want. The clear plastic tape holding the glass together didn't stop us kids from poking at the glass to show Pop Hardy what we wanted from inside. And hidden out of sight in a not so secret space under the candy case was store bought liquor, home brew and white lightning. There was always a good selection of spirits — Wild Irish Rose which we called 'Will I Run', Silver Satin, MD (Mad Dog) 20/20, Boone's Farm, Orange Tommy, Ripple and Sangria. We carried maybe 6 beer brands but most guys preferred Schlitz or Colt 45 while women favored Old Milwaukee or Champale. We also carried the essentials — corn meal, bread, bleach, sardines, potted meat and soda crackers, pork and beans, Tide washing powder, Argo starch, Dixie Crystal sugar, chewing tobacco in little square blocks, snuff, general notions, remedies and whatever. When my grandfather ran the business lard was stored in a big tin vat and flour was ground on site. After my dad took over, Crisco in the can and Gold Medal flour replaced the chores of mucking with the lard box or shoeing away the little, grey flying bugs that were always drawn to the flour inside the bin. And to us kids' joy my father brought in an ice cream box. A hand written cardboard sign was prominently posted up by the wine shelf that wishfully read "Cash Today, Credit Tomorrow," although most days a good number of folk had to get it "on the book."

I hung out at the store as far back as I can remember, although I didn't get to regularly work weekends until I turned 11 or 12. I usually swept, which meant filling a soda bottle with water and sprinkling it over the floor before sweeping to keep down the red clay dust. Every now and then, especially if it was rainy outside, I swept up the dried red mud clogs that came off folks' shoes. I kept coal or wood in the fire, ran the numbers, or tip books as they are called, and looked out for County Sheriff Carl Crane in his Ford Sunbeam (like the one driven by *Mayberry's* Andy and Barney) with the big whip antennae.

It was standing room only on weekends. Folks spilled out onto the steps or hung out in the yard depending on the weather. In the winter an outside fire burned in a 50 gallon gasoline drum just a leap from the front door over by a big drainage ditch. Dancing inside was close up. Inevitably, someone would go through the wooden planked floor and fall 2 feet to the ground, as there was no sub-flooring. It became somewhat of a guessing game as to when a plank would give way and who would be the victim. Yet we were always ready to perform an immediate jack-legged patch job. Such mishaps usually occurred when James Brown was playing on the 'jute' box or piccolo machine as we called it. We had a couple of "JB" wannabees with their hair pressed and the pointy-toed hit top black boots like those worn by Brown. Like Mr. Oliver Ellis, always neatly dressed and old when I met him, who fancied himself a dancer. He'd jack his pants up by his belt just before he did his thing. Any move James Brown did, Mr. Oliver Ellis would attempt to mimic, even going so far as trying to slide across the fragile, uneven wood floor. Mr. Ellis with his shoes was the exception to the rule. Though Brown fined his band members for dirty shoes, most of the people who danced to his music wore dusty or raggedy shoes, and a few 'bare-footed' it.

There are a few theories on how the word funk was born but I think it originated in places like our store. Those who lived in the rural south in the years prior to the mid-seventies can imagine what Gray's Groceries was like. Most black communities had a similar place. During the day it was the typical dry goods store. After the work day was done it was the place to get a beer before heading home, exchange the gossip of the day, get the numbers, complain about white people and talk about the Lincoln High School basketball team. On weekends it was the nightclub. My dad would put brown paper bags over the light bulbs that hung from the ceiling to discourage moths and dim the building. The place always had an old smell about it that was a mixture of stale beer, the oily, vinegary scent from the pickled products, coal and the burlap sack it came in, old petrified wood and the musk of people that worked in the fields, cotton plants or any other job that was dirty. Field workers had a wet, sweaty scent. The "lint heads" who worked the mill would come during the week covered in cotton dust from head to toe accompanied by a dry, dusty aroma. Leroy Jackson, the one-armed auto mechanic, came by the store everyday straight from the grease pit of Glenn Hope's Esso station.

In the summer the building was hot even with both doors open and the two small fans running on high. And you couldn't get too close up on the fans as neither had safety grills. It was always a wonder why the building didn't burn down with the bad electrical wiring that my granddad had rigged up. In the winter, the farther away you were from the stove, the colder you were.

Folks had their favorite artists. Leroy Jackson routinely punched Aretha Franklin's number on the piccolo machine. Franklin was always referred to by her first name — Aretha. My mother liked Sam Cooke, Jackie Wilson, Kitty Lester and Mary Wells. Girls most often punched in The Supremes, Marvin Gaye and Tammi Terrell or Kim Weston, Dee Dee Sharp and The Miracles. Older women preferred Gladys Knight and The Pips, Otis Redding, Al Green, Percy Sledge and Aretha. Kids liked "Little Stevie Wonder" and later on the Jackson 5. Men generally liked whatever girls and women liked but it was usually some male singer pleading for one more chance. But if someone put a quarter in the juke box, one out the three picks was sure to be a James Brown tune.

My father had an older friend by the name of James Montgomery. We respectfully called him Mr. Montgomery. He called himself "Po Roller", especially after he'd been drinking. Montgomery worked for Jack Dobson whom we called "Mr. Jack." Montgomery was his top man. He worked for Mr. Jack from the time he was a boy until his death in his sixties. Montgomery always moved and walked real slow and bent over. Like many older black men of that time, he wore a battered fedora. He generally dressed in overalls and wore an old dark suit jacket. Just as daylight hit you could look out the window and see Montgomery making his way up the road. Or we'd hear my dad who was getting ready for work say, "There goes "Po Roller." Oftentimes my father would leave a bit early so he could give Montgomery a ride and spare him the mile walk to work. Even as Montgomery got older Dobson paid him a weekly stipend and gave him somewhere to go, even though he did little or no work when he finally got there. Drunk or sober, Montgomery was the only person who ever had unlimited credit in my dad's place. Whenever there was trouble of any kind Mr. Montgomery was the person my father went to. I was Montgomery's favorite kid. He couldn't read so he'd give me a quarter and say, "Play James Brown. Play 'I feel good' ("I Got You")." Montgomery moved slow except when it came to cutting at someone who crossed him. He would drink too much, soil himself and appear to be asleep on the bench with his head hung down in his chest. But if someone tried to pick his coat pocket, at the slightest touch, he would instinctively and quickly pull the knife he always carried on him. He also had a little pearl-handled, chrome-plated .22 that he might use on occasion. A person knew they had gotten on the wrong side of Montgomery when he said, "Po Roller don't mess with nobody." That was their cue to make a mad dash out the front door. But the tension died quickly when someone put a dime in the machine and played "I Got that Feeling", "Cold Sweat" or Mr. Montgomery's favorite — "I feel good." Folk would forget the ruckus and start doing the Grind, Shing-a-ling, Boo-ga-loo, Shimmy, Watusi, Bump, Funky Four Corners, Tighten Up, Jerk, Mash Potatoes or Monkey. Or maybe they would select "It's a Man's World" which always sparked a lively conversation.

On Wednesdays the Collin's Music man would come by to divide up the money from the juke box and bring new records. There was always a lot of Brown on the piccolo machine. A perk for our family was the extra copy of "Lickin' Stick" or "Night Train" that the piccolo man would leave us. When a 45 record came off the machine, we got it. He always had to bring an extra disc for Brown's hits because Brown's songs, even the ones released in the late 50s and early 60s, were never stale or out of style. What could the man take off? "Think?" "Caldonia?" "Out of Sight" was hot well into the late sixties. And there are no better 'slow drag' songs (hip hoppers call it the "bump and grind") than "Try Me" or "I Lost Someone."

Brown was a constant presence in our store. He was the low country homeboy who made it big. The state of Georgia and the city of Augusta claim him as their hometown hero and he too claimed the state and city. Yet he never moved more than 40 miles from his family's roots in Barnwell County, South Carolina along the Savannah River establishing a home on Beech Island in Aiken County, South Carolina, adjacent to Strom Thurmond's Edgefield County home. The earliest recorded account of Brown's kin can be found in the 1860 census records of the James C. Brown plantation. Brown's parents and grandparents are included in the 1930 census records of Barnwell. He was born in the South Carolina, jailed here, his last legally questionable marriage was licensed here, and his final resting place is here. Throughout his life he publicly rejected South Carolina, but maintained a private connection to the place that was obviously his home. The conflicted relationship is the story of Brown's music and life. His music shouts out what he was running away from, what he did get away from and what he could never quite escape. The reason we love him is because an awful lot of us see our own story in that dilemma and the persistence to live through it. It's the dilemma of loving someone, some place or something and hating it at the same time, or seeing the good and bad in the same thing. That's why Brown's popularity isn't just about him. It's about South Carolina and the people and a world of joy and pain that he was always close to. That's why it's hard to bury him.

Brown's body lies in a 24 karat gold-plated casket at his daughter Deanna Brown's home in Aiken, South Carolina. Under cover now, he is laid out the way thousands of mourners at his public funeral in Augusta, Georgia, saw him right before New Year 2007, in a black silk tux with tails and silver sequined satin lapels, red shirt, black gloves, black pointed-toe boots with rhinestones on the tip and a little gold #1 pin on his black bow tie. The service was called a homegoing, and the delay in getting the Brown to his final resting place had a lot to do with the nature of home. Given that he is "The Godfather of Soul", that it has took a while to entomb his body is no stranger or surprising than preparing Vladimir Lenin's tomb or the Egyptians building a pyramid for King Tut. Much of the delay is in figuring out to set up 'Brownville' or 'Soulland' or whatever name his 60-acre Beech Island estate will take on for tourists.

I believe Elvis is dead, but just as it hasn't been easy to bury Elvis, it is hard to bury James Brown. At any moment in a day you'll hear his voice, his name, a beat or a song. A Brown phrase crystallizes a situation like when it's time to leave a room — "it's too funky in here" — or when it's time to go to work or party — "you gotta get on the good foot" — or when hearing someone being deceitful or stupid — "talking loud and saying nothing." That he died on Christmas day gives some believers hope that his lingering spirit will one day re-enter his body and he will "get up" and rejoin the living. Still, beyond an improbable resurrection, the substance that fed Brown's music won't decompose. It lingers. For the sake of discussion let's call it soul power.

Soul power is a connection to the people and their lived experience — good, bad and ugly. It means hearing what you feel and feeling what you hear. It's in the call and response, like a preacher and the congregation. It can be one person singing their story alone, like when Otis Redding sings "Sitting on the dock of the bay." It's putting the blue note in a plea, a wail, a moan, a holler or a shout. It's about the process of life with all its messiness, funkiness, bitterness, bewilderment, danger, love, anger, sex , lust, payback, redemption, relapse, stupidity, joy, heartbreak and pain, possession and obsession, shame, loss, pride, good and bad dealings, disappointment, exploitation, struggle, suffering, falling down and gettin' on up. And at some point returning home metaphorically, physically or spiritually. Even when home isn't the best place to be.

Now, this is not about who has or doesn't have soul. It's about where Brown got his supply. I believe there is something cosmically black about South Carolina. My belief arises from the fact that the vast majority of African slaves brought to the United States for life on the plantation disembarked on Sullivan's Island — the 'black Ellis Island' — just off the coast of Charleston. Brown picked up from the vibes the Africans brought off the slave ships and taken out into the fields. He inherited what they sang about and how they sang it. Plantation slaves subversively sang "Jackass rared, Jackass pitch. Throwed ole Marsa in de ditch…" while Brown sang "you can't tell me how to be the boy when you know I'm grown."

The Roma or black Gypsies (not to be confused with the Tinkers) also settled among and intermixed with the Africans in the low country region of South Carolina. Thus a context for Brown's constantly being on the road with his itinerant band of musicians all decked out in their ornate costumes, living free-wheeling lives.

The African beat and rhythm landed on Sullivan's Island. It rolled down the coast to Edisto Island and traveled up the Savannah River to Brown's neck of the woods. It is not surprising that two of the most profound influences on modern popular black music — James Brown and Motown — can so clearly place their historical pedigree from the same region. Edisto Island, one of the barrier islands in the low country swamp area, is where escaped African slaves sought refuge from their would-be masters. Edisto is where bass player and Motown *Funk Brother* James Jamerson found the blue note. Jamerson carried the bottom beat in just about every Diana Ross, Marvin Gaye, Smokey Robinson or Motown tune. In the movie, *Standing in the Shadow of Motown*, Jamerson is quoted as telling a friend he made his first musical instrument by stretching a rubber band on a stick and sticking it into an ant hill so he could, "make the ants dance." It is easy to imagine Brown, the young songwriter, reminiscing on his childhood, recalling a day he sat on an ant hill and wrote, "I got ants in my pants and I need to dance."

Some of us wrote off Brown's dissing South Carolina as his not wanting the world to think "the hardest working man in show business" was a country bumpkin. He could justifiably claim Georgia since his formative years were spent in urban Augusta which, despite the obstacles he would face as a teen, was a slightly better environment than backwater Barnwell. Even 130 years after emancipation, life in rural Barnwell was still pretty much like it was on the plantation. Brown's mother Susie ran away from it in 1936 leaving 3 year old James with his father James Joseph Brown, Sr. Within the first six years of Brown's life his dad left the fields to work in the tar plant. From the turn of the century through the sixties just about every county had a tar plant. It provided tar for roads, railroad ties, house siding and a variety of other uses. The work was hot, black, hard, nasty, sticky, smelly, dirty and dangerous. Small, impoverished, black enclaves of little tar-paper shotgun houses sprung up around these plants. Chain gang camps were located close by so as to provide county road crews. Families of inmates migrated to these communities.

These small black communities also served big white-owned farms, providing the bulk of work in much the same way as when plantation owner James C. Brown was alive. This is what it was like in Freyline. Jack Dobson's big farm, one of the three large farms in our area, employed many of the men in Freyline. A tar and "criso" wood plant was within smelling distance. Relatives would come through with the county prison road crew and were often allowed to visit with kin while in the neighborhood. James Brown came from just such a community. Every winter a couple of those tar paper houses burned to the ground in a flash, often taking their occupants with them. The tar paper would raise the temperature of an already out of control blaze which took on a blue flame and gave off an oily smell.

With his mother gone and his father working, young James, as he recalled, "was pretty much left alone to roam the backwoods of Barnwell to fend for himself." His childhood might have been as idyllic as playing in the fields or running barefoot behind the older kids or 'no tellin' what a young kid alone might have seen or experienced in the woods.

Now, I don't know exactly why Susie ran, and I don't know a lot about James Brown Sr. (James legally dropped the Jr. from his name). Yet before Brown's birth through at least the 60s and 70s, the south was an extremely harsh place for black women. Spousal violence was endemic.

Black women didn't have a rung on the social ladder. They were often on the brutal receiving end of black male's anger at his condition and treatment by white society. A black woman had very little protection from abuse unless she had a special relationship with a white patriarch. Or she could resort to the dreaded "ten-cent pop pistol" which was a mixture of hot grits and lye. Black children too were often victims of abuse and a hard life at an early age.

Brown's music came from a raucous and oftentimes violent environment with all the emotions and contradictions carved into his psyche for better or worse. Maybe Brown was saying something about Susie's life and his when he sings "when we did wrong papa beat the hell out of us" in "Papa Don't Take No Mess." It surely says a lot about the world I witnessed growing up in rural South Carolina at a time when common law marriages were the norm. Back then a man could kill a spouse or mate and was protected by laws recognizing "crimes in the heat of passion." Even a black man who killed his wife or girlfriend, if he was fortunate enough to own property or have money, could sometimes avoid jail time or a long sentence for murder. I had one uncle who only did 4 years on the chain gang for beating his first spouse to death with a 2x4 stud. Another uncle served 12 years on the chain gang for killing "the wrong man" over a woman. My father on occasion would beat my mother. My siblings and I would grab his legs in her defense—two boys to a leg. It was often violent in our home, but he only ran us out the house at gunpoint once or twice. Maybe Susie Brown was escaping such a life.

Still, there were some hard and fast rules folks lived by. The rules dealing with whites boiled down to staying out their business beyond work. The worse place a black person could be was in the middle of white folks' business or to have them in the middle of yours. But rule number one within our own community was 'stay out of married or grown folks' business' or fights between a man and a woman. The second rule—don't interfere with a parent whipping their child—often gave relatives, friends, neighbors and school officials the go ahead to physically "correct" their child. The words "I'm gonna beat some sense into you" came right before a whack or slap across the face, a lick upside the head, a butt lickin'—hand or wooden paddle—a whipping or beating.

Tree switches — the offense determined the number — were used for whipping and belts or barber straps for beatings. Violence is still condoned today. The threat of violence is often used as a punch line in jokes. In a Bill Cosby comic bit Cosby chides his son for some transgression saying, "I brought you into this world and I can take you out." The truth of the matter is the South that Brown and many others grew up in was a very violent place.

Brown continued to live with his father and a host of live-in girlfriends until he was 6 years old, when his father moved to Augusta. There he left the boy to live with his Aunt Honey on Twiggs Street. His aunt, like Richard Pryor's grandmother, ran a whorehouse. Living with his aunt no doubt provided Brown with an abundant array of grunts, groans, squeals, and sexual repartee for his songs. In Augusta he spent more time on his own, hanging out on the streets and hustling to get by. Brown managed to stay in school until he dropped out in the 7th grade. He earned money by picking cotton, racking pool balls, shining shoes, sweeping out stores, washing cars and dishes, singing in talent contests and buck dancing for change to entertain troops from Camp Gordon.

In 1948, at around age 16, Brown was sentenced to 8-to-18 years for burglary and armed robbery. He was sent to a juvenile detention center in Toccoa, located in northeast Georgia just over the state line from South Carolina. Brown, who played the harmonica, formed a gospel quartet while in prison. The quartet performed for the local prison crowd and other prisons around that area. During one of those performances, future band mate Bobby Byrd watched the show from outside of the prison gates. Brown later became friends with Byrd when the prison baseball team played Byrd's team. Brown played pitcher and Byrd played shortstop. Byrd promised to help Brown get out of prison by offering to provide him with a place to live. Byrd's family then helped Brown gain an early release after serving about three years of his sentence, under the condition that he would not return to Augusta or Richmond County, Georgia. By all accounts Brown failed to live up to the 'leave Georgia' terms of his release. After his release Brown did brief stints as a semi-professional boxer and a pitcher in semi-professional baseball, and after a career-ending leg injury Brown turned his full attention to music.

In 1955, Brown and Byrd's sister Sarah performed in a group called "The Gospel Starlighters." Eventually, Brown joined Bobby Byrd's vocal group, the Avons, and Byrd switched the group's sound from gospel to rhythm and blues. Brown's name and story first spread by word of mouth, from community to community. The group changed their name to The Flames and began touring the Southern "chitlin' circuit" eventually signing a deal with the Cincinnati, Ohio-based label Federal Records, a sister label of King Records.

The Flames' first recording in 1956 was the single "Please, Please, Please" which became a #5 R&B hit, selling over a million copies. Five years later, in 1961, "Please, Please, Please" was still on my father's juke box and folks were still slow dragging to it. Hearing someone repeat Brown's plea — "Good God Almighty" — was almost as common as "good morning." The Flames went on to become "James Brown and The Famous Flames." Their music spread from juke box to juke box and on to the airwaves. Brown's black and white photo on bold lettered black, orange and white live show announcement posters popped up on telephone polls or were tacked to the sides of black country stores, including ours, a couple of weeks before a local gig. Through the posters we followed and mimicked Brown's hairstyles from process to afro to process.

Back then (as now), you heard James Brown every day. If you were old enough or knew somebody, you could get in to see Brown at the municipal auditorium or his live club show. Wherever he performed his records were on sale. Seeing a live show meant going to the XL 100 Club in downtown Spartanburg or driving the 35 miles over to The Ghana in Greenville. The Ghana's house band — Moses Dillard and the Textown Display, featuring a young crooner named Peabo Bryson (now a Disney voice artist) — would often open the show. When grown folks wanted to make weekend out of it they drove up to The Bird Cage in Charlotte or the El Matador down in Columbia or over to Augusta to Brown's The Third World which he opened in 1962 with co-owner Charlie Reid, Sr. whose funeral home ended up doing his last rites. In Atlanta they could see him at Le Carousel which was located at Pascal's, a restaurant frequented by Martin Luther King, Jr. and his cohorts or The Royal Peacock about 4 blocks from King's church Ebenezer Baptist on Auburn Avenue.

Our store was always jumpin' in the early sixties, especially since most southern blacks got their first taste of new music on the neighborhood juke box. If the weather was clear you could hear black artists late night on any AM transistor radio beamed in from *Randy Radio* out of Tennessee. We either bought our records locally from Collin's (the white-owned amusement company) or downtown Spartanburg at Oliver's black-owned drug store. If you had patience and a mail box you could mail order from Randy or Ernie's Records out of Tennessee.

Families scheduled Sunday evening television time around seeing him on *The Ed Sullivan Show*. Kids would suffer through Frankie Avalon and Annette Funicello's 1965 movie *Ski Party* just to see him and The Famous Flames dancing and singing "I Feel Good" by the fireplace in ski sweaters. We joked that James and the Flames were "the only negroes on the slopes" or they were "dancing was to stay warm." Still, a whole lot of black boys in the South couldn't wait for winter so they could wear their thick ski sweaters and pistol-legged, shiny, creased "sharkskin" pants. Brown's music was the soundtrack to the black south throughout the sixties and much of the seventies. Kids danced 'to the rhythm of the James Brown band' at high school basketball games and the dances afterwards. Big-thighed drum majorettes bounced down Main Street in the local Christmas parade to the beat of "Papa's Got a Brand New Bag."

Sometimes, like a gypsy, be it on the Southern "chitlin' circuit" or playing Las Vegas, New York or Europe, Brown entered the theater through the backdoor, got his money up front and in cash, put on a show, sold some records, left out the back door and split town on the 'night train.' At other times, he mingled with the people and occasionally took some along with him. Brown worked with hundreds of local musicians and workers during his years on stage. Every kid who played a horn dreamed of being on stage with the James Brown band. "Maceo blow your horn" and "Play it Fred" were as much a part of the slang of the day as Brown's "hit me" or "good God." Boys either wanted to play the trombone like Fred Wesley or the sax like Maceo Parker. Wesley and Parker probably influenced more kids to join their local high school bands than any one else during that era. A few local kids in the school band ended up in Brown's band. Like Coleman Sistrunck who in the sixties started playing the trumpet with the Wilkerson High School band in Orangeburg then on to The Exotics, the local band that opened for Rufus Thomas and many of the Memphis-based Stax acts that came through the state. From there he ended up with Brown's band as a bass player in the mid-seventies. Sistrunck is currently music director at W.G. Sanders Middle School in Columbia, South Carolina.

Mary Duckett, now a public relations consultant for Greenville County knew Brown well. Duckett, who managed Moses Dillard's band, also operated many of the area nightclubs in Georgia, South and North Carolina during the heyday of the southern circuit in the 60s. Duckett spoke with me about her contact with Brown in the days of the "chitlin' circuit." Duckett said, "James would pass out promotional $100 dollar bills with his face on the notes. That was proof you actually met him. And those bills turned up everywhere." She went on to say, "James stayed in touch with people he worked with and met throughout the years. The last time I saw him was when he came to Greenville in the early 1980s to attend the funeral of Cathy Thornton who for many years traveled with him as his private nurse, tending to his exhaustion after performances."

The sixties are when Brown is credited with creating the music genre now called 'funk.' Papa's Got a Brand New Bag" which came out in 1965 was followed by "Money Won't Change You" and "Cold Sweat." Yet songs like "Don't be a Drop Out" and "Money Won't Change You" revealed Brown's social consciousness. He followed the anti-drop out song up by touring schools sponsored by then Vice President Hubert Humphrey, donating scholarship money and performing a benefit concert in Mississippi in 1966 for wounded activist James Meredith.

Brown was the go-to guy after Martin Luther King was killed. He went on stage in front of thousands of black kids at the Boston Garden on April 5, 1968, the night after King delivered his "Mountaintop" speech to hundreds at Mason Temple in Memphis. As word spread across the country of King's murder, instead of canceling his concert, Brown arranged to televise it with the belief that people would rather watch him perform than riot. From the stage he counseled his fans not to destroy their own community in anger and to respect King's memory.

King preached against the Vietnam War in life and Brown stepped into the breach after his death. In June, two months after Memphis, Brown took an integrated band featuring Marva Whitney, Tim Drummond, Clyde Stubblefield, Jimmy Nolen, Maceo Parker and Waymond Reed to Vietnam to help ease the still raw racial tension among the troops over King's death. He offered to go at his own expense to head off the Lyndon B. Johnson-led government from using cost as an excuse for denying his trip. Even though the government ultimately picked up travel expenses, Brown lost hundreds of thousands of dollars in canceled stateside shows to make room for a predictably dangerous trip. Brown and his crew performed deep 'in country' where Bob Hope dared not go. When Brown arrived in Saigon my elementary school bus driver Eugene "Blue" Boyce, drafted right after high school, was alive to greet Brown and his band. Yet Blue, like so many young men, never made it out of Southeast Asia. He was killed in September later that year. Brown's prominence in the aftermath of King's death did not go unnoticed as his face appeared on the cover of *LOOK* magazine in 1968 with the captions — "Is this the most important black man in America?"

Brown went to the war front to help lower the racial thermostat. Meanwhile, back on the home front, his fellow South Carolinian Senator Strom Thurmond raised the mercury by excoriating equal rights' advocates like the recently assassinated King as "troublemakers," "outsiders" and "communist agitators." Thurmond and his campaign manager Lee Atwater were also poised to play a central role in South Carolina's support for Republican presidential candidate Richard Nixon running the first GOP "Southern Strategy" campaign appealing to disaffected southern white voters. Thurmond and Brown came from the same area of South Carolina, yet emerged as the state's spiritual and cultural alter egos. From his 1948 Dixiecrat presidential bid on a platform of perpetual segregation to opposing desegregating Little Rock High School in Arkansas in 1957 to switching party affiliation in 1964 from Democrat to Republican over racial integration and the Civil Rights Act of 1964, Thurmond spoke white supremacy. Yet, 21 years after Thurmond swore "segregation forever" Brown trumped him when he called out, "Say it Loud!" and the kids responded, "I'm Black and I'm Proud!"

For the most, public school desegregation in the late 60s meant the closing of black facilities and the layoff of scores of black teachers. It meant black kids entering a system and culture that was universally assumed to be better than what they were coming from. Blacks integrated a white situation, not vice-versa. Yet, as the official policy of segregation ended, the black children that walked through the school house doors weren't serenely humming "We Shall Overcome." "I'm Black and I'm Proud" was their anthem. It was everywhere. It was at our store. It was in the streets. It was on the juke box and radio. It was in the air as my sister Valerie and I entered all-white Fairforest Elementary School in 1969. Saying it was often accompanied by a clinched, pumped fist — down low, subtle yet subversive, or up high, defiant and proud.

For some "I'm Black and I'm Proud" was an announcement of new found black pride. It straightened out those who confused the demand for equal rights as whites with a desire to be white. Not that I ever heard any black wishing out loud to be white. For those like me, it was simply calling ourselves what we were already calling ourselves. We were saying to white people that there was nothing wrong with being black. Thankfully, Brown knew the difference between "I'm black and I'm proud" and "I'm black but I'm proud." The African slaves were called black. Even as Negro became Colored became Negro and white southerners mangled nigger and Negro to come up with their acidic "nigra," black was and remains the only term accepted with little argument on any side. Without a doubt, "I'm Black and I'm Proud" settled the self-identification debate for many. Even in the era of the African-American tag there's no shaking black — because Brown made it cool to be black.

The seventies were my pubescent, teenage years. Things were changing for me and the folks around me. Tension around full-scale desegregation and busing occupied our minds. The protest against the Vietnam War was having an effect. And the heroin epidemic hit the black community. My oldest brother, who had volunteered for the army in the early-seventies at the tail end of the Vietnam War, narrowly escaped be sent to Southeast Asia. What he didn't escape was the heroin addiction he picked up while stationed in Germany. Brown's 1972 song "King Heroin" spoke to my brother's and many others' predicament.

Many of the artists of the seventies took on the turbulent times. The Temptations sang it was "A Ball of Confusion." Curtis Mayfield sang "Mighty, Mighty (Shade and Whitey)" and "If There's Hell Below (We're All Gonna Go)." Brown went from cementing racial identity to promoting racial uplift to leading the black sexual revolution with songs like "Sexy, Sexy, Sexy" and "Sex Machine" with its' refrain — "shake your money maker." Before there was Tone Loc's nineties' hit "Baby's Got Back" there was Brown's "Hot Pants! (Smoking)".

Brown made bad good and then declared himself "Superbad." He was "Soul Brother Number One" even as black "peace-and-love" groups like Frankie Beverly and Maze, Kool and the Gang, Earth, Wind and Fire came on the scene with a more laid back sound. Sly and the Family Stone, the Ohio Players and George Clinton and Parliament/Funkadelic built on the funk foundation of Brown's "Give it Up or Turn It Loose", "Can't Stand It" and a host of hits. As Curtis Mayfield and Marvin Gaye smoothly laid out the politics of war and race in their music, Brown shouted, "Get on the Goodfoot" and "Papa Don't Take No Mess!" While Aretha was crowned the "Queen of Soul", Elvis the "King of Rock and Roll" and Frank Sinatra was named the "Chairman of the Board", Brown proclaimed himself the both the "King" and "Godfather of Soul" and we accepted it without a fuss.

Brown didn't let anyone, including the 'black nationalists', tell him who to be. They often called him a "black capitalist" but it was deeper than that. Brown believed he and others blacks had a stake in America through the dues his parents and grandparents paid with years of toil. That's what songs like "Say It Loud", "Open Up the Door", "Payback" and "Funky President" spoke too. King spoke of a "promissory note" and a "bounced check." Brown sang, "I don't want nobody to give me nothing. Open up the door and I'll get it myself." And, "you can't tell me how to run my life down and you can't tell me how to keep my business sound…, you can't tell me how to use my voice..," — all lines in "Talkin' Loud and Saying Nothing." In that song Brown was talking to black nationalists, white racists, politicians and the person next door. But the message was the same — James Brown called his own shots and if you can't tend to your own business don't try to tend to his.

When he and Sammy Davis, Jr. endorsed and had their pictures taken with Richard Nixon in late 60s, we forgave them both. At least I did. My mother had a copy of Davis' biography Yes *I Can* that I read as a boy. The title said it all. A few blacks heckled Brown at a couple of concerts with the chant, "James Brown — Nixon's clown," but it wasn't widespread, it didn't last long and it didn't stick.

It is also possible that his flirtations with Nixon may have had something to do with him and other blacks getting the opportunity to buy up AM radio stations in the late-sixties. With greater access to the airwaves, Brown's music, along with Gaye, Mayfield, and The Staple Singers — played on black-owned stations — helped set the mood of the seventies. And the stations did more than play music. They were lifelines. They employed black workers and promoted black business. They informed their listeners on issues, mobilized them around election time and connected them to black folks' doings outside their communities. When Muhammad Ali fought George Foreman in Kinshasa, Zaire in 1974, we heard about the "rope a dope" on black radio. When a black boy in another county or state died a suspicious death or was the victim of a police shooting we heard about it on black radio. In the 1996 movie *When We Were Kings*, Brown, fight promoter Don King, and Ali talked about their plans to economically energize the black community. Brown may have been the only one who tried to make good on the pledge — although King had a fair number of radio stations in the late seventies.

In South Carolina, the seventies saw popular black stations emerge like WHYZ in Greenville, WOIC in Columbia and Brown's station in Augusta, WRDW. This, combined with advances in the civil rights movement, spurred easier access to the music of black artists. It meant the difference between having to wait two weeks to get music through the mail or taking the bus to the Main Street F.W. Woolworths, and buying the song you heard on the black radio station the very day you heard it.

The eighties were tough on Brown. He wasn't putting out hit records and his personal life was heading towards turmoil. Like many, I took his presence for granted, although when he appeared in *The Blue Brothers* film in 1980 I went to the theater to see him as the Reverend Cleotis Brown — shouting, sliding and dancing behind a pulpit, with an inspired congregation to match his energy and Chaka Khan leading the choir. And, for me, the only part of the 1985 movie *Rocky IV* worth seeing is Brown singing "Living in America." Yet beyond a couple of bright spots in the 80s many of us moved away from Brown's music.

Throughout the years I had heard stories about Brown's relations with women, his multiple marriages, his son Teddy dying in a car crash back in 1973, and all the kids — inside and outside of marriage. In 1984, when I heard Brown had married someone from the TV dance show "Solid Gold" I thought it was Darcel, the black lead "Solid Gold Dancer." Turned out that his third wife, Adrianne Rodriquez, was the show's hairdresser.

Although Adrianne filed domestic abuse charges against Brown four times during the early part of their 12 year marriage, it is safe to say that many of us did not view Brown as a domestic abuser. Many of us saw the reported violence between Adrianne and Brown as a two-way street making it easy to invoke the longstanding and sometimes morally problematic "stay out of married folks' business" rule. Then there were those who whispered that Adrianne might be one of those battered women who for some twisted reason didn't think her man loved her if he wasn't beating her. I remember a couple fighting outside our store one afternoon in the late 60s. The young woman was upset because her guy wanted "to quit" her. As she jumped on her man's back she cried out, "I love you, Willie. Beat me." His response was to throw her in the dirt and beat her without mercy. The only thing that stopped the beating, at least temporarily, was my father's demand that they take their fight off his property.

Some of us also worried that Brown was being set up in a way that would result in him losing control of his music rights and fortune. There was an added measure of prejudice by some blacks toward Adrienne who was Latino and later with Tomi Rae Hynie who's white. Some questioned how Hynie would manage Brown's legacy if given the chance. But with or without drugs as an excuse and before his relationships with Rodriquez and Hynie, Brown's harsh moods affected his relationships with those around him, including his band members. "James was bossy and paranoid," said Fred Wesley, the bandleader of Brown's "JBs" in the seventies. "It was ridiculous that somebody of his popularity could be so insecure."

Wesley currently lives about 50 miles east of Columbia, South Carolina in his wife Gwendolyn's small home town of Manning. Wesley added, "James didn't do drugs when I worked with him. Oh, he had his Bali Hi [wine], but you know he did the 'King Heroin' song and James worked all the time. The drug stuff didn't start until after I left."

When rumors surfaced that the man who in "King Heroin" told kids to "get their minds together and get off drugs" was using a bedroom drug like PCP (angel dust) shortly after marrying Adrianne, who was 17 years younger than he was, I can't say I didn't believe the gossip. Yet I empathized with Brown, like a family member stricken with an illness, or in a bad situation. In the 80s, PCP had replaced heroin as the ghetto drug of choice. One of my older brothers did federal time in the late seventies for possession with intent to distribute the drug while serving in the Army at Ft. Knox, Kentucky. PCP was a drug that police claimed gave its user extraordinary strength. This added potency myth of the drug made it easy to believe the stories about an aging 'sex machine.'

Given Brown's experience, his marital difficulties, sexual conflicts, rumors of substance abuse and any other bouts of "escapism" seemed an inescapable part of his journey. Brown was conflicted but he was never a faker. His signature tune is "Sex Machine." The object of soul power is to make it through whatever the dilemma or 'bewilderment' that ensnares its victim. It's where some folk go when they have just about had it and are just holding on. Sometimes escapism becomes a death wish in slow motion. But the idea in one's mind is to be somewhere other than where you are at for whatever reason.

Rumors aside, it has never been publicly proven that Brown had a PCP addiction. The allegation that Brown was on PCP came from a local police analysis of an improperly administered blood test after his initial arrest in October 1987 by the Aiken County, South Carolina Sheriff's Department. First, police claimed the test showed Brown high on cocaine, they later changed their story to PCP. Brown always denied the charge. At the time Adrianne also denied Brown used PCP. It wasn't until Adrianne died in 1996 of heart failure after having liposuction surgery that the public got a fuller picture of the couple's drug use. The Los Angeles Coroner's Office listed Adrianne's official cause of death as due to PCP intake and heart disease. Two years later Brown was sentenced to 90 days in a drug rehabilitation center.

Still, in late 1987, when the story about gunplay between Brown and Adrianne hit the street, it had a tit for tat spin to it. According to the grapevine, the couple were arguing in the bedroom. James pulled out a .22 pistol and demanded that Adrienne leave his house. She refused and did not budge from her spot on the bed. After Mrs. Brown refused to budge Mr. Brown unloaded his .22 into the mattress. Mrs. Brown still didn't budge. Mr. Brown ran out of bullets. Then, as the story goes, she pulled her pistol from under the pillow and he fled in his pick-up truck over to his Augusta office. There he confronted, with an inoperable shotgun, some people who were holding a meeting there about using his private restroom. At some point in the drama the Augusta and South Carolina cops got involved and the story of the two-state "high-speed chase" sped across the globe. Brown always maintained that he fled to Augusta — out of South Carolina — where he would be safe. It saved his life. In South Carolina "he was just another black man." In Augusta he was a hero.

So many of the things that were happening to Brown and his mate were the things that happened in the lives of the people that came up in neighborhoods around the juke joints. We were all familiar with the combustible and sometimes deadly mix of alcohol or drugs, sex and insecurity. We were also familiar with the excesses and unfairness of the police, judges and the courts.

The inside story of the fight between the couple remains in doubt. But the story ends with Brown in jail. In 1988 he was convicted and sentenced to six years in a South Carolina prison for carrying an unlicensed pistol, assaulting a police officer, along with various drug-related and driving offenses. From what I have been able to gather no drugs were found on Brown's person — only what was alleged to be in his blood system — at the time of his arrest. So his conviction amounted to a "blue light violation" — refusing to pull over for the cops. A 19 year old white man, in court on the same day as Brown, charged with a second offense of the same violation, received a suspended sentence.

The '80s were also a time of transition for me. When my dad passed away in 1982, despite the good memories I had of our store, the bad ones took over. I tore the old building down, left my hometown and moved to Houston, Texas. A year later I ended up back in South Carolina in a state job in Columbia with the rural improvement division of Governor Dick Riley's office. Riley later went on to be Secretary of Education under the Bill Clinton Administration. My job was to travel the state to catalog the needs of the poorest communities. I also started working as editor of *The Palmetto Post* and later *Black News* — both weekly black newspapers. In addition, I took on a volunteer job as producer of radio-magazine show at WDPN, an FM radio station owned by the late State Senator I. DeQuincy Newman. Newman was former chairman of the State NAACP in the 1960s. Newman was also head of Riley's rural advocacy office. A year earlier, in 1983, he had become the first black elected to the South Carolina Senate since the 1880s.

This amalgam of experiences and history of community organizing led me to Jesse Jackson's campaign in 1984 as a field coordinator and South Carolina state campaign coordinator in 1988. In '88 Jackson won the state with 64% of the vote. After the campaign I traveled to Africa, opened an art gallery in Columbia and ultimately returned to work with *Black News*.

It was as editor of *Black News* that I met James Brown for the second time in my life. This time it was face-to-face while he was incarcerated at the State Park Correctional Center in Columbia shortly after his November 1988 conviction after his car chase on Interstate 20 along the Georgia-South Carolina state border.

Black News had covered the initial 1987 incident and arrest of Brown by the Aiken County Sheriff's Department prior to my returning to the paper. The police claimed they only shot at Brown's tires. But the paper sent a photographer to Augusta to take pictures of the truck while it was still at the police department — up on cinder blocks with all the tires removed — and then ran a front page photo of Brown's white Ford F150 short bed pick-up truck with the 21 bullet holes in the driver's side door and bed.

Bernard Legette, a reporter with the paper, had somehow managed to interview a jailed Brown over the phone and asked him, "Why were you trying to flee?' to which Brown responded, "Man, they [the police] were trying to kill me." Brown was pissed off about being in jail. He rhetorically asked Legette, "Would they shoot at and lock up Elvis?" Brown's mug shot was all over the television screens and in the white newspapers. So we took up the task of telling the untold part of the story and building community support for a pardon for the singer. Our paper also covered the many trips Al Sharpton made to the prison to picket over Brown's lockup. It is no overstatement that Brown considered Sharpton as one of his sons.

On Legette's insistence I set up a visit with Brown at the prison hospital located in Columbia. Brown was placed at the minimum security facility with the hope he would be granted early release.

The day I met Brown he was wearing a plastic beautician's cap over his fresh do with a red bandana wrapped around the cap. Being in jail didn't make Brown any less a star, especially at a co-ed facility where the majority of the inmates were women on work release. Several ladies at the facility kept Brown's hair freshly pressed and there were also two male inmate barbers at the facility. Brown arrived at our meeting wearing a pair of freshly starched prison-issued jeans. His light blue shirt, tucked neatly in his pants was also pressed and perfectly creased. The top two buttons of his shirt were undone. Brown preferred to be called Mr. Brown and that's what I called him. He was "Mr. Brown"— in control and dignified. We sat in a classroom reserved for our use, by a big window, in a couple of those old wooden school desks. We didn't talk about his music or his personal business. He spoke of how the Aiken, South Carolina and Richmond County Georgia police had harassed him over an eighteen month period prior to his "high-speed" chase and the bullet holes in his truck. I asked him what help he thought he needed from the paper and the outside world.

Brown claimed that Aiken police officers — about two years prior to his incarceration — had thrown him on the ground, handcuffed him and placed him on his knees in the back of a police car. The police claimed he had left the scene of fender bender on the Interstate. Brown claimed he had only stopped to help a distressed motorist on the side of the road and left when his presence began to cause a commotion. He told me that the local police "had it in for him." He disputed the "high-speed chase" story (the police later recanted) and complained that following his arrest on the night of November '88, a white, plain-clothes Richmond County, Georgia policeman had hit him in the mouth breaking a denture. Brown conveyed both a sense of anger and restraint. He never uttered the word racism to me. When I asked him what he thought of those who put him behind bars he said, "Some of us are traveling by planes, some of us are traveling by bus or in a car, some got to walk and there might be some in covered wagons. But we're all going the same place."

After my first visit the paper began publishing regular updates on Brown. We sponsored "Free James Brown" events at a couple of area clubs. I appeared on MTV with the black rock group Living Color, who were opening for the Rolling Stones' 1989 tour at Clemson University and provided updates on Brown to the *Arsenio Hall Show*. I once talked to the French Minister of Culture's office, which tried in vain to encourage Republican Governor Carroll Campbell to release Brown so that he could perform on Bastille Day in July of 1989. South Carolina Senator Strom Thurmond even called Campbell to ask that Allen University, a small, black AME college in Columbia, be granted custody of Brown so that he could attend the French event. Governor Campbell refused his request.

In the early months of 1989 Jackson asked me to arrange a meeting with Brown. Jackson, fresh off the 1988 presidential campaign and at the height of his political power, wanted to meet with Governor Campbell to seek a pardon or early release, and wanted to talk to Brown first. Jackson was concerned that all the hell-raising by Sharpton and Brown's wife might hinder Brown's early release. But Brown was still angry that Georgia had dropped its charges while South Carolina hadn't. In a meeting room the warden set up for us Jackson said to Brown, "James, when you have your head in the jaws of a lion you have to pull it out carefully and you surely ought not to help the lion."

Jackson never met with Campbell, as the governor felt that releasing Brown early was favoritism. I visited Brown two or three more times after his transfer from the hospital to a Broad River Road reception and evaluation facility also in Columbia to check on Brown's well-being for our newspaper updates and to coordinate a couple of Jackson visits. Brown was released about 4 years early after the mainstream publicity died down. He ended up serving 15 months at the Broad River facility and 10 months in a work-release program in Aiken before being paroled on Feb. 27, 1991. I didn't see Brown again until after his death.

In 1992 while attending the Democratic Convention in New York as the southern political director for presidential candidate Iowa Senator Tom Harkin, I ventured out to The Blue Note nightclub in Greenwich Village. There I met rock impresario Phil Spector. Spector, who was wearing a big Ross Perot campaign button, eyed my Harkin button. We immediately struck up a conversation. When I told him I was from South Carolina, Spector says to me, "You people helped James Brown but you didn't help Ike Turner. Why didn't you help Ike?" My immediate response was that Ike was beating Tina. Everyone had heard the stories through the years. We loved Tina. Maybe not as much as Aretha. But Tina represented raw, gritty, black female sexuality. I told him that the difference between Brown and Turner was that the community didn't view Brown as cruel. That we knew Brown too well, and knew how close many of us have been or could be to the situation that had befallen him. Ike Turner was never as close to the people as James Brown.

Through the grapevine I was aware of Brown's doings after his release. I knew he was spending more time in South Carolina and whenever he would appear on television I made a point to watch. I read the wire reports covering Adrianne's death in 1996 with a bit of sadness. I was tickled when I heard Brown was dating talk-show host Rowanda. As 2000 rolled around I was happy to hear that Brown was starting to pay more attention to his Augusta radio station.

On May 20, 2003, the South Carolina Department of Probation, Parole and Pardon Services pardoned Brown for his past crimes in the state. After the decision Brown sang "God Bless America". "God bless America on this beautiful day. I hope my pardon shows the youth that America is a beautiful country," said the 70-year-old singer. "I feel good!" That same year Michael Jackson presented Brown with a lifetime achievement award at a Black Entertainment Television bash, and Brown received one of the prestigious Kennedy Center Honors.

Brown died on Christmas day, December 25, 2006 at age 73. I immediately thought, dying on Christmas Day, what good timing! I was concerned Brown wouldn't get his due respects from the country as President Gerald Ford died the day after Brown, so I called Al Sharpton to talk about the funeral.

Family members said their first good-byes to Brown in a private service at Carpentersville Baptist Church in North Augusta, South Carolina the day before he made his last trip out the South. After the service Sharpton put Brown's body in a van and drove all night to New York. There, tens of thousands followed Brown's horse-drawn hearse down 125th Street, Adam Clayton Powell Jr. and Frederick Douglass Boulevards. Reminiscent of when Martin Luther King, a lettered-man born of elite, middle-class parents, was taken through the streets in the center of the black South in a mule-drawn wagon. Now, here was Brown, born poor with a 7th grade education taken through the streets in the heart of the black North in a horse-drawn, gilded carriage. Instead of lining up outside Ebenezer Baptist Church, the people stood outside Brown's church, the Apollo Theater.

The night before the Augusta funeral on December 30, 2006, Michael Jackson made a late night visit to C.A. Reid's Funeral Home. The "King of Pop" spent a little more than an hour alone with Brown after his body had been prepared for the next day's trip downtown. Upon seeing Brown in repose Jackson, softly quipped, "He didn't wear his hair like that." He then, according to a couple of workers, proceeded to fix Brown's coiffure, poofing out his bangs so that Brown's new hairdo was a bit freer, and parting his hair the way he remembered. The workers fretted as Michael mussed up the Godfather's newly pressed 'process' one man saying to the other, "We can't let James go out with his hair looking like that." After Jackson left, the beautician was called back in. Later that night Jackson returned to the funeral home to spend a little more time alone with Brown. "You know, Michael was really sincere in his affection for James," said Charlie Reid, owner of the funeral home. "I think he had to be at James' funeral because James was a big part of his life in a real way. It was like if he had missed the funeral he would have missed a part of himself."

On December 30, 2006, the day of Brown's public memorial service, I drove over with a couple of carloads of friends to the James Brown Arena in Augusta. Brown had told his family to call Sharpton if anything happened to him. Brown left his body in the hands of the son of his old business partner Charlie Reid, Sr. who started the Third World nightclub with him in the 60s. He wanted to be buried in the place and by the people he got his power from. He planned it that way. Sharpton kept Brown's homegoing from being taken over by the bigwigs.

Brown's final service wasn't like that of Ray Charles where the entertainment community came out in full force. It wasn't a government-sponsored state funeral like Rosa Parks' or a pompous national one like Coretta Scott King's. Brown's death didn't seem to make America pause like it did when Elvis died. There was no international mourning such as when John Lennon was killed.

Bootsy Collins, Fred Wesley and many of the old band members that had worked with Brown through the years were at his funeral. Rapper turned preacher Stanley Kirk Burrell, aka MC Hammer, stayed around Georgia and South Carolina for both private and public services as did Carlton Douglas "Chuck D" Ridenhour, Atlanta comedian Bruce Bruce and activist Dick Gregory.

There was a sense of family and forgiveness at Brown's funeral in spite of the awkward moment when Hynie sang and lingered over Brown's open coffin. The women of the Ladies' Auxiliary dressed in white or the church 'sympathy club" women were sure ready to fan anyone one who might pass out, but no woman really 'showed out' at the Godfather's funeral.

It was impossible to mourn Brown while watching him dancing and singing "Sex Machine" on the jumbotron. Like the thousands of other folks in attendance, I danced standing on my chair. Brown often said a line which was included on his funeral program, "I'd rather die on my feet than live on my knees." Even on his back James Brown brought people to their feet.

That's why we loved Brown. He never became nostalgic about sex or sexuality and the joy of expressing it in a song or dance or life. He believed that dancing and freedom were one and the same. That's why those who care about him never judged him harshly. As a friend of mine put it: "When you're listening to Brown, and all that funk—it's an assertion of dominance, mastery, cool and an absolutely fierce expression of need, satisfied and arising again, over and over as long as we're alive. Freedom is connecting with the life force — soul, and the struggle to keep it glowing, keep the coals or "Bodyheat" hot, when everything in the world seems determined to extinguish the embers. Freedom is let loose with a big howl, a scream, or "Eeeee Yowlll!" as Brown would express it. And however it comes out it always translates to; No, damn it! I will not be extinguished. Sex is one of the few and best ways to express that howl, at the level that can be expressed any time even if one has no money, no status, nothing. Oftentimes it's the thing that allows one to say, I'm a man or a woman, and I'm alive—not just plodding through the day, not just getting by, but alive, glowing coals, hand of god, 'I'm Superbad.' It's what lets us be both animal and god for a moment, so we can go on being human the rest of the time." For a lot of the folk who walked in the streets and stood in line to say goodbye to Brown, this is their life's ethos. Brown's life says that there is very little difference between the plantation, the streets and the penitentiary. He experienced all three and never lost touch with any of them or the people there.

Shortly after Brown's funeral I met a young fellow by the name of Sinclair McDonald who met Brown at the R and E (reception and evaluation) center in Columbia. McDonald, in jail from 1989 to 94 on a 7 year sentence for cocaine trafficking, proudly told me, "I was transferred to State Park in Aiken along with him and served his food to him everyday when I was assigned to the kitchen. We were together for about 7 months." He went on to say, "I got to talk to Mr. Brown everyday and you know we were kinda going through the same thing with that drug thing. Mr. Brown told me, 'you got to live one day at a time, brother.'"

During the public memorial service Dr. Shirley A.R. Lewis, president of Paine College, a historically black college in Augusta, GA, posthumously bestowed an honorary doctorate upon Brown, the 7th grade dropout. In one of his last taped interviews, when asked what he thought was the most important thing Brown responded, "We've got to educate our people. We've got to educate our people. You can't do it if you don't know it." And even after death, his will provided for a scholarship fund for underprivileged kids in South Carolina and Georgia.

When I was growing up in South Carolina everyone had a Strom Thurmond or James Brown story to tell. The two men were a lot alike. They were both driven. Both saw themselves as "sex machines," although Brown wasn't a hypocrite about it as Thurmond was. Brown fathered a bi-racial son bearing his name and urged his black kids to do DNA testing, not for his benefit but for theirs. Thurmond went to his grave without recognizing his bi-racial offspring. Ironically, Strom Thurmond Jr., the senator's son, is the singer's Aiken probate attorney.

One day I picked up *The State* newspaper, South Carolina's largest paper and the headline read: "Rebel soldier's tooth found" with a subhead equally disturbing: "Memorial service will be held in Saluda for S.C. Confederate."

Now, I'm not into monuments. That is due to the annoying number of Confederate markers and monument in my home state of South Carolina and throughout the south. But thank goodness there's a statute of Brown in his adopted home town of Augusta, Georgia. His real home, South Carolina, ought to erect a statute, monument, or memorial to Brown. But if it never happens, Brown will still always be around. His bottom beats will always drive R&B and hip hop. His body rests in South Carolina but his presence is everywhere there is music. In the middle of the field at halftime at a high school or college football game, or in the stands with the basketball teams pep band. It's in George Clinton's beats and Prince's feet. You can't escape Brown, nor do you want to. "You know you want — Soul Power. You gotta have some — Soul Power. What you need — Soul Power. Give it to me — Soul Power."

Why Does Barack Obama Hate My Family?

ADDRESSING A CONGREGATION AT THE APOSTOLIC CHURCH OF God, one of Chicago's largest black churches, on Father's Day, Barack Obama said:

> Too many fathers are M.I.A., too many fathers are AWOL, missing from too many lives and too many homes. They have abandoned their responsibilities, acting like boys instead of men.

This was his "Sister Souljah" moment. Just as Bill Clinton during his 1992 campaign tried to reassure whites that he wasn't too cozy with blacks by denouncing a rapper, Obama was appealing to whites by condemning his own.

Even so, I wasn't surprised to hear him referred to black men as "boys."

Obama has often taken to "playin' blacks." Playin' in blackspeak means to fool or use a person or persons. (George Bush's selling of a war on the Iraqi people to America is an example that readily comes to mind or — "Bush played us cheap" or "he played us for fools.")

Early in the campaign year, Obama used one of the oldest racial stereotypes in a speech to black South Carolina state legislators: "In Chicago, sometimes when I talk to the black chambers of commerce, I say, 'You know what would be a good economic development plan for our community would be if we make sure folks weren't throwing their garbage out of their cars.'" Translation: black people are dirty and lazy.

One would think getting money is a better plan.

Then, the day before the Texas primary, he let loose again, in a predominantly black venue: "Y'all have Popeyes out in Beaumont? I know some of y'all, you got that cold Popeyes out for breakfast. I know. That's why y'all laughing. ... You can't do that. Children have to have proper

nutrition. That affects also how they study, how they learn in school."
Translation; black people are fat, stupid and lazy.

How would people respond if John McCain (or any person of a different race, nationality or ethnicity) threw out stereotypes like these?
What would we say if a white person had stood in the pulpit of a black church, or anywhere else for that matter, and referred to black men as "boys," in any context?

But since it's Obama, sounding like Bill Clinton before his fall from black grace, or Bill Cosby speaking out of his own personal pain, the change candidate's remarks were met with hosannas mostly by a vapid, racist, white-dominated corporate media, the black people who say what their white bosses want to hear, and blacks and whites alike who shout amen even when Obama's saying something plainly contradicted by their own life experiences.

It was no big surprise that after the speech those critical of Obama were dismissed "as out touch" with the new "post-racial" illusion. Bob Herbert of the *New York Times* appearing on MSNBC's *Hardball* went so far as to say that anyone who disagreed with Obama's Father's Day admonition to black men was living in a racial "fog" of the past. Newspapers across the county affirmed the smear with headlines like "Obama tells black men to shape up" or "Obama speaks 'inconvenient truth' to black men" or "Obama calls black men irresponsible" or "He's saying things people don't want to hear"— with the inference that truth was flowing from his tongue.

I saw no headline lead with the word "some" black men.

Playin' folk on any day is bad enough. But, as a father, grandfather and a black person, I see playin' black men on Father's Day as even more repulsive. The day is for honoring fathers. We don't honor the vets on Veteran's Day by pointing out those who choose not to fight, or the cowards, or even the enemy.

The Obama life narrative highlights that his dad abandoned him as a kid. So, maybe it's his abandonment issues that he's laying on the rest of us. That would explain why he kicked his father "under the bus" implying he had acted like a "boy" when he and his wife divorced each other. Was she acting like a "girl" at the time? It is as simple as one parent being good or a victim and the other a bad victimizer? And, what of the fact that both his mother and father remarried? Is it his wish that his mom and biological dad had remained unhappily married? Does he wish his half-sister had never been born? Is he against divorce? How does he feel about forced or even loveless marriages? Maybe he believes there should be a required economic declaration before a woman gives birth and that two signatures on paper are required before conception?

No doubt, there's a difference between being a sperm donor and being a nurturing, involved parent. But you don't have to share a living space with a child to have an influence on him or her. And you can share a living space and be a lousy father or mother. That's life. I was very young when I first heard the phrase "staying together for the good of the kids." As I grew I learned that oftentimes living arrangements between ex-lovers have to change for the good of the kids.

I'm not claiming to know the story behind the picture of Obama and his father at the airport, but I suspect that joint custody between Hawaii, Indonesia, Massachusetts, Kansas, New York, Illinois and Africa would have been tough.

Writing about Obama's speech gave me a headache. I found myself getting testy just thinking it through and what it means to me and those around me. A lot of people have approached me to talk about Obama's speech. People walk up to me at the gas checkout line and strike up a conversation about Obama. Just the other day, a black woman behind me in line pipes up and says, "Things sho' gonna be better when Obama gets elected." She was not pleased with my response to her uninvited optimism. But I don't think what she said was or is helpful in real terms.

I was speaking to a single, black woman lawyer about my unease with the speech and she immediately went off on black men in general. Now, my lawyer friend is a smart, progressive person. She's a former New York State prosecutor but I've never consciously deducted points from her humanity for her past employment choice. But in our conversation she threw out all the standard lines, "black men aren't taking care of their kids," and "they are sorry." I countered by saying most

243

social psychologists believe that an adolescent girl is more mature than an adolescent boy, so, who do we pin being the most irresponsible on? I asked her: If we believe that it is a woman's right to chose whether or not to be a mother, then why should irresponsible black fathers be the sole point of Obama's attack? And why should any aspect of black male-female relations be grist for the campaign mill?

What Obama's "bash the black man" game leads to is an environment where black people — separate and not equal — is the issue.

Moreover, it passes on one of the lowest of all the smears and stereotypes: the lie that black men have no morals. It reinforces the white supremacists' notion of blacks as irresponsible, overly sexual beasts; a notion that far too many black folk as well as white unwittingly buy into.

I happened to have what turned out to be a very short breakfast meeting with a white female friend who was also a former Hillary Clinton supporter. She's now onboard with Obama. As we spoke, after not seeing each other for more than a month or so, the topic quickly went to Obama with me telling her I didn't plan to vote for him, his speech being just one of the reasons. She responded by threatening never to speak to me again if I supported Ralph Nader or Cynthia McKinney. I don't know if she was serious or not.

On the subject of the Father's Day speech she followed up by asking in a somewhat careful way, "Aren't black women more responsible than black men? That's what I've always heard."

She's been married 3 times and has kids by her first husband.

But I didn't mention that. Instead, what I think might have ended our breakfast prematurely was my black man race card response to the "irresponsibility" question. It's the answer I give to anyone — black or white - who raises the question: A black man would have to be full of self or group hate to believe that black men are more irresponsible than white men or men of other races or ethnic backgrounds. George Bush, Dick Cheney, and a host of other white guys who lied America into the Iraqi war, which has resulted in countless deaths, prove the point. And that's just the most recent example of white, male irresponsibility. The history of the United States is drenched in blood due to the decisions of immoral, irresponsible white men.

A couple of weeks after the Father's Day speech while waiting for a plane at Chicago's O'Hare airport, I found myself in a conversation with a white, female airport worker. The woman, also a mother of mixed-race children, worked out on the pad, most likely unloading baggage and other such laborious tasks. She was sitting down resting between flights in the employee section, just a couple of seats away from me. She overheard me talking to a friend about the Lorraine Motel in Memphis and the 40th anniversary of Martin Luther King's death. This prompted her to tell me about her taking her two kids on a trip to the historic site. I felt her pride as she told her story of her trip. She remembered how she welled up with tears looking up at the balcony, and her kids asked why she was crying. She recalled how her kids responded when they got on the old '50s city bus and the recording yelled out, "Niggers move to the back of the bus!" She said it was then her kids understood why she had cried earlier. It presented her the opportunity to tell them how far things have come and what it took to get here. It was one of those moments when a parent feels like they're teaching their kids something important.

At some point we started talking about Obama's black man speech. She supports Obama. She told me of the pride her mixed-race kids felt in Obama's success, him being mixed race like them. But at the end of our conversation she too concluded that Obama's speech was aimed at white people.

When I first heard Obama's Father's Day speech, my immediate thoughts were of Camille, my recently married 30-year-old daughter. Around the time she turned 25, she informed me and her mother that she planned to have a baby. I simply told her it was her choice since she had to bear the primary burden of raising a child. Or, as the song goes, "if you dance to the music, ya gotta pay to the piper..."

When my daughter came to us, as parents, what we consciously didn't do was lay a single-parent stigma on her, since nobody really raises a child alone. At least where I come from. So, we got a granddaughter to help raise and nurture along with our two other grandkids by my son and his wife who, coincidently, was a teenage mother before she and my son began dating in high school.

One of the jobs of a parent or grandparent is to prevent a child in their care from being saddled with guilt, self-hate or any other baggage society would strap on their backs — regardless of the circumstance of their birth, which a child has no say in. I see our job as rejecting the stigma, which paints a child as "a mistake." Or, in political terms, it's as simple as reinforcing Jesse Jackson's "I am somebody" in a kid.

You don't need to be Alvin Poussaint to know that a child — any child, regardless of color or economic status — who doesn't value their life or feel their worth as a human or feels unloved grows up to be an adult who doesn't value life — theirs or anyone else's.

When Camille and her child's father were going through their breakup, I had one of those heartfelt talks with the both of them. She and the young man had dated since middle school. And, although they had a child together, they were at a fork in the road with one another. It was one of those moments when young people learn adult things, such as the fact that a child does not always make a relationship better nor can it keep an unhealthy or loveless relationship together. And, when a couple splits, in the heat of it all, it's important not to do or say something stupid that would scar not only their individual lives, but their child's future as well. We told the young man that he was the father of our grandchild and nothing could alter that fact. We assured him that we didn't expect anything less than him having a full relationship with his child. He has done just that over the years. But we didn't call him an irresponsible boy. That seemed not only counter-productive but holier than thou. Of course, we weren't running for president; we were just trying to give a kid a chance.

Camille married 5 years after NyAshia's birth, but it wasn't to her child's biological dad. It was to a fellow who has three children of his own. He also shares joint parental custody with his ex-lovers. In the three or four years of his courtship of my daughter, his kids called my wife and me grandmama and granddaddy. While a marriage license and church service made it official, it didn't take all that for us to be family. Everyone in this blended situation — the biological father of my granddaughter, the biological mother of our blended grandkids, and the rest of us — have always shared parental responsibilities.

Now, I'm not trying to universalize my family's experience. But I sure wouldn't lay Obama's take about responsibility on the people around me. Nor would I suggest that they adopt his worldview of what a family is or should be. Because by his two-biological, heterosexual parents residing in same household definition of a family, every other type of family setup is inherently deficient in every sense of the word: economic, social, moral.

In the days after Obama's speech, Ishmael Reed, Dr. Ron Walters and others rebutted the candidate's targeting of black men with the Boston College study which revealed — surprisingly to some — that black fathers not living in the same domicile as their children are more likely to have a relationship with their kids than white fathers in similar circumstances. Walters, an Obama supporter, warned his candidate, "Black people are not voting for a moralist-in-chief."

So, in light of the Boston College study should we conclude that white men are more irresponsible than black men when it comes to spending time with their kids? Maybe Obama should find a white church and offer white men advice on Father's Day? Can we expect to hear him call them "boys?"

Or maybe he should take a trip to the hollows of Appalachia and tell the "trailer park crowd" that if they would just "pick up the garbage" from around their trailers and "stop engaging in incest" (or whatever other stereotype that comes to mind) they would not have it so bad.

And shouldn't he be advising the polygamist families out west? Or, hopping on a plane to Massachusetts to lecture the fathers and parents of the pregnant teens in Gloucester?

According to Health and Human Services, "throughout the 1990s, black teens have had the largest declines in teen childbearing rates of any group" while "Latinas have had the highest teen birth rate of any major ethnic/racial minority in the country since 1995." Why doesn't Obama take his message to the barrios? Maybe he could go to a Catholic Cathedral in the heart of an East L.A. Latino community and challenge

Latino men's machismo. He should use "boys" in his speech and admonish the parishioners not to eat so many burritos.

Truth be told, I don't wish to see a particular racial, sexual, religious or ethnic group singled out for derision or used as a campaign prop. Stereotypical remarks about blacks, Latinos and whites in Appalachia are just as inappropriate and stupid as remarks about Jewish materialism or Irish drunkenness.

I'm old fashioned about some things. My mother is prone to say, "Keep your business off the streets." I'm only putting out my family's personal stories to illustrate why I'm leery about Obama.

Many of those around me plan to vote for him. For the most part, my response is to ask folks to look at their lives and check whether or not what Obama is saying squares with their reality. Never mind how they "should" be living — never mind how Obama's "current" family looks. I just ask if, with all the troubles of getting along day to day, is it helpful to have his polish on how they should be living piled on top?

My new son-in-law has two young boys and a daughter. Like so many other black teens who weren't as lucky as Obama, he got busted in his teen years and did a little time on a drug arrest. Obviously his life has turned around. Luckily, he's a brick mason. If he didn't work for himself in a skilled trade, it would be hard for him to find work. He knows that because he went to jail, his sons also have a 60 per cent likelihood of going to jail. He has to fight extra hard to make sure his kids are not that statistic. And it's a tricky thing. You want your kids to understand the many race traps but not be defined by them.

After Obama won the South Carolina primary, whenever I was asked, I'd say that in the general election my vote was his to lose. Prior to and after their wedding, my ex-offender son-in-law, somewhat of a race man (he planned to vote for Obama "because he is black"), who just recently found out he could vote despite his conviction, constantly reminded me of what I had said, "Remember, you said your vote was his to lose."

Shortly after his and my daughter's wedding, a couple of day after Obama's Father's Day speech, we were sitting together with a friend of his, a young, married father of one, who was in their wedding party. Once again he reminded me of what I had said about "my vote to lose." I let loose with just about everything I've said in this article. I told him to look at his own life and then tell me what he thinks about Obama.

I asked my son-in-law to think about his wedding and the people who were there. There were lots of young mothers and fathers and children, divorcees, second marriages, common-law arrangements, ex-lovers, step-parents and grandparents, etc. Many of those people, if they believed Obama, could be passed off as being "irresponsible" and their kids dismissed as "mistakes." I asked him: Did he truly believe that many of the people in that church, whose lives he knew, were less moral or responsible than others, as Obama inferred? Ex-offender, former unmarried father of three, rap music producer, isn't he one of those whom Obama is condemning? On paper, anyway. Yet, he has raised three good kids.

Whenever I suggest to Obama insiders that he's a lot like Bill Clinton, they go apoplectic. Yet, as race-baiting and race politics goes, Obama has proven himself to be as good, if not better than Clinton, long considered the modern master of race politics. If you believe, as I do, that he "played black men to court white voters," then all Obama's protestations about Bill Clinton's race-baiting were just a ruse. And, in that light he is no better than Clinton when it comes to using race fears. He may even be worse than Clinton because he plays it both ways assaulted and assailant. I'll be willing to bet that if Clinton were honest in revealing how he really felt about Obama, that would be at the heart of his grievance.

No doubt, people are excited about the prospect of a young, vibrant, black person as president. They see their choice as between John McCain and Obama, and conclude that Obama is "the only option," or say "He will never be as bad as Bush. He will never be bad as Reagan." Or they say their man Obama "has a chance to win. We need to give him some latitude." "We need to let the man do what he needs to do to win." "We should trust him." "Barack is one of us, no matter what he sounds like right now."

As critical as I am, I actually want to believe he's "one of us." But I don't see it.

That isn't necessarily a bad thing for Obama. If people like me don't see Obama as "one of us," that strengthens the belief of the powerful that he is "one of them."

For sure, Obama has most black voters in the bag. I'm pretty sure that my vote falls in the "doesn't matter so much" column. And from listening to Obama, a whole lot of my family members' lives don't matter much either.

I'm not really looking for change from Obama should he win. I'm looking for the fight to come.

Index

About the author

Kevin Alexander Gray & his younger sister Valerie were among the first blacks to attend the local all-white elementary school in rural, upstate South Carolina in 1968. Since then he has been involved in community organizing working on a variety of issues ranging from racial politics, police violence, third-world politics & relations, union organizing & workers' rights, grassroots political campaigns, marches, actions & political events.

He is currently organizing the Harriet Tubman Freedom House Project in Columbia, South Carolina which focuses on community based political and cultural education.

Founding member of the National Rainbow Coalition in 1986. Former co-chair of the Southern Rainbow Education Project — a coalition of southern activists. Former contributing editor — *Independent Political Action Bulletin.*

Gray was the South Carolina coordinator for the 1988 presidential campaign of Jesse Jackson & 1992 southern political director for the presidential campaign of Iowa Senator Tom Harkin. Gray was also the 2002 SC United Citizens' Party & Green Party Gubernatorial candidate.

Former managing editor of *The Palmetto Post* and *Black News in* Columbia, South Carolina. He served as a national board member of the American Civil Liberties Union for 4 years & is a past eight-term president of the South Carolina affiliate of the ACLU. Advisory board member of DRC Net (Drug Policy Reform Coalition).

AK Press

Ordering Information

AK Press
674-A 23rd Street
Oakland, CA 94612-1163
U.S.A
(510) 208-1700
www.akpress.org
akpress@akpress.org

AK Press
PO Box 12766
Edinburgh, EH8 9YE
Scotland
(0131) 555-5165
www.akuk.com
ak@akedin.demon.uk

The addresses above would be delighted to provide you with the latest complete AK catalog, featuring several thousand books, pamphlets, zines, audio products, video products, and stylish apparel published & distributed by AK Press. Alternatively, check out our websites for the complete catalog, latest news and updates, events, and secure ordering.

Also Available from AK Press

The first audio collection from Alexander Cockburn on compact disc.

Beating the Devil

Alexander Cockburn, ISBN 13: 9781902593494 • CD • $14.98

In this collection of recent talks, maverick commentator Alexander Cockburn defiles subjects ranging from Colombia to the American presidency to the Missile Defense System. Whether he's skewering the fallacies of the war on drugs or illuminating the dark crevices of secret government, his erudite and extemporaneous style warms the hearts of even the stodgiest cynics of the left.

Available from CounterPunch/AK Press

Call 1-800-840-3683 or order online from
www.counterpunch.org or www.akpress.org

The Case Against Israel
by Michael Neumann

Wielding a buzzsaw of logic, Professor Neumann dismantles plank-by-plank the Zionist rationale for Israel as religious state entitled to trample upon the basic human rights of non-Jews. Along the way, Neumann also offers a passionate amicus brief for the plight of the Palestinian people.

Other Lands Have Dreams: From Baghdad to Pekin Prison
by Kathy Kelly

At a moment when so many despairing peace activists have thrown in the towel, Kathy Kelly, a witness to some of history's worst crimes, never relinquishes hope. Other Lands Have Dreams is literary testimony of the highest order, vividly recording the secret casualties of our era, from the hundreds of thousands of Iraqi children inhumanely denied basic medical care, clean water and food by the US overlords to young mothers sealed inside the sterile dungeons of American prisons in the name of the merciless war on drugs.

Dime's Worth of Difference: Beyond the Lesser of Two Evils
Edited by Alexander Cockburn and Jeffrey St. Clair

Everything you wanted to know about one-party rule in America.

Whiteout: the CIA, Drugs and the Press
by Alexander Cockburn and Jeffrey St. Clair, Verso.

The involvement of the CIA with drug traffickers is a story that has slouched into the limelight every decade or so since the creation of the Agency. In Whiteout, here at last is the full saga.

Been Brown So Long It Looked Like Green to Me: the Politics of Nature
by Jeffrey St. Clair, Common Courage Press.

Covering everything from toxics to electric power plays, St. Clair draws a savage profile of how money and power determine the state of our environment, gives a vivid account of where the environment stands today and what to do about it.

Imperial Crusades: Iraq, Afghanistan and Yugoslavia
by Alexander Cockburn and Jeffrey St. Clair, Verso.

A chronicle of the lies that are now returning each and every day to haunt the deceivers in Washington and London, the secret agendas and the underreported carnage of these wars. We were right and they were wrong, and this book proves the case. Never leave home without it.

Why We Publish CounterPunch

By Alexander Cockburn and Jeffrey St. Clair

TEN YEARS AGO WE FELT UNHAPPY ABOUT THE STATE OF RADICAL JOURNALISM. It didn't have much edge. It didn't have many facts. It was politically timid. It was dull. CounterPunch was founded. We wanted it to be the best muckraking newsletter in the country. We wanted it to take aim at the consensus of received wisdom about what can and cannot be reported. We wanted to give our readers a political roadmap they could trust.

A decade later we stand firm on these same beliefs and hopes. We think we've restored honor to muckraking journalism in the tradition of our favorite radical pamphleteers: Edward Abbey, Peter Maurin and Ammon Hennacy, Appeal to Reason, Jacques René Hébert, Tom Paine and John Lilburne.

Every two weeks CounterPunch gives you jaw-dropping exposés on: Congress and lobbyists; the environment; labor; the National Security State.

"CounterPunch kicks through the floorboards of lies and gets to the foundation of what is really going on in this country", says Michael Ratner, attorney at the Center for Constitutional Rights. "At our house, we fight over who gets to read CounterPunch first. Each issue is like spring after a cold, dark winter."

YOU CANNOT MISS ANOTHER ISSUE

Name _____

Address _____

City _____ State _____ Zip _____

Email _____ Phone _____

Credit Card # _____

Exp. Date _____ Signature _____

☐ 1 year **$45**   ☐ 2 year **$80**   ☐ Donation Any Amount
☐ 1 year email **$35**   ☐ 2 year email **$65**   ☐ Low-income/student/senior **$35**
☐ 1 year both **$50**   ☐ 2 year both **$90**   ☐ Low-income/student/senior email **$30**

A one year subscription consists of 22 issues. The email version is a PDF emailed to the email address you include. Please notify CounterPunch of email and mailing address changes. Low-income/student/senior subscriptions are 1 year only.

Send Check/Money Order to: **CounterPunch, P.O. Box 228, Petrolia, CA 95558**
Canada add $12.50 per year postage. Others outside US add $17.50 per year.

Visit our website for more information: **www.counterpunch.org**

The Secret Language of the Crossroads
How the Irish Invented Slang

By Daniel Cassidy

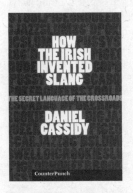

In *How the Irish Invented Slang: The Secret Language of the Crossroad*, Daniel Cassidy co-director and founder of the Irish Studies Program at New College of California cuts through two hundred years worth of Anglo academic "baloney" and reveals the massive, hidden influence of the Irish language on the American language.

Irish words and phrases are scattered all across the American language, regional and class dialects, colloquialism, slang, and specialized jargons like gambling, in the same way Irish-Americans have been scattered across the crossroads of North America for five hundred years.

In a series of essays, including: "Decoding the Gangs of New York," "How the Irish Invented Poker and American Gambling Slang," "The Sanas (Etymology) of Jazz," "Boliver of Brooklyn," and in a *First Dictionary of Irish-American Vernacular*, Cassidy provides the hidden histories and etymologies of hundreds of so-called slang words that have defined the American language and culture like *dude, sucker, swell, poker, faro, cop, scab, fink, moolah, fluke, knack, ballyhoo, baloney,* as well as the hottest word of the 20th century, *jazz.*

Available from CounterPunch.org and AK Press
Call 1-800-840-3683
$18.95

Spell Albuquerque
Memoir of a "Difficult" Student

By Tennessee Reed

"Tennessee Reed is a brand new star in the galaxy of our spirit-shining for all of our people."—Simon Ortiz, author of *Telling and Showing Her*

"Reed writes with clarity, wit, and wonder-and with an open-hearted passion that disarms, refreshes, and delights."—Al Young, author of *Something About the Blues*

"I'm not like them," Tennessee Reed would tell her teachers to get them to see that the approach they used for students with "normal" brains didn't always work for her. As it turned out, she was different in quite a few other ways as well, including the great reserves of courage she could call upon to fight an educational system that often defined her disabilities as laziness or stupidity.

The daughter of writer/choreographer Carla Blank and novelist Ishmael Reed, Tennessee was diagnosed at an early age with several language-based learning disorders. The bottom line, the experts agreed, was that she would never read or write. Within a few years, however, she published her first book of poetry. By the time she was a teenager, she was writing the text for Meredith Monk performances and traveling the world to read her poems. Spell Albuquerque is an inspiring memoir of one woman's struggle to overcome racism and institutional authority and to achieve what everyone said was impossible.

Tennessee Reed is the author of five books of poetry, including *City Beautiful, Airborne,* and *Electric Chocolate*. She is a graduate of the University of California at Berkeley, and has a master's degree from Mills College.